WOMEN@INTERNET

Creating New Cultures in Cyberspace

Edited by

WENDY HARCOURT

SID
Society for International Development

ZED BOOKS
LONDON & NEW YORK

UNESCO

For

Amir Yanir Michael,

Emma Claire,

Sherry Njeri and

Silas Jan,

little WoN cyborgs of the future, born during the project

Women@Internet was first published by
Zed Books Ltd, 7 Cynthia Street, London N1 9JF, UK, and
and Room 400, 175 Fifth Avenue, New York, NY 10010, USA
in 1999

Distributed in the USA exclusively by
St. Martin's Press Inc., 175 Fifth Avenue, New York NY10010, USA.

Cover designed by Andrew Corbett.
Cover illustration by Katherine Kirkwood
Laserset by Long House, Cumbria, UK.
Printed and bound in the United Kingdom
by Biddles Ltd, Guildford and King's Lynn

A catalogue record for this book
is available from the British Library.

ISBN 1 85649 571 X Cased
ISBN 1 85649 572 8 Limp

CONTENTS

ABBREVIATIONS

AAAS	American Accord for the Advancement of Science
AJN	Asia–Japan Network
ALAI	Agencia Latinoamericana de Información
APC	Association for Progressive Communications
ASAFE	Association pour le Soutien et l'Appui a la Femme Entrepreneur
ASEAN	Association of South East Asian Nations
AT&T	American Telephone & Telegraph
AWORE	Asian Women's Resource Exchange
BT	British Telecom
CBOs	Community-based organizations
CIDA	Canadian International Development Agency
CIHRS	Cairo Institute for Human Rights Studies
CWIS	Centre for World Indigenous Studies
DAW	(UN) Division for the Advancement of Women
DAWN	Development Alternatives for Women in a New Era
EZLN	Ejercito Zapatista para la liberación Nacional
EU	European Union
FAWE	Forum for African Women Educationalists
FIRE	Feminist International Radio Endeavour
FSL	Family Status Law
GEF	Global Environment Facility
GIS	Geographic Information Systems
GK97	Global Knowledge 97 Conference
GNP	Gross National Product
GPS	Global Positioning Systems
HDR	Human Development Report
IC	Information Communication
ICCBWSI	International Cross-Cultural Black Women's Studies Institute
ICT	Information and Communications Technology
ICWGK	Independent Committee on Women and Global Knowledge
IDC	Standing Committee on Information, Documentation and Communication
IDRC	International Development Reseach Centre
IMF	International Monetary Fund
ISP	Internet Service Provider
IT	Information Technology
ITU	International Telecommunications Union
IUAES	International Union of Anthropological and Ethnological Sciences
IWTC	International Women's Tribune Centre
KCSE	Kenya Certificate of Secondary Education

METRAC	Metro Action Committee for Women
NEWW	Network of East–West Women
NGO	Non-governmental organization
NGORC	NGO Resource Centre
RAW	Ramfourt Action Network
RHLA	Red de Humanistas Latinoamericano (Latin American Humanist Network)
SEAFDA	South-East Asia Forum for Development Alternatives
SID	Society for International Development
SOO	State-owned operator
SYNFEV-ENDA	Synergy, Gender and Development – Environment and Development in the Third World
TAMWA	Tanzania Media Women's Association
TIL	Technology and Interactive Learning Ltd
UNAM	National Autonomous University of Mexico
UNCED	UN Conference on Environment and Development
UNCHR-IWG	UN Commission on Human Rights Inter-sessional Working Group
UNCTAD	UN Conference on Trade and Development
UNCSTD	UN Commission on Science and Technology for Development
UNDP	UN Development Programme
UNECA	UN Economic Commission for Africa
UNESCO	UN Educational, Scientific and Cultural Organization
UNIFEM	UN Development Fund for Women
UNU/INTECH	UN University for New Technologies
UVLA	Universidad Virtual Latinoamericana
UNWCW	UN World Conference on Women
WICC-ISIS	Women's International Cross-Cultural Exchange
WID	Women in Development
WIF	Women, Information and the Future
WIGSAT	Women in Global Science and Technology
WOM	Women's On-line Media
WoN	Women on the Net
WTO	World Trade Organization
WWW	World Wide Web

CONTRIBUTORS

Laura Agustín is a popular educator and student of migrations, *mestizaje* and cultural hybridism. Her work in recent years has focused on sex tourism and the migrations of Latin American and Caribbean women to Europe to work in the domestic and sex industries. She has participated in international fora on prostitution and trafficking and is currently rethinking concepts of sexuality, work and victimization. A perpetual migrant, she is now working in Spain.

Fatma Alloo founded the Tanzania Media Women's Association (TAMWA) which brought together female journalists working on issues of concern to women and society. One of the first issues launched by the campaign was Violence Against Women. After ten years of continuous work and advocacy the Sexual Offence Bill was passed in Tanzania where offenders receive life imprisonment for rape and defilement. Presently she is the Director of the NGO Resource Centre (NGORC), a project of the Aga Khan Foundation based in Zanzibar, Tanzania. The NGORC, established in 1996, provides support to communities in order to build capacity, access and share information, promote advocacy and debates on development issues and provide training in capacity building to civil society organizations. The Centre works with NGOs and Community Based Organizations (CBOs) in order to strengthen them and promote the advocacy role of civil society.

Lamis Alshejni, from Yemen, is currently studying for a double BA at John Cabot University in Rome, Italy, and is a volunteer for the Women in Development network at the Society for International Development (SID-WID). Her main concerns include women's issues, human rights and Islamic philosophy. She has been active with Amnesty International, and worked at the Cairo Institute for Human Rights Studies (CIHRS), Egypt.

Lourdes Arizpe, a cultural anthropologist from Mexico, has held several distinguished positions in the field of culture and international development, including: Director of the Institute of Anthropological Research, National Autonomous University of Mexico (UNAM), 1991–4; President of the International Union of Anthropological and Ethnological Sciences (IUAES), 1988–93; member of the Steering Committee of the Development Alternatives for Women in a New Era (DAWN); Executive Commissioner of the World Commission on Culture and Development, 1992–4, and Assistant Director-General for Culture at UNESCO, 1996–8. Her publications in English include: *Culture and Global Change: Social Perceptions of Deforestation in the Lacandona Rain Forest* (University of Michigan Press, Ann Arbor,

1995) and (as editor) *The Cultural Dimensions of Global Change: An Anthropological Approach*, (Paris, UNESCO Publishing, 1996).

Silvia Austerlic studied Graphic Design at the University of Buenos Aires, Argentina and has been a teacher of Art History since 1990. In 1997 she helped to set up a Virtual University of Latin America (http://www.ldc.lu.se/latinam/uvla/uvla1.htm). Since 1995 she has been working on a design conceptual framework to counteract the cultural impacts caused by changes in the use of information and communication technologies. She is interested in design education from the perspective of developing countries and is a member of the SID-WID network.

Rhona O. Bautista holds a BA in Library Science from the University of the Philippines, where she is currently studying for a masters degree in Women and Development. As Resource Centre and Information officer of Isis International–Manila, Rhona is also in charge of improving the electronic information and communication work of Isis. She manages the Women's Resource Centre and conducts training workshops for women's NGOs on setting up and managing resource centres. Isis International–Manila's work includes research, publications and information networking.

Marisa Belausteguigoitia Rius is a doctoral candidate in Ethnic Studies, with an emphasis on gender and sexuality, at the University of Berkeley. She is presently completing a dissertation on 'Cultural scenarios at the border: construction of subjectivity and cultural forms of representation at the limit of the nation and nationalisms'. In Mexico, she has been involved in the organization and coordination of an NGO that deals with urban disenfranchised women's legal and health issues. She has also taught and researched at UNAM since 1984.

Kekula P. Bray-Crawford focuses on Indigenous Peoples issues, learning through grassroots organizing and international strategies. In the last three years she has worked on the Internet on the UN Draft Declaration on the Rights of Indigenous Peoples and for the UNCHR Special Rapporteur on International Treaties, Agreements and Other Constructive Arrangements between States and Indigenous Peoples. Her work on the Net aims to facilitate access in remote and rural areas of the Pacific, identifying and learning solutions to the numerous issues affecting electronic multi-media communications technologies. Through cybertechnology she is also mapping out the history of her culture and islands.

Sally Burch is a journalist, born in the UK, who has lived in Ecuador for 15 years. She is Executive Director of Agencia Latinoamericana de Información (ALAI), a communication organization dedicated to the promotion of human rights and democratic participation by social movements in the development of Latin America. ALAI runs a Women's Programme, committed to developing the communicational processes of women's movements and networks as an indispensable element for organization, advocacy and social protagonism. ALAI also defends women's right to communicate, and actively promotes women's access to a strategic use of new communication technologies as a tool for networking and fostering gender equality and as a means of empowerment.

Arturo Escobar is Professor of Anthropology at the University of Massachusetts, Amherst, and author of the influential *Encountering Development – The Making and Unmaking of the Third World* (Princeton University Press, 1995). He has undertaken research for the past five years in the Colombian Pacific rainforest region, looking at the intersection of development, capital and social movements in the region in the context of transnational debates on biodiversity conservation. He is a member of the SID *Development* editorial board and was guest editor of *Development* 42.2 on 'Globalism and the Politics of Place'.

Farideh Farhi is a leading voice challenging the forces of classical socialism, capitalism and Islamic fundamentalism in Iran. Since 1993 she has been the English editor and a member of the editorial board of *Iranian Journal of International Affair*s published by the Institute for Political and International Studies based in Tehran, Iran. Her three major areas of interest are foreign policy, women's issues and development. On women's issues she is seeking to lift the taboo on talking about the problems posed for women after the Iranian revolution – with particular attention to needed legal changes. She is the author of *State and Urban-Based Revolutions: Iran and Nicaragua* (University of Illinois Press, Urbana, 1990) and has published extensively on women, Islam and the politics of revolution in Iran.

Edie Farwell, **Peregrine Wood**, **Maureen James** and **Karen Banks** are members of the Women's Networking Support Programme of the Association for Progressive Communications (APC). The programme is a network of networks whose mission is to empower and support organizations, social movements and individuals in the use of information and communication technologies. It aims to build strategic community initiatives fostering human development, environmental preservation, social justice, participatory democracies and sustainable societies. Composed of a consortium of 25 international member networks, APC offers vital links of communication to over 50,000 NGOs, activists, educators, policy makers, and community leaders in 133 countries.

Wendy Harcourt coordinates the Women on the Net project as one of her tasks as Director of Programmes at SID. She was awarded a PhD by the Australian National University in 1987 and joined SID in 1988 as editor of the journal *Development* and coordinator of the Women in Development programme. Her research and advocacy work focuses on gender relations in the fields of environment, alternative economics, culture, international development, reproductive rights and European women's issues. All her work is undertaken as part of the collective international exploration of alternatives to mainstream thinking on gender, culture, economics, sustainable development and population. She has edited two other Zed books: *Feminist Perspectives on Sustainable Development* (1993) and *Power, Reproduction and Gender* (1997).

Sophia Huyer works with Women in Global Science and Technology (WIGSAT), which facilitates global networking among women scientists and technologists (both formal and non-formal) for collaboration and coalition building around the world. Current areas of focus include women's use of information and communications technologies for empowerment (especially economic) through mobilization, organization, information sharing and knowledge production *vis-à-vis* both indigenous knowledge and creative technology development. She is also a doctoral candidate at the Faculty of Environmental Studies at York University, working on social movement strategies in response to the globalization of economies and information.

Sohail Inayatullah is currently senior research fellow at the Communication Centre, Queensland University of Technology. Associate editor of *New Renaissance* and senior writer for *Global Times: The Alternative World Journal,* he is also on the editorial boards of the journals *Futures, Periodica Islamica* and *Futures Studies.* He has published widely in the area of futures studies and culture studies. He recently published *Macrohistory and Macrohistorians* (Praeger) and a CD-ROM, *Futures Studies: Methods, Emerging Issues and Civilizational Visions* (Prosperity and Adamantine). In process are *Theorizing Futures* (Grey Seal) and *The Knowledge Base of Futures Studies,* Volume 4 (Futures Study Centre).

June Lennie, Margaret Grace, Leonie Daws and **Lyn Simpson** are members of the research team coordinating the project 'Enhancing Rural Women's Access to Interactive Communication Technologies' based at the Communication Centre and the Centre for Policy and Leadership Studies at Queensland University of Technology in Brisbane, Australia (http://www.fbs.qut.edu/rwp/). Project activities begun in 1996 have included workshops held around Queensland, on-line discussion groups, a 'virtual conference', and a major seminar held in the state capital city. The project has highlighted the significant role of rural women in the uptake of new interactive communication technologies and the importance of taking 'soft technology' factors into account. Policy recommendations are being developed to ensure that rural communities can benefit from the new communication technologies.

Alice Mastrangelo Gittler was Programme Associate with the International Women's Tribune Centre, a small women's NGO based in New York, until she chose to work at home, take care of her small son, and 'test the limits of global telecommuting'. From 1990 to 1997 she was managing programmes related to science, technology and information technology. She also designed and conducted computer training, and wrote and edited science and technology publications for IWTC. She presently works independently on issues of equity and diversity in technology, particularly those relating to the use of electronic tools for community-based and global NGO organizing and activism.

Ivana Milojevic previously lectured at the University of Novi Sad, Yugoslavia, and is currently living in Brisbane, Australia. Her education and interests are in sociology, women's studies and futures studies. She has completed a book on violence against women and is, in between taking care of two young children, trying to do research in the area of women's futures and feminist utopias. She has recently contributed articles to *The Futurist*, *Futures* and various books including the *1998 Yearbook on Education* (Kogan Page).

Nidhi Tandon is an economist and activist from East Africa, currently based in Toronto, Canada. She has over ten years' experience in research and technical assistance management in the UK with the Commonwealth Secretariat and the Overseas Development Institute. She is a co-founder of both ABANTU for Development, an African women's organization based in Kenya and the UK, and the Independent Committee on Women and Global Knowledge, who made a stand on behalf of women at the Global Knowledge conference in Toronto in 1997. She has conducted a pilot training workshop on policy and technical aspects of the Internet for 25 women's organizations in East Africa coordinated by ABANTU for Development. Her interests span international trade policy and e-commerce; employment and investment implications for Africa; distance education and rural schools – all in the context of the evolving information technologies.

Gillian Youngs is a lecturer at the Centre for Mass Communication Research, University of Leicester, UK. She has taught at Syracuse University (New York), the Hong Kong Centre, and Nottingham Trent University, UK. She is currently working on the theory and practice of feminist possibilities on the Net and is active in a number of international networks. Her other research interests are globalization, technology and culture, and inequality and identity. Her publications include *From International Relations to Global Relations* (Cambridge: Polity Press, forthcoming) and, as co-editor with Eleonore Kofman, *Globalization: Theory and Practice* (London: Pinter, 1996).

PREFACE

Freedom to Create: Women's Agenda for Cyberspace

Lourdes Arizpe

Reaching out to the new cyberworld

In the Internet, we look through screens, darkly, sensing others, finding the contours of their selves, as we pick words here, images there, for this prodigious piecing together of a new reality. To see this new cyber-world, we need to interpret it – collectively, reaching out for new words, bouncing off symbols, crafting new metaphors. That is what the cyber-explorers in this book are doing.

When Wendy and I decided to throw a women's project into the Net-future, we did not expect such a prolific, image-filled outburst of enthusiasm and expertise. Magic: over one hundred women, and men, re-materialized through virtual space saying, yes, we will create this new mythology of cyberspace with you, as we run deeper into the cracks of nowhere. But we will make it somewhere, a place-based global community in which women are active agents.

What happens to gender when it goes through the hardware? We do not know yet but we will see. We do know that in other civilizational transitions, such as the Industrial Revolution, women were taken off the rails of the advances in technology. Are women really not interested in technology? Perhaps, but this might have been conditioned by the gender division of labour adapted to agriculturalism and industrial capitalism. Equality, in building technology or in handling it, however, does not erase gender differences. Which ones are they? Do they change, according to the medium of communication? This, indeed, is what we shall see. It is well known that in all societies women are keenly interested in communication. A touching, feeling, hopefully loving kind of communication. In fact, both women and men need this kind of communication. Can this soft dialogue filter through the metal machines and optic fibers? Or will it take women to soft-wear the new technologies?

The main thing is that women must now be active agents in experimenting and interpreting the new forms of communication that the new technologies offer us. I believe that creativity is, today, the key process that will allow us to reinvent the world. The way forward cannot be to follow blindly the unregulated global market or uninformed data technologies – which are not the same thing as true information technologies – but, rather, to work together for a future which we have freely chosen. If we cannot even do that, what would be the point of zapping like mad from one cyberimage to another?

Taking hold of the imagination

Imagination without technology can lead to utopias in the desert; technology without imagination can end up shredding our soul. How do we get the right mix of imagination and technology? We know that the new information and communication technologies will bring changes we cannot conceive of today, both in the way we think, in cognitive structures and in social and economic transactions. If present trends continue, most of the negotiations, adaptations and creative solutions to emerging problems will be dealt with in cyberspace.

This is why knowing and understanding cyberculture is so important. Rarely have generations, such as ours, been present at the birth of a new culture. Perhaps it should not be called a 'culture' because what is being created in cyberspace is merely a framework for communicating: netiquette, codes, navigating terms and maps. In fact, one could argue that the medium of the new information technologies opens up the greatest opportunities that small, isolated cultures have ever had to communicate among themselves. Certainly this is the case for many island cultures of the Pacific, or for diasporic peoples, from Lithuanians to Mixtec Indians from Mexico.

Very rapidly we are finding more and more different languages and scripts in cyberspace. So what would be the culture image for such a new territory? Paraphrasing Kekula Bray-Crawford, are we going towards an *archipilago* of linguistic and cultural islands in the liquid continent of cyberspace?

Self-awareness on the part of cyborgs will be a key factor in shaping the way in which virtual communities will evolve. Developing a women@internet community is already a statement of self-awareness which leads to identity. In a world in which humans have become mobile geographically as never before, they may carry their cultures with them, like internalized software, but they must also find new ties to bind them to communities across countries and continents. The Internet may be the site for these new virtual identities.

Women, especially, have made a quantum jump in identity in the last three decades. Feminism has created a global room of our own. Beijing was simply the visible demonstration of the new allegiances that millions of women around the world share. There is not one movement, nor one single image of how women should be in the future across the globe, but there is the certainty that basic components of women's daily lives in all cultures in all countries have changed in the last thirty years. Most of them now choose the number and spacing of their children, live longer and have a new feeling of selfhood that drives them to want to participate more actively in social, spiritual or political processes. Out of this shared perception of fundamental changes have come many different strategies and aims in mobilizing women. This is excellent, because we need the diversity of women's experiences to open up many different roads to the future. The old cultural diversity is being threatened by the overwhelming amount of new information but the new cultural diversity will be coming out of this new cuisine.

We are thinking as we are running. We are learning as we are creating. What an extraordinary collective experience! And this applies not only to the information technologies but to all areas of life being affected by economic interdependence, political shifts and the cultural redrawing of social maps. A new world is being built, one characterized by globality, which is something we do not properly understand as yet, and for the very reason that we are still building it.

Finding *convivencia*

To begin with, we need what I have called *convivencia*, capacity building to live together with a multiplicity of cultures and religions. There can be no sustainability without *convivencia*, as controversy over the environment has profusely demonstrated in the past few years.

In this transition, how are women to exercise their creativity most effectively? The answer, clearly, is by shaping and putting the new information and communication technologies to work from women's points of view to organize tomorrow's societies – except that, as never before in history, these societies will be globally linked.

A headline in the *Herald Tribune*, 18 May 1998, announced that a constellation of 66 satellites had just been put in place that could connect everyone in any corner of the world through the telephone system. This means that to the images which first gave us our initial feeling of belonging to one planet – the photographs of Earth taken from space, or the live coverage of events happening on the other side of the globe through TV cable networks – will now be added direct, personal, immediate contact, even through live images in the near future, with anyone in the world. Indeed, the Global Age has quietly been ushered in.

Women who have been forced to live in a confined space, in their houses or in their heads, get the shock we all received when suddenly facing images of other women freely organizing their lives with their partners, participating in political processes, and giving voice to their demands and dreams. This may be frightening if one's culture has no values to deal with cultural diversity, or with different ways of constructing gender between women and men. The first reaction, understandably, is one of fear and denial. In such a state women may take refuge behind their traditional customs and be manipulated easily by patriarchs or politicians afraid of losing their hold over them. Can virtual communication break down these new borders of cultural and gender fear?

Feminist challenges in the virtual world

As many of the chapters that follow confirm, the feminist challenges in the Webworld may be summarized in four points. First, women must not be left behind in the gap between those that have access to the new information technologies and those that do not. There is the danger of sliding into a world divided between the info-poor and the info-rich, with women, as we know only too well, ending up at the gates of technology and information.

Second, women should be active agents in ensuring that the star-like potential of information technologies is directed towards enhancing human well-being rather than strengthening existing power monopolies.

Third, the meanings of tomorrow must be created today and women, especially young women, now have greater freedom of spirit and of experience to be creative. As authors in other chapters also state, it is not only a question of having large numbers of women users of information technologies, but of their being partners with men in fashioning basic concepts and cyberspace.

Fourth, the possibilities that new forms of communication and expression have placed in our hands at this start of a millennium are awesome. It is up to us now to navigate them for our place-based knowledge and action.

A certain context is needed to be able to work in the direction just mentioned: democracy and human rights are important, but so is the freedom to create. This goes further than freedom of expression, because it implies the ability to overstep old frames of mind to create new values and to build new institutions.

Cyberspace will greatly accelerate our capacity to create and build. This will have important effects in encouraging women to participate in designing and implementing models of economic development, constructing stable democracies, ensuring that different cultures can exist side by side without violent conflict and providing the sense of trust, partnership and solidarity that are necessary to any society in which people cooperate for mutual well-being. Such a vision calls for women cyberzens who are rooted in their local cultures yet have a stake in national and global civil society. Will women@internet work in this direction?

In the last three centuries many things that seemed immutable have been changing: women were thought to have an 'eternal feminine nature', yet, as Galileo would have said, this so-called 'nature' seems to have moved; cultures were carved out in our minds to coincide with political borders, and yet cultures have shrunk and expanded borders; how do we build a frame of mind that starts out from reason and equality to define gender-balanced, cultural citizenships within and across nations in this new global *polis*? How do we strengthen resilient yet stable, complementary yet loving, relationships between genders, generations and communities? In any case, we have an extraordinary new tool with which to build all this. So read on. It is quite fascinating.

CYBORG MELODY

An Introduction to Women on the Net (WoN)

Wendy Harcourt

Introducing WoN

This book emerges from the cyberculture created by a group of women and men meeting together in cyberspace in the project Women on the Net (WoN), set up originally by the Society for International Development (SID) with UNESCO funding.[1] WoN had several aims. First, to encourage women, particularly in the South and in marginal groups in the North (and Central and East Europe), to use the Internet more easily as their space, thereby empowering women to use technology as a political tool. Second, to open up and contribute to the new culture that was being set up on the Internet from a gender perspective at once local and global. Third, to bring together individual women and men working from different institutional bases (women's NGOs, information technology networks, academe, women activists) to explore a transnational women's movement agenda in response to and shaping evolving telecommunication policies. And fourth, to create a resource (community and support) base which could be tapped into by different women's groups in terms of analysis, knowledge and skills in navigating the Internet.

The group is made up of individuals, many with strong institutional affiliations, who have been dialoguing with one another for just over one year. The main mechanism for communication has been a 'cyborg list' which was set up in mid-1997 following an initial meeting of members of the group in Santiago de Compostela, Spain.[2]

The term 'cyborg' has been borrowed loosely from Donna Haraway for whom this is:

a hybrid creature, composed of organisms and machine ... appropriate to

the late twentieth century ... made of, first, ourselves and other organic
creatures in our unchosen 'high-technological' guise as information systems
... and reproductive systems ... communication systems ... and self-acting,
ergonomically designed apparatuses (Haraway, 1991, p. 1).

The image lends itself to a group which communicates as women
through their computers in cyberspace. The second image of Haraway's
cyborg, the 'feminist cyborg,' is still being debated by the group. But in
the sense that both political, professional and personal lives are part of
the list's discussions there is certainly a strongly woman-centred and
gender-centred sense of identity being built on the list. The discussions
on technical and political agendas are intermixed with personal and
intimate histories and happenings. The frustrations of being women
working in a male environment are shared along with the pleasures: two
babies have been born during the group's existence and one more is
expected by the time the book is published. Health difficulties,
managing professional and political life with children, and new and old
partners are part of the culture being created, with an intimacy which
the solitary act of typing into a keyboard in front of a screen belies, but
which the image of cyborg embraces.

The book is one outcome of the discussions on the cyborg list, in
particular the meeting at Santiago and the preparations for a second
meeting at a conference on 'Gender and Globalization' in March 1998
at the University of California, Berkeley. The group is now developing
various working mechanisms to embark on other projects.

In over 2,000 messages sent and received as part of the cyborg list
between the Santiago and Berkeley meetings there have been some
fascinating conversations, particularly in preparation for moving from
cyberspace conversations to 'fleshly' conversations in Berkeley.

We present here a selection of these conversations leading up to the
Berkeley meeting in order to illustrate the type of culture that an
Internet dialogue produces. The dynamic which has evolved on the
cyborg list is somewhere between the personal, the political and the professional. There have been intense discussions over the crossing of
academic and activist knowledge terrain, over language and meanings,
over concepts, of place and identity. The lively discussion brought out
new ideas and concepts but most of all it created a dynamic – a cyborg
list culture – that helped people to start working together as a group,
communicating with one another as technicians, academics, activists and
UN professionals from nearly 40 countries.

In this introductory chapter we aim to give readers a sense of the
spirit of the discussions which underlie the chapters in the book. The
conversations map out some of the ways in which WoN is trying to

cross different boundaries: geographical, political, professional, spatial and personal. In a somewhat experimental style the chapter aims to combine a narrative with the direct e-mail speech of participants in the dialogue (most of whom contribute a chapter in the book). It is an experiment in the politics of communication as well – moving the e-mail conversations with their sense of immediacy and intimacy to the printed page – an experiment that challenges our traditional notions of writing and analysis in space and time.[3] The narrative aims to guide the reader through the dialogue while still capturing the different voices and therefore the richness of tone as well as ideas. Such a mix of styles aims to retain the sense of personal sharing and oral communication which the Internet uniquely generates.

Mediating borders

The conversation was generated around discussions at the second meeting the group held as part of a conference on 'Gender and Globalization' held at the University of California, Berkeley, early in 1998. The group had met once before in 1997 and the aim of the second meeting was to bring the sharing of experiences, conversations and enthusiasm of the first meeting to a new environment – women working in academe. This was a postmodernist conference of largely US-based feminist theorists, radically different from the majority of the group who are Southern-based or work in international contexts as activists or policy makers. Strong initial interest was expressed by both the Berkeley organizers and WoN, but also some concern about how these two worlds could meet usefully – as the conversation unfolded below indicates.

The discussion on the list serve kicked off with the description proposed by Marisa – a Mexican anthropologist doing her PhD in Berkeley, and myself – an Australian researcher living in Italy who was co-ordinating the group – for the agenda of the WoN workshop. The WoN workshop was to be conducted in two public sessions which would open the whole conference.

The first session was entitled 'Mediating the Borders' and would aim to open up a discussion on how the culture of feminists, ecologists, NGOs, indigenous groups, information technology, progressive groups, and migrant women is shifting traditional borders through cyberspace interactions. The discussion was to focus on the new forms of knowledge creation and communication linked to different political agendas, 'building on our collective knowledge of the challenges, ruptures and changes'.

The session would aim to look at processes of mediation and ventriloquism involving different women's voices on the Net, not only in 'patriarchal' cyberdiscourses but in those of theorists and the group itself. It would look at the construction and questioning of a theoretical framework to analyze cyberspace and women surfing into it, with a parallel analysis of concrete experiences. The key questions proposed were: 'Who is to speak or remain silent? How do we move in and out of theory strategically in order to respond to the changes in reality? How are women creating knowledge, forming circuits of meaning which defy academic classification? What boundaries are we feminists, ecologists and the like entitled to cross?

WoN's proposed second session on 'New Paradigms for Globalization' would look at how women and other social movements in their creative use of information communication technologies (ICTs) both defend and transform local cultures and how these strategies point the way towards a new paradigm of globalization.

From this initial posting a very vigorous debate emerged, first among the academics in the group – who quite possibly felt more comfortable with the language and space within which the conference was framed.

Marisa immediately suggested the notion of place as a way to frame the WoN sessions, moving away from the polarities she suspected might emerge between concepts of the local and the global in the Conference. In her message to the list she stated:

> I am thinking of concentrating on: place-consciousness, the socialized conception of place and overall the political use of global/local, space/ place con-fusions, parallel to a careful, microscopic analysis of the demands for going 'back into place'. I think that focusing this from a complex academic angle and also from our activist and institutional experience we will 're-conciliate' the visions of academia, activism and government institutions in the necessity of grounding our analysis and projects 'from below' but with a profound analysis of the many and various complications of the notions of place and reality. This may lead us to frame the analysis 'creating transformative spaces for alternative futures'. And through this, also help us to locate a hyphen, a mark (scar?) in this alternative (alter-native) and figure out what is 'other' (alter) and what is native (place-bound).[5]

Marisa immediately placed the group as border crossers in her postmodernist feminist style. **Arturo**, an anthropologist from Colombia also working in the US, responded by asking:

> I wonder how WoN/us will 'interface' with the more academic-oriented rest of the meeting. I am sure ... that our project will be welcome as a

much-needed practical side of their Conference.... One of the challenges facing our discussions in Berkeley ... is to examine how women's appropriation of the Internet counteracts or differs from the social/ cultural basis, practices and impacts of dominant uses of cyberspace and new information technology and information communication technology. For Virilio, for instance, new information technologies, in their reliance on real time, tele-communication at a distance, elimination of the 'here' and 'now', transform radically the nature of communication, space, time, life.[6] In Virilio's dystopian view, concrete places and peoples disappear, duration and extension are rendered meaningless. It is a powerful argument (not unmarked by a certain eurocentric and male perspective).

How shall WoN respond to global delocalization? Which practices are needed (of place, local culture, local/global connections, communities, etc.) to counteract the delocalizing tendencies of the new information technologies? How to balance 'activity and interactivity, presence and telepresence, existence and tele-existence'? Said differently, how to defend AND transform place, community and place-based cultures without the entrapment that they have often entailed for women?

Gillian, a British international political economist lecturing in communication at the University of Leicester set up a further area for discussion within the list, feminist versus masculinist ways of thinking:

The established feminist critiques and all the contradictions around long-established public/private debates in feminism should be central to radical thinking about the Net and women's/feminist possibilities. Masculinist philosophies of 'being' have in-built and if you like 'gendered' notions of time and space. My sense is that cyber possibilities require us to go back to some philosophical basics in this area and ask fundamental questions about how much women have actually worked to theorize time and space in their own interests. For me this is a fascinating theme which can be enhanced by the use of cyberspace to share and build new imaginings about potentially radical concepts and practices.... What I am concentrating on increasingly are the deeper philosophical implications of gendered articulations of space and time, particularly through the highly masculinist traditions of philosophy.... I want to think with other women working on the Net in various ways about its possibilities in this respect. Does the space it represents offer any new and radical challenges to these powerful masculinist forms of 'knowing'?...[7]

Translations

The debate had become quite intense, and confined to those who felt comfortable or not with abstract language and philosophy. There seemed to some, however, to be a danger of spinning off into abstractions that did not root the group's work clearly enough in the stated aim to empower women working in the South. There was considerable anxiety about discussing issues as activists and women of colour in an academic setting. People also voiced concern about the perils of using theory, given its links with imperialism and Western philosophical traditions.

Among the responses to the initial conversations involving Marisa, Gillian and Arturo – including some straightforward questions such as 'please translate' – was **Pi**, a technician working in Isis International–Manila, a feminist resource centre with a new but strong IT base.[8] Pi brought the debate back to the question of who is speaking, and for whom.

> I am quite torn about those big words that have been chosen to frame the discussion in Berkeley. Not that the way we have framed our discussion in Berkeley does not make sense to me, or is not relevant to my work. Definitely, 'Mediating Borders' is a good metaphor for the work we are doing.
>
> But 'we' are also different from one another. 'We' have different points of reference. The members and collaborators of WoN are women working in women's resource and information centres (mediating between local and national, regional and global, etc.), women working in international agencies (mediating between national and global, between academe and policy makers, etc.) women in academia (mediating between academe and the rest of civil society, etc.), women in Internet Service Providers (ISPs) (mediating between the Internet and information users, etc.), etc. Then there are also the men whose role in an initiative called 'Women on the Net' is presumed but not necessarily clear to everyone. (I don't mean the individual men who are already part of WoN, but men as a group. I raise this query in part because it is not clear to me how WoN will and should respond if other men would like to join the network.)
>
> We are also mediating borders inside WoN. Take, for example, some of the words used to frame the proposed Berkeley discussion: ventriloquism, patriarchal cyberdiscourses. Even the word cyborg, the name of our mailing list (cyborg and its connotation of a cyberspace inhabited by genderless, raceless, ageless, transformed identities may be fascinating but they are also potentially dangerous and retrogressive). These are words not normally used by individual women and women's groups I work with. Which, again, does not necessarily mean that they are not relevant to my context. Only, I have to 'mediate' between these words (literal, metaphor and all) and my context. What do these words evoke, provoke, invoke in me? What are their equivalents in my own tongue and symbolic world? Should I appropriate them, and why? As

'mediators of borders' we are asked to name, to describe, to abstract – powers that are not to be taken lightly. But we ourselves; that is, our own experiences are also constantly being named, described and abstracted by those who mediate other borders.

[Can we look] at the 'borders' being mediated within the group, and between WoN and the rest of the world (real-time and cyber)? Is it possible for us to arrive at a consensus about WoN's main focus of work?

Lis, from her work at the headquarters of a UN agency, added to that critique:

I have been following the deliberations on the Berkeley meeting with interest, and Pi's contribution gives me the impulse to react. I agree very much with her about how to focus the discussion. We work at different levels, and while being interested in theoretical debates, my main concern is now to make the link with the practical day to day lives and realities of women, some of whom don't even know yet that the Internet exists or what it could mean to them.

My main interest is ... to learn about the different uses of the Internet and how this medium serves and could serve for women's empowerment. Specifically, how to make the Internet useful (and accessible of course) for women in remote urban or rural areas of developing countries, and how they can make optimal use of the medium in support of their process of (economic) empowerment. Thus, I am looking very much forward to ... the exchange of experiences, to the dialogue and to strategizing on how to make this 'electronic empowerment' happen! (oops, what does this mean – do we want electronic empowerment as a means for political and economic empowerment? I am afraid I got into a theoretical issue).

Ventriloquism

The group then began to question quite seriously its use of language, the sense of inclusion and exclusion and the possibility of opening up a new way of dialoguing that could allow for diversity while building solidarity and identity.

To the question of defining the use of 'ventriloquism', **Marisa** responds:

We are using 'ventriloquism' in the context of our meeting at Berkeley to give a metaphor or an example to the 'performance of voices that are not ours'. A ventriloquist offers her/his body to the expression of the voices, concerns, dramas, etc. of others. This may be willingly so, in case of forms of representation (elected members of communities) or unwillingly, when you reproduce positions that you have not analyzed carefully. The Internet as a complex communication media may be used productively as another vehicle to ventriloquism in both senses. Are we as users conscious of both: our ventriloquist techniques (active circulation of our voice through others' cyberspace) and our ventriloquized selves (passive impersonation of others' concerns)? I guess what I want to stress is the actual circulation in cyberspace of information without a body, which can be appropriated for many uses. In this precise case 'ventriloquism' alludes to the politics of voice and impersonation of 'voices'.

It is the same old story of kidnapping others' voices or reproducing others' concerns, disregarding politics of place-based experiences, which may be swallowed by such powerful media as the Internet. Thank you very much for asking: sometimes academia does not give us a break in the invention of meta-meta-phors (for who? from whom? what for?)

Some of the discussions stimulated by the list happened outside the main forum, especially those involving participants who felt intimidated by the language being used, and needed encouragement to come on-line. A very poignant contribution came from **Kekula**, an indigenous woman activist with a strong technical and lobbying background.[9]

In this discussion ... I sense an old paradigm encounter which I would like to be able to comprehend ... I've struggled with academia [in order] to challenge the borders, recognizing the gap as a large part of our problem (globally). I need messages loaded with academic terminology when it is thick to [be interpreted] for me in my own poetic language so I can understand where the discussion or people themselves are coming from. This does give life, appreciation and light to a world I thought was without.

The general concern I speak of is the boundaries academia has presented throughout the colonial period of our existence as indigenous peoples. It was our very first encounter across the board with colonial settlers which were missionaries. Their Bible was the academic imposition (because it was taught like a classroom) upon traditional spirituality, practices and belief systems, coupled with a new language. These impositions created a negative IQ upon native thinking and immediately what were ancient astronomers became heathen and unintelligent. That is the origin of the thought and becomes the neocolonial framework today upon which a Western system is built.

On this same timeline now we have encountered Internet technology which creates the very first window to escape that imposition. My own thoughts only. Where thinkers meet scholars, actors activists and indigenous, Western level communication, creating a new level to the political, social, economic and cultural framework – now crossing regions.

Education must come in innovative and creative ways, with relevant objectives and the desire to overcome challenges. The categories we encounter, both positive and negative are: (a) survival and vision; (b) utilization and access; (c) education and development; (d) stable infra-structure; and (e) economic empowerment. Often the utilization of Inter-net communications has been slowed not only due to concepts and economics, but indigenous perspectives and the neocolonial experience.

When Arturo asks: 'How shall WoN respond to global delocalization?' he points to my own indigenous concern/fear in the 'academic-oriented rest' because I also know that through an appropriate or inspiring interaction and hopeful interface we can bridge the gaps.... I also fear the encounters if I do not understand them, and have been often in that seat at the UN or formal regional study groups. This was my training ground as a delegate of our independence movement and as a member of the UN global indigenous caucus.

I am trying to develop a position on this in a grassroots manner of thinking. I can learn terminology – but how do I bridge terminology and inspire a meeting of it? WoN has definitely taken up the same challenge, and I am Amazed. I am looking very forward to bringing recognition to it as we develop these relationships.

... I am looking for interpretation of the concerns Arturo raises ... so that I can explore my own global indigenous position to add to it, to bridge within it, if needed and to counter what is conflictual in that world for my work which endeavours to break free....

... I relate to Marisa's 'ventriloquism' in a very feminist sense. The uses of the technology has opened up the creative minds of women to be free – I shy away from or combat, competitiveness, protectiveness and barriers of academia. I want to interact with other women on-line to establish a space very shortly that has the power to challenge the actual system of the world and impress global change in our own women's collective direction....

Another person who felt disconcerted for different but equally strong political reasons, working in the Americas, was **Laura** from Argentina, who for many years travelled the world working with migrant women and sex workers.[10]

The recent messages on the list have made me a bit nervous.... Obviously we can't all speak or understand the same way, I hope we are not dreaming about a utopian 'unity.' On the other hand I don't like being in the position of having to ask 'What does that mean?' over and over. My heart seems to go somewhere else while I read such things. If I say that, will some people feel they need to 'silence' themselves?

Pi says:

These are words not normally used by individual women and women's groups I work with. Which, again, does not necessarily mean that they are not relevant to my context. Maybe they are relevant, but I don't like to divide myself up in pieces that talk one way in one place and another in another. And knowing I can't talk this way with my friends is alienating to me.

Kekula says:

I am trying to develop a position on this in a grassroots manner of thinking. I can learn terminology – but how do I bridge terminology and inspire a meeting of it? Most of the women I am working with don't know about the Internet. Many don't have telephones in their countries of origin or access to telephones abroad. They are not 'indigenous' and are only written about in the *New York Times* as 'victims of trafficking' or 'carriers of HIV'.

In a later message Laura continued to question 'thick language' and to underline the need for translations:

I believe the issue is not whether we have a job in the academy or a job on the street but whether we can understand each other at the most fundamental level, where the specific words we use *can* be chosen. I hear two problems being addressed within this: unfamiliar vocabulary and concepts, and abstract thinking.

The unfamiliar words problem should be easily adjusted. A chemist doesn't use her most technical words to explain what she does to a non-scientist. On this list we have people who don't know what words like 'dystopic' mean, and I was one of them. I believe it's better for people who 'have' words like that to try to find replacements for them when talking with those that don't – making a conscious effort as part of their work – than for everyone else to be confused, stop listening, or asked to interrupt constantly to ask 'What does that mean?' Isn't this what we do kindly when talking to someone who is a beginner at our own language? We slow down and choose easier words.

There is a power relationship in these situations, it isn't just about diversity. I will not interrupt over and over to say 'I don't follow or understand' because I don't want to feel like a student with a professor or like an ignorant person with a more intelligent one.

The second problem, about abstract thinking, doesn't have such an easy solution, and that's where we have to tolerate and accept differences. People who have never been to school haven't learned to 'tell a story in order', they tell it in circles, they repeat or skip things. More 'educated' people who expect a clear chronology (line) perceive this as faulty, but it's the way the person thinks. Those who think abstractly often can't easily give concrete examples of what they mean.

Both Kekula and Laura raise the issue of heart and head, of knowing and not knowing and of feeling excluded and silenced. **Marisa** pushed these feelings further, returning to her metaphor of ventriloquism:

> Maybe we need more discussion centred in the erasures of 'place' and 'here' (Escobar/Virilio), by global and the 'now.' Ventriloquism stresses the politics of voice and the erasure of body and with it location and also compression of time, speed, place. In Gillian's words: 'How much have women worked to theorize time and place in their own interests?' We will give evidence at the conference of the possibility of using the Internet to locate and underline 'women' questions and responses in precise places. We will show how time and place may be 'gendered', with the use of high tech. I love it, the most difficult of the assignments ever (Third World women voices circulating) done by the most sophisticated technique.

Marrying the technical, the theoretical and the practical

In these conversations an emerging sense of community and identity within the group started to emerge, with the different groups – academics, activists and technical people – willing to offer new ideas, to react to responses and to open up spaces for diversity, acknowledging the power differentials and the personal needs while still staying with the political project of creating a new culture on the Internet. Following these exchanges, more people came in offering their points of view.

Marie-Hélène was the coordinator of a women's programme in Synergie Genre et Développement (SYNFEV-ENDA)[11] a large environmental and community NGO in Senegal:

> I am very impressed by the issue of translation from the 'thick theoretical/conceptual language' to poetic comprehension from Kekula as well as the connection between the conceptual discussion and the daily lives of the women in Asia as Pi says! [There is] a need for translation, in my ... case from English to French as English is not my mother tongue and I am very far from understanding the whole meaning of a loaded conceptual discussion in English (I would even say that even if it were in French I would not be at my ease [as] I do not have an academic profile). But I see now that 'translation' may have very other meanings than 'simply' going from one language to another.

Nidhi, an East African now living in Canada as an advocate and activist, added, along the same lines:[12]

I think the last few comments on language are very important. If I am honest, my eyes tend to skip past those passages which I deem either to be too 'academic/theoretical' which is probably one of the reasons why I loved biology but couldn't fathom physics, or where I perceive the details to be beyond my immediate interests.

The Berkeley meeting could be a challenge because (I may be wrong of course) the rest of the programme within which our workshop is situated will most probably be heavily academic, Western (Californian) biased, and it will be important I think that we can bond to ensure that whatever we put across is a message which is tangible and relevant to us as women and that we see Berkeley and the context that it has situated as an opportunity (rather than as a threat) for us to put across that message.

This assumption does mean ... that we should continue to use this medium to air our interpretations and meanings and to realize that we are a diverse group plucked out, as it were, from thin air.

If by carrying on the conversations for the next four weeks, we progress towards a marriage of the technical with the theoretical and the practical, then that will be four weeks well used and we can use Berkeley for other things.

The dynamic of the conversation picked up as the academics who had initiated the conversations ventured in again to help with this marriage of the technical, theoretical and practical. Gillian, in an intensely personal statement, brought out how women can find ways to communicate in a new way on the Internet which can be political, personal and public:

Dualisms of emotion and thought are fascinatingly central to the incredible conversations on the list about this problem of 'understanding' and the 'academic' in the last few days. One of the areas which our project can explore because of the people involved is the pain and potential of such situations. Knowledge boundaries, it seems to me, count in such complex ways in the operation of the contemporary global economy and our whole understanding of 'knowledge' needs so much more work.

I would feel very sad if anyone thought that my comments identify me as someone locked in a world of academic non-communication.... I spend a large chunk of my life working with women and others in various ways on the Net and via e-mail and the amount of time I am using complicated academic language is tiny. Communicating is what it is all about for me, sharing why and how we are doing what we are doing, the problems we face, and the ideas we can collaborate on. Learning about one another and the lives we lead and their diverse meanings is what I'm here for.

The incredible exchanges about language in the last few days moved me intellectually as well as emotionally.... I find it hard to separate my practical desires and imaginings from my intellectual and emotional ones, I have all my life, and that's why academic life and its different dimensions including teaching and educational teamwork as well as thinking, sharing ideas and writing, is comfortable for me. There are important ways that I feel at home in it. It is not an abstract realm to me, it is very practical in so many ways....

The Net is highlighting and challenging multiple knowledge boundaries, including those dividing women on so many bases. Communication is not something I assume. I know it has to be worked at and I feel that this is what we are doing as part of this project. We cannot assume we understand one another whether we use complicated or simple language. There are many barriers to understanding even between people with similar ideas working on a joint venture like this.

... I feel I am striving with others for 'voices' to be heard to produce collectively possibilities which might not otherwise be imagined. For me there are theory/practice dimensions to this. I consider practice and engage in it as well as reading and thinking about historical forms, particularly of feminist theory, and more recent forms. I find this productive and exciting. It is part of what makes me feel alive, including in academia where I share such sentiments with colleagues who have chosen and often fought for such a life for similar reasons.

Arturo also came in with:

It is worrisome, if not sad, to know that many academics produce knowledge that fails to transform anything, including their lives. At the same time, I do not think theoretical/'academic' knowledge is necessarily disembodied and disembedded from reality. For me, producing theory about the world and about concrete situations is an intensely emotional, even bodily, process. I never understood those who insist that it (abstract knowledge) is only a product of the mind.... Perhaps because I believe that there is another way of thinking about our intellectual work as a political practice, one that is not delinked from the world and that seeks to transform it, in conjunction with those who are actively engaged in struggles to do just that. In the ethics of transformation is where we meet – and this might encompass physicists as well as biologists, peasants as well as ecologists, indigenous peoples as well as their NGO allies (even if the meeting place, as Gillian also says, always has to be constructed and its terms consciously thought out). Perhaps it was Nidhi who said that it is from a position of self-confidence (and strength, actually) that WoN practitioners have to approach the Berkeley encounter with an academic world that will hopefully understand and support our efforts.

At this point, in my own contribution as coordinator, I reviewed what was being said on language, politics and reaching out across borders from a personal perspective:

I too, like Gillian and Arturo, feel challenged and moved. The bridging/ crossing of these borders is precisely what I spend my life doing in the SID and my feminist work as an intellectual by inclination, forever pulling myself down to the ground. It is very exciting to have this dilemma erupting so spontaneously in this group which Nidhi says is pulled from thin air. Well, not quite – I think there have been connections that do weave from concrete meetings and exchanges of ideas and recognition of potential ways to work together. My image is rather of circles, or of throwing a stone in a lake and watching the circle widen and increase. Or the wind blowing with many voices intertwined and trying hard to hear and bring them together. Or of finding a political space which is both local and global/feminine and safe.

I see we are trying hard to listen and respect our differences – careful to involve cultural with practical with abstract, and to see that we all have different strengths. I am very glad to see how we are translating to each other, trying to use different languages and not trying to impose any particular approach. As Laura says, it is a question not of new voices but of listening to those who are speaking. And if we can explore and go deeper as a group learning from the other, not afraid and being able to ask, that is the most important thing.

I don't want to flow too much on all that is said – the temptation is to try and be more poetic in order to respond to Kekula's message (it is how I felt after Santiago when I wrote that poem on our meeting) – but it is hard to marry technical, theoretical and activist knowledge without searching for another way to do it. What I did want to do is suggest ways we can prepare for Berkeley as well as having this free flow and sharing.

I appreciate the honesty of Gillian and Arturo and Marisa, who are the academics in this group, who for me are far from boring but super inspiring, building of others and also vulnerable.

The message was also about coordinating the meeting and in that I also wanted to start to visualize the concrete place:

For the public event I am trying to get a sense of that space the academics among us know better. Marisa described the room as a beautiful one with a view of the sea and we would sit in a half circle in front of the audience. Which I think I am right in saying could be up to 250 people.... This is daunting for all of us, but all of us are thinkers and writers and have things to say, and this audience is opening out the hands and minds to us so we can accept that we have authority and things to share and say. We are coming as guests and equals and in a strong group. So we should put aside our fears and enjoy learning and meeting others, even if US Western academics – though I don't know if that is entirely true – in spirit they are feminist and that is the positive beginning. We after all begin the show, and it is not ours to worry about: we are important contributions – the delicatessen, to use the evocative language of Marisa (for me an image of the corner shop with all the delicious things to see and eat from around the world, a very safe but spicy idea).[13]

Moving to the poetic and political

Interestingly, the language and dynamic of the group had moved in the course of a few weeks from abstract concepts and setting meeting agendas to more poetical, personal and political language. Also, as Berkeley was approaching, we were trying to grapple with how we could meet 'in the flesh' and beyond our cyberspace-determined conversations. There was, though, a marked excitement and a sense of pooling difficulties as a group, which stayed with participants as they found a way to communicate across boundaries. This spirit is evident in the last conversations recorded here. Tellingly, the sign-offs to each posting became more individualized and personalized – with a switch to sending love and warm wishes and descriptions of home life and the weather in an attempt to share more vividly people's 'here' and 'now'.

Fatma from the NGO Resource Centre, writing from what she affectionately calls her 'steaming island of Zanzibar' enters the debate with the comment:[14]

It is rare that I use the cyborg as I am overwhelmed at the kind of information that goes to and fro.... I want to say that my most innovative and stimulating work has been as a result of my interaction with academics on the one hand and the grounded community on the other hand. When I say academics I mean intellectuals who have NOT remained in ivory towers of theories that never plays a part in mobilizing communities or impacting change.

In Tanzania we have renowned intellectuals who have radical ideas but have failed miserably to create a viable force for economic or social enhancement of the nation and as a result leadership too. We remain with this group of academicians who rub shoulders with leaders who have failed miserably and continue to invite World Bank and IMF to 'solve' our problems when the people know where the problem lies. As a result on the one hand we have a highly intellectual/academic exercise nationwide (debates-press), so an outsider gets impressed at where we are as a nation, and on the other hand we have empty vessels of the common people who know what they do not want – poverty.

In this scenario, then, who mobilizes and who are the agents of change – alliance of what I see as popular democratic forces – these are organized groups at community level, like health, education etc., musicians, artists, intellectuals who write from the pulse of people's plight (activists), media personnel, medical field whereby they debate on medical ethics and human rights and take on the corporate world, land issues activists, violence against women campaigners, parliamentarians who dare to ask questions although they are within the system and non-corrupt leaders (few but they are there).

Now my dears I have spoken of my country and analyzed it as I see it. I am on the cyborg. What does this make me? A journalist, an IT freak? An intellectual? a feminist? – you got it! We have to move out of compartmentalization and incorporate a movement with a pulse and feel the ripples and if we are to be the delicatessen so be it!

Fatma brought home the need to establish a multiple and flexible identity within the list. **Erika**, a trainer and communication technician working in a women's resource group in Mexico, continues with enthusiasm:

I've so appreciated and enjoyed the exchange on the different ways we communicate, translate, mediate, think, dream.... I particularly identify with what Pi and Laura expressed, but, unlike Laura, I am not nervous about the Berkeley meeting – our sharing demonstrates just how rich our time together can be, and, as many have said, how diverse we are. Our respect for each other and the different worlds we move in, and our attempts to listen, have also been quite eloquently expressed. All of this energizes me for our time together in planning sessions in Berkeley and takes away nervousness.... Reading everything that people have said about bridges and borders and our different styles of expression, as well as the different worlds we move in, made me recall how I felt going into the Santiago meeting. I remember when I first received the initial invitation to Santiago to explore the meaning of women and cyberculture. I was fascinated with Wendy's description of the agenda and what the meeting would accomplish. I was particularly fascinated with the term 'cyber-culture' and anxious to gain a deeper understanding of what it could mean. This is because I have great difficulty finding time to get beyond my daily activities of getting women interested in Internet, getting them on-line, giving user support in less-than-ideal connectivity situations, training, etc. I seldom have the time or energy – and certainly I lack some elements – to connect my daily practice to a deeper reflection or theoretical debate. The workshop represented a challenge for me to be less practical and, perhaps, more creative and imaginative in my thinking about Internet and a forming cyberculture. In part, when we were called together to reflect on 'women and cyberculture' I anxiously awaited 'the answers' from an academic/philosphical/theoretical standpoint. I was surprised when a lot of our time was dedicated to hearing about women getting on-line in very diverse situations – the nuts and bolts of MY work – and in general so many of us in so many different regions facing the same problems (women don't have telephones – let alone computers – where we are working, yet women are getting on-line and doing incredible things). It was great to hear about all of those experiences (and hearing them also helped me validate more my own work) but I still had trouble seeing in a more philosophical and critical way the larger concept of women and cyberculture, and felt we barely scratched the surface. (After all – it was only one day!) I mean to say, it was clear that those who are more academically focused were interested and able to learn a lot from those who are doing, for example, trainings, and vice versa. Again, we all wanted to go deeper and further and the book that everyone is working on so diligently is an expression of that. I quite look forward to it because I hope it will give me more perspectives for reflection.

I'm interested in WoN precisely because of the way our diverse work can inform each and all of us in our development of ideas and on-the-ground practice, and how we can turn that all around to have a broader impact. However, from my understanding of the Berkeley schedule, there will be very limited time to hear about more 'case studies' as Lis mentions (the practice side) and also limited time to check in and see what we are all understanding about women and cyberculture as a concept, and Women on the Net's mission. Nidhi's suggestion to take advantage of our time on-line before Berkeley is important, and it is great to see us doing that.

... Amazingly I live and breathe Internet but participating in a list as active and thought-provoking as this is difficult. I no sooner get one message redacted in my brain to you all than the debate roars on before I can hit Queue. (Do you all have Queues in your brains?) I liked the way you helped me to visualize the Berkeley event, Wendy – it made the whole agenda come alive! It will be quite fun if we can have a riotous presentation and time while we are there, as Fatma says.

The final comment comes from **Alice**, working in New York and unable to travel to Berkeley:[15]

These discussions are making me feel all the more sorry that I will miss the Berkeley meeting! Erika's point about rarely having time for reflection is one that I share and one which is often overlooked. I was thinking about just that when I read Erika's message. In my years at the International Women's Tribune Centre, the practical demands of the work made it extremely difficult to find places and opportunities for reflection. The fact that our discussions are related to technology adds another dimension. Because the practical problems with using information and communications technologies are often so daunting, getting beyond them is a challenge. I also think people often see practical (or technical) people and thinking people as two different types. I disagree (my mother is a scientist, artist, gardener, among other things, so I have always resisted these kinds of distinctions): it is a matter of finding the space to put them together.

I admit to having some of the same reactions as others expressed when the discussion got more theoretical – I get the feeling that I have had in the past – that I have forgotten how to reflect and to see the work in its larger context. The problem is that I often feel this as a personal shortcoming rather than something that I think is actually an issue for many activists. Meetings like Berkeley can be a good antidote. I have found that to participate in encounters with people who don't do quite the same things I do, or who are working in different contexts – but who share some common ideas and philosophies and commitments – are those which are most enriching. This is how I would characterize our group.

And this all points back to how, with new technologies, we are finding ways around these dilemmas and barriers/borders that keep diverse ideas and people from having the opportunity to collide, change and grow. Now if we can only keep it up....

Epilogue

Many of the ideas raised in this dialogue resurface in the book – so do keep on reading – and of course were debated in Berkeley and are continuing to be explored on the cyborg list. The point of the chapter, though, has been to introduce some of the dynamics, the different voices and tones, and the sense of striving to create new ways of communicating that the Internet is opening up for people in this group. It was an exciting series of conversations. But the tantalizingly fast conversation flung around the globe on list serves can be a trap – as you type into the screen, thinking you are having conversations, in fact you are communicating in quite a particular way as a 'cyborg', missing many cues that personal communication provides. In Berkeley new 'fleshly' dynamics were created that were intense and challenging about differential access to power and knowledge and silences within the group – all part of a loss of innocence and a growth that is no doubt required for such a group to maintain its dynamism.

Putting together this book has been part of the first phase of the group – its sharing of experiences, analysis and visions on new forms of communication in cyberculture that can embrace the political, professional and personal levels. We hope you enjoy reading about the experiences and experiments individual members of WoN are creating in cyberculture.

NOTES

1 As well as thanking all the members of the WoN project for their support in the making of this book, I wish to thank Gillian Youngs and Marisa Belausteguigoitia Rius in particular for their comments on this chapter and tremendous support throughout this voyage in cyberspace. A very special thank you also goes to Elena Mancusi-Materi for her careful and hard work on the manuscript – without her this book would not have happened. Three other people have been vital from the start: Lourdes Arizpe, whose brilliance and inspiration gave birth to the entire project; Paola Leoncini-Bartoli, whose busy and cheerful attention to the project kept it ticking along between Paris and Rome; and Lamis Alshejni, whose truly sisterly support made sure the WoN project has continued.

2 The name was adopted first by Sophia Huyer, who has managed the list serve and who has a keen interest in Donna Haraway's work, shared by several of the researchers in the group.

3 Continuing the conversations, Gillian Youngs on reading the introduction contributed this comment related to the politics of communication:

> Reading through the conversation again the cybermoments and thoughts came back to me, the sense of others in our group, of questions about their perspectives on all the ideas expressed. The political immediacy of our communications endeavour was relived. And it reminded me starkly that WoN is one example of how new forms of cyberpolitics create their own times and spaces and that these are concrete in our memories as well as our activities and agendas. It also made me wonder how these conversations, transferred from their times and spaces on to the printed page, would communicate to others reading the book. This is of course a crucial dimension of the wider cyberpolitical potential of endeavours such as WoN's and stresses the importance of the ongoing and expanding 'conversations'.

4 In her comments on the chapter Marisa Belausteguigoitia Rius recalls how complicated it was for her to navigate daily the reactions of the two groups and how the concept of 'delicatessen', became a metaphor for these manoeuvres between the US ivory tower of knowledge and the cyber women entering its gates.

5 Belausteguigoitia Rius raises these issues in Chapter 1 in this volume, in her observations of Mexican shifts in lifestyle.

6 For more on Virilio, see Escobar in Chapter 2 and also Inayatullah and Milojevic in Chapter 5 of this volume.

7　Issues which Youngs raises in depth in Chapter 3 of this volume.

8　See Bautista, Chapter 13 in this volume, for a description of how Isis International is opening up the cyberworld in Asia.

9　A description of Netwarriors and Kekula Bray-Crawford's work in the Liquid Continent can be found in Chapter 12 of this volume.

10　See Agustín in Chapter 10 of this volume on the issues migrant women are encountering in their lives and the potential of technology for them.

11　See Tandon in Chapter 9 of this volume for a description of SYNFEV-ENDA's work.

12　See Tandon in Chapter 9 of this volume for more on her work.

13　Again, in continuing the conversation on reading the chapter Marisa gives a much more profound reading of 'delicatessen':

> Wendy, fortunately the 'delicatessen' metaphor erupted and showed many different layers of its meaning. I did use it ironically and not to show 'diversity' and exoticism but specific forms of representation and capture, the way women of color may be made exotic and semi-tokens. We study and we deconstruct that and sometimes we use it in our favour. Of course the context of the conference could not be compacted in one single intention, this is Berkeley. But the delicatessen syndrome is – in the US – very powerful, so much so that academics are devoting programmes, lives to study and unpack it.

This is an interesting comment also in relation to the Conclusion of this book.

14　See Alloo in Chapter 11 of this volume for a description of her past and current work.

15　See Gittler in Chapter 6 of this volume for a description of her activities.

PART ONE

Moving from Cyberspace to Cyberculture

THIS FIRST SECTION sets out the analytical questions explored in the book as the authors examine the new cultures being created in cyberspace by women's groups on the Net. From the Cyborg Melody we already have a sense of the types of theoretical issues concerning the group – including the relationship between theory and activism and between academe and other forms of knowledge. Part One asks whether women working on the Internet are indeed challenging male ways of knowing and in doing so breaking the traditional silence of women in public discourse. This part also looks critically at the implications of women learning the 'master tools' to create new languages and new vision as potentially skilled users of the cyberworld.

As Internet is such a new sphere the chapters focus as much on the questions as on providing answers. All of the authors are intrigued by what the Internet might offer women's groups working for alternative knowledge systems. At the same time they convey a deep sense of unease about the travellers women encounter in the corridors of cyberspace, the asymmetries of access to the cyberworld and the sheer power of global technocapitalism. Even as they warn that the mystery and surrounding hype has to be stripped away, there is a sense of enthusiasm and hope for a new type of communication and culture to be found on the Internet that can build and support women's political work. The chapters capture the sense of a new engagement among women's groups as they network, weave different worlds and bring their culturally place-based knowledge to others through the medium of the Internet.

Marisa Belausteguigoita Rius introduces the dangers, mysteries and fascinations cyberspace offers as it changes into a cyberculture that unravels local traditions in ways that include or exclude women. Her analysis takes in the varieties of today's female cyborg – hamburger flipper, little girls playing with Barbie dolls masquerading as Aztec warriors, the 15-year-old Mexican peasant girl clad in jeans and T-shirt ritually unwrapping the computer and modem as her dowry/passport into cyber womanhood, and the Chiapas women silenced in the WWW campaign of their people's cause. Her chapter brings out the importance of women needing to be in command of their cyberdreams so that they are speaking in their voices rather than others impersonating them. Arturo Escobar has a similar vision of the need for women to be engaged in the 'meaning making of techno-scientific world building'. He looks at the transnational movements – women, ecologists and political intellectuals – who are deploying cyberspatial technologies in the networking and defence of the politics of place. He argues that the use of the Internet to help in the alternative construction of politics, knowledge and identity can only occur if it is embedded in struggles which provide the reasons for this global networking. Cyberculture, for him, connects people to the real world of political resistance through a virtual envisioning of how gender and ecological relations can be transformed.

Gillian Youngs in her contribution sees the Internet as a place where women can share knowledge across boundaries, creating safe environments which disrupt the public/private divides. She sees virtual space as a communicative space that could provide an environment that enables women to move beyond male domination. Cyberculture then becomes an extension of women's historical work together, building on knowledge of diverse women's lives and taking into account the different positions from which they are speaking, while at the same time helping them to form a social location which invites new links and associations.

Silvia Austerlic, working on the cutting edge of virtual knowledge creation techniques, indicates how the Internet can be seen as a 'culture of design' in the envisioning of new worlds and innovative communication. She looks at the complex management required to create a new cyberculture that would include women and men from the Third World, beginning with the need for education and a knowledge base that enables people to use cyberculture to design new lives. Sohail Inayatullah and Ivana Milojevic underscore the insidious side of the Net and the Web. They are deeply cautious about the potential for exclusion and silencing, particularly of the people living in cultures already perceived by the elites as marginal. They ask how can these people and others engage in global conversations without losing their identities? For them a cyberculture has to be open to communication between all cultures, in order to become a 'gaia of cultures' allowing for a multiplicity of voices and not a monologue of cybertech speak.

CROSSING BORDERS
From Crystal Slippers to Tennis Shoes

Marisa Belausteguigoitia Rius

Potentials and resistance

The challenges that new technologies such as cyberspace are posing for women need to be framed by two overlapping scenarios. The first depicts the many related problems that the politics of access to new technologies presents and the second the diverse forms of resistance that women all over the world have constructed *vis-à-vis* this communication medium.

The basic challenges that women have had to face to create, sustain and circulate their versions of her/histories in their own languages – and against systems of interpretation, kidnapping and ventriloquizing of their voices – are much older than the invention of computers, modems and superhighways. The problem is related not only to gaining access to this technology despite new gatekeepers who restrict access through old prejudices and 'oppressive' orders in new disguises, but also to the ways in which women use this medium. New technologies have readapted and reinforced systems for capturing the voices at the margins so smoothly that the systems have escaped notice along with the voices. In this way the political question of access to the knowledge offered by new technologies of information is masked by a carnival of so-called communication possibilities. In the history of the oppression of women, gays, slaves, colonies, and any other group on the margins of society, the instruments of the 'master' – language, tools, and concepts – have consolidated different types of subordination, but also forced the creation of zones of resistance.

It is on these sometimes fragile but always productive zones of resistance that I would like to focus in this chapter. Resistance does not mean rejection of access to the new technologies of communication, as this would be suicidal. It means a cautious, conscious and microscopic approach to the new form in which language is being used and communication is being deployed, and the new ways in which women are interpellated to form part of this Internet cybersociety. Resistance may also respond to the way in which technical commands are given; the polemic established between 'easy to use' technologies and technologies of control; the diverse gatekeepers that select, delete and connect cybernauts; asymmetries between cyberspace zones of information in the Northern and Southern hemispheres; and, finally, the problems posed by the politics of access and use, with vectors of difference such as race, gender, class and sexuality.

We need to do more than empower women to use this technology and convince them that it is available to them. In general it is not. This new technology has to be conquered and it will not be conquered only by increasing the number of users. The master's cybertool needs to be deconstructed and dismantled in order to be used not only by female cyborgs expert in technical languages, but also by subjects that are capable of interpreting multiple systems of mediation, translation, impersonation and representation of the voices of 'others'.

Adopting a vision from below

Parallel to the notion of resistance – this microscopic approach to macroscopic technologies – we need to develop user-experts conscious of and sensitive to the problems of appropriation and representation. The 'I' that travels within cyberspace is not the Cartesian 'I'. The 'I' of the cyborg, half-machine and half-person, is never monolithic. The technologies that are constituted from above need users trained in adjusting the powers of the 'vision from below' (Haraway, 1991, pp. 188–96).

Cyberspace needs to be invaded and conquered by systems that allow the constant and differential repositioning necessary to 'see from below'. Cyberspace, as used by female cyborgs, needs systems of language and communication that represent the 'standpoint of the subjugated' (Haraway, 1991, p. 193). Women who are different in class, race, sexuality, nationality, age, physical ability and religious affiliation need to be represented inside the languages that cyberspace is producing. Cyberspace needs to be transformed into cyberculture, into an infinite number of ways of representing diversity.

Challenging the transnational

This challenge is particularly hard since transnational economic models have created an illusion of diversity and multiculturalism totally devoted to the reinforcement of the market and the technologies of buy and sell. In relation to the possibilities of open markets, to the expectancies of accumulation of capital and multiplication of corporations that control nations, cyberspace could not possibly be more diverse. The global adapts to the local: 'think globally, act locally'. Barbie changes colours, varies the texture and forms of garments (but never hips and waist dimensions or facial lines) to represents diversity and multiculturalism: Barbie dressed as a Mongolian, Barbie impersonating a Zapotec woman, Barbie dressed as 'Adelita' or Indian women.

There is an intimate connection between the mechanisms of transnational models of capital and capital accumulation, and the way cyberspace functions. Information travels without regard for national borders and state controls; corporations settle in export zones and camouflage their products with the local culture at hand; cybernauts impersonate the voiceless and are experts in the most sophisticated technologies of ventriloquism. Welfare states are leeched away in the process of dissolution that impacts on groups of disenfranchised women. It transforms the workforce into 'maquiladoras' and those who find formal employment in the transnational export zones. The mechanism of cyberspace, its fluency and time-space compression, mirrors the transnational models of capital accumulation offering illusions of democracy, opportunity and agency for some. But the cyborg is not generally the person sitting in front of the computer, half-machine, half-subject, wondering about the 'power to see from below' (Sandoval, 1995). The cyborg is the 'other', flipping hamburgers and talking the 'cyborg speech' of McDonalds.

Fleshly encounters

The SID/UNESCO workshop 'Women and Cyberculture' allowed for the presentation of diverse experiences related by women as users and entrepreneurs of cyberspace services and advantages.[1] The participants felt empowered and encouraged by many of these accounts. They learnt and probably adapted and implemented some of these successful events in personal or public environments. Other accounts made us shiver, situating treasured romantic or utopian missions in more complicated scenarios. In this chapter I want to share presentation of two of these accounts. Neither gives rise simply to a shiver or a celebration; rather, both are experiences which mingle hope and confidence with pain and distrust. One happened in the North, the other at the southern border of Mexico.

Transformation of the *quinceañera* to cyber debutante

In early 1997 I travelled to Mexico in order to obtain the visa that would bring me to Santiago de Compostela, Spain. I needed to cross the border and process my visa in one of the Mexican interstices, those liminal zones of resistance and also of market opportunism: Tijuana, right at the border between Mexico and the US. In the endless queue of people standing in the sun at the American consulate, I met a peasant who worked in the fields in San Diego County, Rancho San Bernardo. As happens many times in queues and in Mexico, I was invited to a party. His daughter was going to celebrate her fifteenth birthday. In Mexico and more so in rural areas, becoming 15 years old is a big event. Families spend years of savings to honour guests and the debutante. Cinderella-like dance performances with 15 charming *chambelanes* (male dance companions) are orchestrated. *Chambelanes* are requested to wear a tuxedo, dance and court the *quinceañera*, who is dressed in pink, yellow or blue. Her hair is tied in a bun with blue ribbons that could touch the sky, resembling her dreams. These parties normally mean a presentation of the daughter to society. The ritual represents a developing woman, ready to marry.

I arrived at the party and began to look for the *quinceañera* in some sort of anthropological, moved but also troubled way. I was waiting to see her emerge from a cloud of dry ice. No clouds emerged, no blue dress appeared, no *chambelanes* dressed in tuxedos to court her through the room. She was dressed in black pants, her black hair loose over her shoulders. Black tennis shoes were worn instead of the feminine crystal slippers. I arrived precisely at the moment when her father was about to give her the present that normally represents her entrance into society as a female. The room went silent as two men carried two big boxes. Amanda confidently walked to the centre of the room and began to unpack her present. From the distance I saw what appeared as a cord, metal, a rectangular device, a square artifact, a screen: a computer with modem (I learned later)!

What does it take to change crystal slippers for tennis shoes, what does it take to transform a rite of passage ending in marriage into a cyberritual of entry into other structures of knowledge, power, language and life? Well-financed public schools? An alternative curriculum? A feminist father? A border? A sensitive teacher?

The story of the cyber-*quinceañera* does not end here. Will Amanda negotiate more confidently, with more power over her destiny, having access to cyberspace? What are the imaginary scenes that are linked to the computer in such areas (crossed by difference in multicultural locations)? How does the school empower women with their diversities (class, race and sexuality) to inscribe their personal ways of communicating their concerns, their doubts and their desires within cyberspace? Are young 'minoritized' women entering cyberspace as another space 'centripetated' by the powers of masculine economies of meaning? What kind of negotiations will Amanda undergo between cultural expectancies and cyber-possibilities?

Has her father's dream of delivering his daughter to a 'good man' ended with the computer as present, or is he just expecting her to marry *better*? How do cultural scenarios change when dining rooms are 'crowned' with a computer next to the refrigerator? How do women deal with their cyberskills *vis-à-vis* patriarchal laws and patriarchal language in mixed cultural locations? What happens to women at the border, at the limits of cultural hybridity and frontier technologies?

Cyborg Indians?

The South submerges us in other scenarios. As we all know, the Zapatistas – the indigenous rebels in the state of Chiapas – have made a very interesting and innovative use of cyberspace as guerrillas. Nevertheless, it is difficult to find cyborg Indians in the jungle. They are too busy moving from place to place in the jungle to protect their lives, and technologies such as computers and modems are not easy to preserve in the middle of the jungle. What is extremely empowering is the kind of national and transnational cybercoalitions and alliances that the Zapatistas have succeeded in constructing. Zapatistas lists and home pages travel freely within cyberspace. International *encuentros* (gatherings) against neoliberalism and espousing a broad humanity are organized inside cyberspace. The Zapatistas phenomenon is an extremely interesting demonstration of the uses and the range of new technologies in rural, marginal and border zones.

Realities of the Chiapas

Notwithstanding the fact that Chiapas has been penetrated by the most diverse technologies to extract its wealth (oil, gas, energy, mineral resources, forests, agriculture), the majority of its population and the entire Indian population still live in misery. Modernity has come to Indian lives in other ways than through the advent of commodities, alternative forms of democracy (e-mail your local congressman) or buying and selling delirious options in a diverse and open market. Modernity has forced Indians to lose their land; to migrate; to be displaced into ghettoes, reservations and barracks, to incarcerate their agricultural production; to sell their workforce for ridiculous prices; to negotiate their culture without land (an oxymoron), without power (an impossibility), without a welfare state and citizenship to mitigate the perverse effects of economic models (a cruelty). Finally, it has forced them to live without a national project that could guarantee specific forms of cultural and governmental autonomy (the ultimate good of transnational economic models). Amazingly, the poorest of the poor in the south have found a way to circulate inside the Mexican symbolic orders, inside the Mexican imaginary of citizenship and inside cyberspace. In this case the methodology developed by the oppressed is complex – and it is not free of exclusions, technologies of mediation and ventriloquist discourses.

Representation, resistance and mediation

Indian rebels in cyberspace need to be looked at carefully. There is definitely a methodology, a technology developed by the oppressed in order to be heard and also to circulate internationally, but there is also a national and transnational order, formula, language, and political economy, an economy of significance that partially captures their forms of resistance. As I mentioned above, mixed experiences in cyberspace (not only celebratory ones) are needed to underline and analyze issues related to representation, resistance and mediation. I only want to point out one issue and frame it as an opening concern in the context of our interest: women in cyberspace.

Ultimately, one group of people has suffered from the consequences of mediation, and the complications of the rituals and mechanisms of access and circulation within cyberspace and new technologies of communication and information: indigenous women. Where in this cyberwar are the voices of indigenous women represented? In which of the agreements signed by rebels and government are their demands even alluded to?[2]

The silence of indigenous women is not only a product of the perverse economic machinery of capital accumulation and open markets. This silence is also the product of mediations, a ventriloquist technology orchestrated inside the rebel movement. The voices and discourses of the Indian rebels face the problems and advantages of circulation inside cyberspace through the 'disfigurations' imposed by a complex and sophisticated machinery of translation into the languages that dominate the superhighways of cyberspace. The voices of the indigenous women, however, are simply not there – or are present as babbling, whispers, or in such infinitesimal measure that they are difficult to hear.

There are methodologies to deal with the translation and expropriation of the Zapatista discourse inside cyberspace, such as deconstruction or meta-ideologization (Sandoval, 1995), but what do we do with silence? How do we deal with an absence inside national projects, nationalist discourses, transnational technologies? Indigenous women rebels have been able to create an Indigenous Women's Law, concentrating the demands of the national and indigenous cultures of more than ten different ethnic groups. Their discourse, however, is not considered inside the negotiations about indigenous culture and national autonomy between rebels and government. Nor is cyberspace proving to be a terrain where the Indigenous Women's Law and its associated demands can circulate and be empowered.

Indigenous women talk among themselves, to some brave journalists, to the daring feminist representatives of some NGOs; but their voices fade, they are stripped of the 'consistency', the power, the quality of enunciation that would allow them to travel inside citizenship's imaginary scenarios, inside the rebel-government agreement, inside national and constitutional symbolic orders, inside economic models, and finally inside the superhighways of cyberculture (Belausteguigoitia Rius, 1998).

Women, language and desire

Both Amanda's cyberritual of womanhood and the absence and cyber-exclusion of indigenous women are located at the borders and in the margins of fragile zones of resistance that lie at the limits of the Mexican nation. Both represent different challenges faced by women: the problems of access not only to new technologies as complicated or easy-to-use artifact, but also to symbolic, imaginary and economic orders already captured by hegemonic languages, economies of meaning and systems of power. Both experiences bring to the forefront the problems of representation, mediation and resistance that women's voices and concerns face, some in order to circulate in cyberspace, others simply to be heard.

If this conference can help us to analyze and understand what it takes to change fictions of marriage and dreams of femininity in blue into fictions of the power of communication, knowledge and information, dreamt across multicoloured screens, and to analyze and understand highly sophisticated forms of erasing women's voices, we will be closer to our dream: women in cyberspace in command of their needs, aware of the diverse forms in which their voices are kidnapped, endowed with power, and enjoying the freedom of their own languages and multiple desires.

NOTES

1 See Harcourt's Introduction to this volume.
2 An important development within the Zapatista rebellion has been the emergence of the revolutionary Indigenous Women's Law. It was released to the mass media in early January 1994. The Law synthesizes the demands of indigenous women belonging to the different ethnic groups integrated under the EZLN. The ten laws refer to: right to participation in the revolutionary struggle regardless of race, creed, colour or political affiliation; right to work and receive a just salary; right to decide the number of children they will have and care for; right to participate in the affairs of the community and hold positions of authority if democratically elected; right to health and education; right to choose their partner and not be forced into marriage; right not to be beaten or physically mistreated. They also call for rape to be severely punished, for women to be able to hold positions of leadership, and for all the rights and obligations to be elaborated in the revolutionary laws and regulations. The process of integration of the voices of indigenous women – who speak more than ten dialects – was undertaken by two Zapatista women who functioned as mediators and translators. For reasons given in this chapter this Law was not considered when indigenous rights and cultural autonomy were discussed during the official negotiations with the government.

2

GENDER, PLACE AND NETWORKS
A Political Ecology of Cyberculture

Arturo Escobar

Networks, gender and the environment

There is no doubt that 'networks' are 'in' today in our descriptions of
the present and our image of the future. Networks – particularly electronic networks – have become central to the rise of a new type of
society (the 'network society'), the coproduction of technoscience and
society (actor–network theory), and the politics of social transformation
('global networking for change'). Networks are essential to a new type of
'virtual-imagined transnational community'; to new political actors, such
as Women on the Net (WoN), to which this book is devoted; and to the
utopia of a democratic, allegedly globalized world. In all of these
conceptions, networks are facilitated by electronic and information
technologies, particularly the Internet. A good deal of our lives and our
hopes now resides in the networks linked to cyberspace.

Networks, however, are only as good as the ensemble of human,
natural and non-human elements they bring together and organize.
Similarly, they are part of a larger world that might be inimical to their
aims. Does the enlargement of opportunities for cultural resistance
afforded by some technological networks, for instance, balance out with
the narrowing down of real spaces by the forces of a transnational
capitalism fuelled by the same technologies? Is cyberspace a source of
new identities and knowledge of self and the world, as some propose, or
rather the medium where a 'terminal-citizen', increasingly isolated from
the rest of the world and mired in consumption, is being produced at a
world scale, as others argue? Is the activism at a distance made possible
by cyberspace not counteracted and vastly surpassed by the repressive
powers of global technocapitalism?

There are no clear answers to these questions yet. As in earlier periods, our ability to conceptualize the worlds coming into place and to articulate a corresponding politics of transformation leaves much to be desired. Yet there have been significant changes in how we go about it. In some fields, we now seek to derive theory from practical experience, look at everyday life as a source of theoretical insights, and enlist the company of local actors and social movements in their efforts to understand both the world and how we fit into it.

I am invoking here a loose 'we' – the we, let us say for now, of gender-aware academics and intellectuals struggling to develop a new politics of expert knowledge in conjunction with the political projects of subaltern groups. I also write this as I think about the activists of the social movement of the Pacific rainforest region of Colombia, with whom I have been working for some years, and who – I believe, and they increasingly know – would benefit greatly from having access to environmental and ethnic resources in Internet and biodiversity networks. I also think about the excitement of a small and progressive NGO for popular communications in Cali, Colombia which has just inaugurated its first Web page, despite the fact that most of its members can hardly follow a discussion in English. And I think about the vast networks of environmentalist and indigenous rights activists whose voices and concerns I encounter daily on the Internet as I research the rapidly changing debates about biodiversity conservation. I have in mind, finally, the growing groups of women travelling in the nets cast by women networkers, or netweavers, particularly in the pre- and post-Beijing climate.

In this chapter I want to make the following argument. Networks – such as women's, environmental, ethnic and other social movements networks – are the location of new political actors and the source of promising cultural practices and possibilities. It is thus possible to speak of a cultural politics of cyberspace and the production of cybercultures that resist, transform or present alternatives to the dominant virtual and real worlds. This cybercultural politics can be most effective if it fulfils two conditions: awareness of the dominant worlds that are being created by the same technologies on which the progressive networks rely (including awareness of how power works in the world of transnational networks and flows); and an ongoing tacking back and forth between cyberpolitics (political activism on the Internet) and what I will call place politics, or political activism in the physical locations at which the networker sits and lives.

Women, environmentalists and social movement activists on the Net are thrown into this double type of activism, with its contrasting demands: over the character of the Internet and new information and communications technologies (ICTs) in general, on one hand; and over the character of the restructuring of the world being effected by new ICTs-led transnational capitalism, on the other. From the corridors of cyberspace can thus be launched a defence of place and place-based ecological and cultural practices which might, in turn, transform the worlds that the dominant networks help to create. Because of their historical attachment to places and the cultural and ecological differences they constitute, women, environmentalists and social movements in the Third World are particularly suited to this double task. In the end, it might become possible to think about a political ecology of cyberspace that weaves the real and the virtual, gender, environment and development into a complex political and cultural practice.

The first part of the chapter discusses the idea of a contemporary society based on networks and flows; it highlights the tendencies and perils of cyberculture as they are visualized by a number of prominent academics. Missing from this discussion, as we will see, is precisely the place-based uses and appropriation of technological resources by actors such as women, environmentalists and social movements in many parts of the world. What is defining about these practices is their link to concrete places. A conceptualization of 'place' is thus introduced in the second part, with examples of place-based struggles in the environmental field. The last part suggests that new modes of knowing, being and doing based on the principles of interactivity, positionality and connectivity are emerging from the engagement of place-based political actors with new technologies. These principles provide guides for new practices of social and biological design – new combinations of place, nature, culture, and technology.

Flows, networks and real-time technologies

Networks of various kinds have existed for centuries. What is special about today's networks is not only that they seem to have become the backbone of society and the economy, but that they take on novel features and modes of operation. For some, we are faced with a new type of society – a global network society for Castells (1996); a modern society of long networks and hybrids for Latour (1993); a society under the tyranny of real-time technologies for Virilio (1997); a 'virtual-imagined' transnational community for Ribeiro (1998) – precisely because of the novel features networks adopt. The new ICTs are the pivotal element in this profound transformation.[1] It is the rise of a new technological paradigm, and not social, economic or political changes *per se*, that are driving it. This paradigm began gestation with the development of integrated circuits in the 1950s and microprocessors in the 1970s and has seen a progressive expansion into ever more powerful interacting networks at a global scale.

In this view, informational capitalism can be described as 'an economy with the capacity to work as a unit in real time and on a planetary scale' (Castells, 1996, p. 92). Capital, labour, trade and management become organized on a global scale and take the form of a flexible global web. There are limits to this global economy, of course (national states are still relevant actors; labour markets are not truly global; etc.). Moreover, the global economy is differentiated in geographical terms, highly exclusionary, and unstable in its boundaries. Most people in the planet do not yet work for or buy from the informational/global economy. A new international division of labour settles in around four positions: producers of high value, based on informational labour (the interdependent network between USA, Japan and Western Europe, also a triad of wealth, power and technology); producers of high volume, based on low-cost labour; producers of raw materials, based on natural endowments; and redundant producers, reduced to devalued labour (Castells, 1996, pp. 66–150). These positions do not necessarily coincide with countries, but are organized in networks and flows according to the infrastructure of the informational economy.

Of interest for our purposes in Castells's eloquent explanation is the impact of networks and flows on daily life. As interactive networks continue to expand, there is a growing divorce between spatial proximity and everyday life functions, such as work, entertainment, education, and so forth. Networks foster a new kind of space, the space of flows. Cities become 'globally connected and locally disconnected, physically and socially' (Castells, 1996, p. 404). Organized increasingly around flows – of capital, information, technology, images, symbols, etc. – this creates a new type of spatial reality that redefines places. For Castells,

> in this network, no place exists by itself, since the positions are defined by flows. Thus, the network of communication is the fundamental spatial configuration: places do not disappear, but their logic and their meaning become absorbed in the network.... In some instances, some places may be switched off the network, their disconnection resulting in instant decline, and thus in economic, social and physical deterioration (Castells, 1996, pp. 412–13).

Network or perish, seems to be the motto emerging from this view. Castells's view gets darker:

Articulation of the elites, segmentation and differentiation of the masses seem to be the twin mechanisms of social domination in our societies. Space plays a fundamental role in this mechanism. In short: elites are cosmopolitan, people are local (Castells, 1996, p. 415).

To the networked elites belongs the world, culturally connected by new lifestyles and spatially secluded in expensive enclave communities. The impact of this networked space of flows on the space of places is noticeable: segmented from each other, places are less and less able to maintain a shared culture. Real (timeless) time rules in the space of flows, while linear, biological or socially determined time continues to determine places.

> Not that people, locales, or activities disappear. But their structural meaning does, subsumed in the unseen logic of the metanetwork where value is produced, cultural codes are created, and power is decided (Castells, 1996, p. 477).

Can we deny that some of this is happening when we think about many places in the world, particularly in the so-called Third World? And yet, is this all that is happening? As we shall see, Castells's view is questionable precisely because it is derived from a globalocentric perspective, that is, one that finds agency only at the levels at which so-called global actors operate. Yet there is a real novelty to the network society, which arises in great part from the salience of real time. This aspect has been best analyzed recently by Paul Virilio. For this author, the essence of the current transformation is the effect that the new ICTs – operating at the speed of light and under the principle of real time – are having on the regime of time and space that has governed the world until now. Real-time technologies of communication kill the present by 'isolating it from its here and now, in favour of a communicative elsewhere that no longer has anything to do with "our concrete presence" in the world' (Virilio, 1997, p. 10).

> Real-time technologies – continuing with Virilio's caustic analysis – efface duration and extension. Working at the speed of light, communication 'no longer depends on the interval between places and things and so on the world's very extension, but on the interface of an instantaneous transmission of remote appearances....' (Virilio, 1997, p. 33). The 'tele-existence' enabled by optoelectronics promotes a split between the real time of our immediate activities – the here and now – and the real time of media interactivity that privileges the 'now' to the detriment of the 'here'.

How can we live if there is no more here and if everything is now? How can we survive the instantaneous telescoping of a reality that has become ubiquitous, breaking up into two orders of time, each as real as the other: that of presence here and now, and that of telepresence at a distance, beyond the horizon of tangible appearances? (Virilio, 1997, p. 37).

In a similarly insightful way, he announces 'a split between activity and interactivity, presence and telepresence, existence and tele-existence' (Virilio, 1997, p. 44). Material density is replaced by information density. The 'globalization of the present' reduces the ability of local time to make history and geography. The split between place and time (the age-old localization of the *hic et nunc*) is consummated as real-time events detach themselves from the place where they happen. The borders of the near and the distant become blurred, transforming our sense of our experience of the here and now. Embodied, grounded, rooted action loses a great deal of its social importance. Teletopia induces a generalized atopia. Places become newly precarious. Global dimensions are redefined as a consequence. There is an even more radical divide between those who live in the virtual community of real time of the global city, and the 'have-nots' who survive in the margins of the real space of local cities, 'the great planetary wasteland that in the future brings together the only too real community of those who no longer have a job or a place to live that are likely to promote harmonious and lasting socialization' (Virilio, 1997, p. 71).

Responding to cyberspatial technologies

How are we to gauge these visions from the perspective of those who want to use the same technologies for different social and ecological aims? Is it possible for women, social movements and others to deploy cyberspatial technologies in ways that do not marginalize place? The aims can be contradictory: a feminist goal of creating bonds among women through cyberspace might contribute to the erosion of place by detaching women from their locations. The question then becomes: how can women (1) defend place against the delocalization of globalization that erodes local cultures; (2) transform place(s) away from their patriarchal/domineering practices (since places, like the family and the body, have also operated to incarcerate women and control them; since places have their own forms of domination and even terror); (3) venture into the realm of real-time technologies and worldwide coalitions in search of allies and insights for gender struggles? It is important to see the contradictions involved at each step. To maintain the connection to place, to local actors, and the need for proximity while engaging increasingly in exchanges at a distance requires careful balancing acts. How can WoN defend places as they embrace the information highway?

Said differently, this entails conflicting demands: (1) to maintain the value of rootedness and place; the importance of face-to-face interaction for the creation of cultures; the viability of local times; the organicity of certain relations to the natural; and yet (2) to affirm the transformative potential of places and the need to transform them; finally, (3) to advance both processes through a critical engagement with cyberculture (among other means). To articulate the density of place with the density of information; real-time and local-time activism; tele-elsewheres with embodied and embedded places; hybrid cultures created in cyberspace and local hybrid cultures; etc. – these are other ways of expressing the needs confronting those who want to appropriate critically and creatively the set of new computer, communications and biological technologies. What kinds of worlds are we in a position to weave?

For Castells and Virilio, places will become delocalized and radically transformed under the pressures of real-time networks. But what is really the nature of the networks in question? If it is true that networks redefine places, are not places nevertheless essential to their working? These are some of the questions Bruno Latour tries to answer in a provocative work on networks and modern culture. In Latour's view, what separates modern cultures from the rest is that they are based on a 'double divide', between nature and society, and between 'us' and 'them'. These divides, however, are largely spurious, since in reality there are always links between nature and culture, and between us and them. No matter how hard moderns have tried to keep them separate, the same divides have fostered a proliferation of hybrids of the seemingly opposed pairs. Open a newspaper and you will realize that this is the case: the ozone layer (nature) is linked up with corporations, consumers, scientists, government policies (culture); biodiversity is at once biological, social, political, cultural; cloning involves real creatures, new technologies, ethics, regulations, economics. What most defines the moderns is that they have been able to mobilize nature for the creation of culture through networks of hybrids as never before. There is, of course, one factor essential to the success of this process: science.

An analogy with the railroad makes understanding networks seemingly easier. A railroad is neither local nor global. It is, in fact, local at all points; yet it is global, since it takes you to many places (which is different from being universal, since it does not take you just anywhere). Latour uses this metaphor to explain technological networks and the dominance of the moderns. Technological networks enlist the aid of machines like computers, tools like laboratories, inventions like the engine, discoveries like Pasteur's – plus, of course, a collection of diverse subjects. In these networks lies the modern specificity:

> the moderns have simply invented longer networks by enlisting a certain type of nonhumans [machines, science and technology, etc.].... This enlistment of new beings had enormous scaling effects by causing relations to vary from local to global.... Thus, in the case of technological networks, we have no difficulty reconciling their local aspect and their global dimension. They are composed of particular places, aligned by a series of branchings that cross to other places.... (Latour, 1993, p. 117).

And what about those other societies that have failed to invent such 'long networks'? These societies, which Latour refers to as 'premodern', have an advantage over the moderns in that they do not deceive themselves by thinking that nature and culture are separate. This advantage, however, is also their weakness, since by insisting that every transformation of nature be in harmony with a social transformation – by insisting on being ecological, one could say – they gave up their ability to make hybrids proliferate, that is, to build longer and more powerful networks. This feature made 'experimentation on a large scale impossible' (Latour, 1993, p. 140), so that premodern societies remained 'forever imprisoned within the narrow confines of their regional peculiarities and their local knowledge' (Latour, 1993, p. 118). While the premoderns built territories (and places, I assume), the moderns built networks that were ever longer and more connected. The universality of modern networks, however, is an ideological effect of rationalism backed science. In the long run, moderns and premoderns differ only in the size and scale of the networks they invent. For what we all produce – moderns and premoderns alike – is communities of natures and societies: 'all natures-cultures are similar in that they simultaneously construct humans, divinities and nonhumans' (Latour, 1993, p. 106). Moderns only add more and more hybrids to their networks in order to reconstitute social systems and extend their scale. 'Science and technologies are remarkable not because they are true or efficient ... but because they multiply the nonhumans enrolled in the manufacturing of collectives and because they make the community that we form with these beings a more intimate one' (Latour, 1993, p. 108).

A nonmodern constitution

This view is seductive for the so-called premoderns. To accept it would mean that the future, and 'catching up', would become just a matter of building longer and more connected networks. But networks of what kind? And for what purposes? To evaluate this possibility, it is necessary to examine briefly Latour's proposal for what he calls 'a nonmodern constitution', a sort of synthesis of the best the moderns and the pre-moderns have to offer. This constitution, or agreement, is based on the following features: it retains from the premoderns their recognition of the links between nature and culture, while rejecting their imperative to always link the social and natural worlds (their organicity, let us say). It retains from the moderns their ability to construct long networks through experimentation. The nonmodern constitution must also reject the limits the premoderns 'impose on the scaling of collectives, localization by territory, the scapegoating process, ethnocentrism, and finally the lasting nondifferentiation of natures and societies' (Latour, 1993, p. 133). Latour adds a paradoxical step for the nonmodern constitution, and this is that it must reintroduce the separation of nature and culture, but allowing consciously for the proliferation of hybrids and the coproduction of technoscience and society – in other words, to make the idea of a separation between objective nature and free society work once and for all. This amounts to accepting that 'the production of hybrids, by becoming explicit and collective, becomes the object of an enlarged democracy that regulates or slows down its cadence' (Latour, 1993, p. 141).

To be sure, Latour is aware that modern networks have effected 'a veritable bulldozer operation' on most of the world's cultures and natures. Even more, modern societies can no longer incorporate effectively the natures it tends to destroy or the peoples it has degraded; hence his call for a form of nonmodernity that nevertheless is to be based much more clearly on what he considers important modern accomplishments than on any redeemable cultural practices the 'pre-moderns' might have to offer. His proposal, in addition, is problematic on many grounds; to reduce the difference between moderns and premoderns to a question of network size and scale not only con-veniently overlooks the conditions of unequal exchange between networks, it avoids looking into hybridity's contradictions, their links to power and their denigration of places. It is also questionable if Latour's nonmodern constitution solves the contradiction between nature and culture, and between moderns and others, and whether its call for a new democracy will assuage modernity's appetite for conquest and accumulation (Dirlik, 1997). Even more, it says nothing about how living nonmoderns (including many of those he labels premodern) can both deal with modern networks and build different networks of their own.

From Latour, however, we have important lessons to learn about the nature of modern networks. Modern networks (1) include human and nonhuman elements; they are made of, and produce, hybrids; (2) enact connections and translations between the local and the global, the human and the nonhuman; (3) produce large effects (due to scale, size and scope) without being out of the ordinary; (4) do not rely on essential identities (unchanging humans or nature) but on process, movement, and passages without fixed meaning. Humans and nonhumans, techno-science and society, are coproduced through these networks. Latour's, perhaps, could be called a technoanarchist vision that glosses over many of the practices through which networks operate to destroy natures and cultures.

Does it offer lessons for those wishing to construct networks that enlist other types of humans and nonhumans? Does it offer hope for constructing other natures and cultures? As we survey the spectrum of forms of protest against threats to life, health and the environment; as we pay attention to struggles to re/construct society and nature in everyday life; and as we focus on emerging forms of cooperation and coalition building – for instance among women, indigenous peoples and social movements; or in community networks and Free-Nets in many parts of the world (Schuler, 1996) – we come to realize that networks can and do take on new meanings and dimensions, and that they can serve other political and life projects. Essential to this possibility at this juncture in the history of globalizing networks and flows, I believe, is an understanding of what is at stake in the politics of networking for concrete places and environments. I now turn to this issue before drawing some general conclusions about the modes of knowing based on interactivity and positionality that networks might be fostering.

Networks and the defence of place and nature

In the last two months of 1997, Internet list serves on Amazon indigenous issues included reports on the following, among many other topics: denunciation of government concessions for forest exploitation by foreign companies in Brazil and Guyana; a successful claim to lands by the Guarani Kaiowa in Mato Grosso do Sul, Brazil; a passionate speech by Davi Kopenawa, Yanomami chief, against gold miners on their lands, proclaiming their desire for progress without destruction and the right to defend their land; assassination of, or threats to, environmental and indigenous activists in Brazil, Colombia, and other countries; opposition to a large waterways project (the *hidriovía* Paraguay–Paraná) in Uruguay,

Brazil and Bolivia by a coalition of US and South American NGOs; accusations of biopiracy against a Swiss-based organization (Selva Viva) in Acre, Brazil, also involving a London-based NGO and indigenous, Catholic, and local organizations; denunciations by a French NGO of the firm Chanel for endangering the existence of a rare Brazilian tree used in its products; the formation of regional indigenous councils in Brazil to oppose mining and for the titling of indigenous territories; a meeting of rural women leaders of the Americas against neoliberalism; approval of the claims to land and identity by descendants of escaped slaves in Brazil; updates on the class-action suit against Texaco on behalf of a coalition of indigenous peoples in Ecuador for years of devastation of their lands; a statement by indigenous women of the Ecuadorian Amazon against the presence of oil companies in their territories; a massive march by Ecuadorian indigenous organizations on Quito to demand the inclusion of unprecedented indigenous rights in the new national constitution; a report on alarming deforestation in Venezuela (600,000 hectares a year during the 1980s, continuing into the 1990s).

Similarly, during 1997 the biodiversity conference of the network EcoNet, run by the San Francisco-based Institute for Global Communications, carried (among other items) detailed and sustained information and debates on the follow-up meetings to the Convention on Biological Diversity; biodiversity programmes in various countries; opposition to intellectual property rights regimes by national and international NGOs; meetings on biodiversity in various parts of the world and with sets of disparate actors; information on patenting of cell lines; opposition to mega-development projects in the name of biodiversity; new forms of grassroots activism throughout the world linked to the defence of nature; innovations by women in biodiversity conservation; and warning of a pending agreement for bioprospecting between the government of Colombia and a transnational pharmaceutical company.

Internet, locality and networking

There is no doubt that the Internet has fostered a ferment of activity on a vast set of issues that is yet to be understood in terms of its contents, scope, politics and modes of operation. What does this ferment of activity suggest in terms of networks? Who are the actors involved, what demands do they articulate, and which practices do they create? What views of nature and culture do they espouse or defend? If they do in fact constitute networks, what is the effect of these networks in terms of redefining social power, and at what levels? Conversely, what risks, if any, does the participation of, say, indigenous and grassroots groups in biodiversity networks entail for local meanings and practices of nature and culture?

A sporadic but symbolically important posting provides some clues for exploring these questions. In August and September 1997, various Internet sites sparked with an unprecedented message: an indigenous group in Eastern Colombia numbering 5,000, the U'wa, had threatened to commit massive suicide by jumping off a sacred cliff if the US corporation Occidental Petroleum carried out their planned oil exploration in any part of the 100,000 hectares remaining of their ancestral lands. Before its debut on the Internet, the U'wa struggle had seen the formation of a solidarity committee of environmentalists and indigenous rights activists in Colombia, failed negotiations with the government and the oil company, debates on the militarization and violence that the proposed oil exploration would entail, and mobilization by the U'wa themselves. As a result of the Internet postings, the U'wa struggle branched out in many directions – from lengthy newspaper articles in the world press that highlighted the U'wa's alleged traditional non-violence and ecological knowledge, to the establishment of inter-national support groups. Adopted by several international NGOs, the U'wa's struggle spread spatially and socially in unexpected directions. This included international travel by U'wa leaders themselves to disseminate knowledge of their struggle and gather support for it. They arrived with their concerns even at the door of Occidental's head-quarters in Los Angeles, with the support of a transnational U'wa Defence Project.[3]

The U'wa and similar cases suggest a number of emergent grassroots practices enabled by the Internet, particularly the following: the inter-related involvement of a multiplicity of actors in various parts of the world – from grassroots groups themselves to local, national and trans-national NGOs in both 'North' and 'South'; coalitions among these actors with various aims, intensities, and degrees of trust; conjunctural responses to ongoing or particularly acute threats to local natures–cultures; expressions of cultural and ecological resistance; ongoing opposition to destructive development projects, neoliberal reforms, and destructive technologies (such as mining, logging and dam construc-tion); opposition to the apparatuses of death set in motion to put down protest or opposition; translation of local cultures into the language of global environmentalism (from which unfortunately they often emerge as another version of the noble savage); and the irruption of collective identities claiming a place in the world theatre of environment, culture, gender and development.

The processes behind all of these elements and events are very complex – ranging from the remaking of local and national identities to globalization, environmental destruction, gender and ethnic struggles. In biodiversity discussions, which constitute to some extent an exemplary case in the politics of networks, it is possible to see several processes at work: (1) the discourse of biodiversity itself constitutes a network of its own, linking humans and nonhumans in particular ways; (2) in this network, the stake for local actors can be seen in terms of the defence of culturally specific practices of constructing natures and cultures; (3) these practices can be said to be embedded in what I referred to above as the defence of place.

Let us say, then, that biodiversity is a discourse that articulates a new relation between nature and society in global contexts of science, cultures and economies. The biodiversity discourse has resulted in an increasingly vast network – from the United Nations, the World Bank's Global Environment Facility (GEF) and the Northern environmental NGOs to Third World governments, Southern NGOs and social movements – which systematically organizes the production of forms of knowledge and types of power, linking one to the other through concrete strategies and programmes. This network is composed of heterogeneous actors and sites, each with its own culturally specific interpretive system, and with dominant and subaltern sites and knowledges. As they circulate through the network, truths are transformed, reinscribed into other knowledge–power constellations, resisted, subverted, or recreated to serve other ends, for instance, by social movements, which become, themselves, the sites of important counter-discourses. Technoscientifically oriented networks such as biodiversity are continuously being transformed in the light of translations, travel, transfers and mediations among and across sites. In fact, several contrasting conceptualizations of biodiversity have emerged in recent years from distinct network sites and processes.[4]

It can thus be said that 'biodiversity', far from being the neutral conservation arena of science and management that is often assumed, underlies one of the most important networks for the production of nature in the late twentieth century. As places become entangled with the network, contestation over conceptions of nature–culture follow. The U'wa project, like many social movements in biodiversity-rich regions, makes it clear that the aim of their struggle is to defend a particular way of relating to nature, rooted in their culture. Ethnographic studies document entirely different natures–cultures among many groups with increasing eloquence and detail. For instance, one of the most commonly accepted notions is that many local models do not rely on a nature–society dichotomy. Unlike modern constructions, local models in non-Western contexts are often predicated on links of continuity between the three spheres. This continuity – which might nevertheless be experienced as problematic or uncertain – is culturally established through symbols, rituals and practices embedded in social relations that differ from the capitalist type.[5]

Local models of nature exist in transnational contexts of power yet cannot be accounted for without some reference to groundedness, boundaries and local cultures. They are based on historical, linguistic and cultural processes that retain a certain place specificity despite their engagement with translocal processes. From this perspective, a theoretical and utopian question suggests itself: *Can the world be redefined and reconstructed from the perspective of the multiple cultural, ecological and social practices embedded in local models and places?* This is perhaps the most profound question that can be posed from a radical networks perspective. What types of networks would be most conducive to this reconstruction? The question requires, however, that we look a bit closer into places and their defence.

Place-based practices

As Arif Dirlik has pointed out (1998), place and place-based practices have been marginalized in debates on the local and the global. This is regrettable because place is essential for thinking about alternative construction of politics, knowledge and identity. The erasure of place is a reflection of the asymmetry that exists between the global and the local in much of contemporary literature on globalization, in which the global is associated with space, capital, history and agency while the local, conversely, is linked to place, labour, tradition, women, minorities, the poor and, one might add, local cultures.[6] Some feminist geographers have attempted to correct this asymmetry by arguing that place can also lead to articulations across space – for instance through networks of various kinds (Massey, 1994; Chernaik, 1996). In resisting the marginalization of place, other authors focus on place as a form of lived and grounded space, the reappropriation of which must be part of any radical political agenda against capitalism and spaceless, timeless globalization. Politics is also located in place, not only in the supra-levels of capital and space.[7] A parallel step entails recognizing that place – as the ecological conceptions discussed above make patently clear –

continues to be a grounded experience with some sort of boundaries, however porous and intersected with the global.[8]

Contemporary theories of globalization tend to assume the existence of a global power to which the local is necessarily subordinated. Under these conditions, is it possible to launch a defence of place in which place and the local do not derive their meaning only from their juxtaposition to the global? Who speaks for 'place'? Who defends it? Can place be reconceived as a project? For this to happen, we need a new language. To return to Dirlik, 'glocal' is a first approximation that suggests equal attention to the localization of the global and the globalization of the local. The concrete forms in which this two-way traffic takes place are not so easily conceptualized. As Massey puts it well, 'the global is in the local in the very process of the formation of the local ... the understanding of any locality must precisely draw on the links beyond its boundaries' (1994, p. 120). Conversely, many forms of the local are offered for global consumption, from crafts to ecotourism. The point here would be to identify those forms of globalization of the local that can become effective political forces in defence of place and place-based identities, as well as those forms of localization of the global that locals can use to their own ends.

To be sure, 'place' and 'local knowledge' are no panaceas that will solve the world's problems. Local knowledge is not 'pure' or free of domination; places might have their own forms of oppression and even terror; they are historical and connected to the wider world through relations of power. They as easily originate reactionary and regressive changes as they might progressive politics. Women have often been subordinated through restrictions linked to place and home (Massey, 1994), and of course native groups have been spatially incarcerated and segregated. These factors have to be taken seriously. But against those who think that the defence of place and local knowledge is undeniably 'romantic', one could say, with Jacobs (1996, p. 161) that 'it is a form of imperial nostalgia, a desire for the "untouched Native", which presumes that such encounters [between local and global] only ever mark yet another phase of imperialism'. What changes occur in particular places as a result of globalization? Conversely, what new ways of thinking about the world emerge from places as a result of such an encounter?

The defence of place is an increasingly felt need on the part of those working at the intersection of environment and development, precisely because the development experience has meant for most people a sundering of local life from place of greater depth than ever before. Not only are scholars and activists in environmental studies confronted with social movements that maintain a strong reference to place – veritable movements of ecological and cultural attachment to places and terri-tories – but faced also with the growing realization that any alternative course of action must take into account place-based models of nature with their accompanying cultural, ecological, and economic practices. Debates on postdevelopment (Rahnema and Bawtree, eds, 1997), local knowledge, and cultural models of nature are having to face this problematic of place. Reconceived in this fashion, ecology, cyberculture and postdevelopment would facilitate the incorporation of place-based practices and modes of knowledge into the process of outlining alternative orders. Said differently, a reassertion of place, non-capitalism and local culture should result in theories that make visible possibilities for reconceiving and reconstructing the world from the perspective of place-based practices.

Interactivity and positionality: a feminist political ecology of cyberculture

It seems paradoxical to build a link between place and cyberculture. But if it is true that we are witnessing the emergence of a virtual-imagined transnational community which alters the conditions for activism in a shrinking world (Ribeiro, 1998), then we must recognize the necessity of building just such a link. Activism at a distance makes perfect political sense in cyberculture. But this activism, as Ribeiro also points out, must be based on a further link, between cyberactivism and face-to-face activism in physical space – what I called here place-based political practice. To be sure, this link is to be thought about in terms of the interplay between different actors at local, regional, national and trans-national levels of network integration – that is, according to new forms of relating space, place and politics. It must also consider the discourses that relate those levels of integration and which might enhance the effectivity of transnationalism (environmentalist, feminist, and indige-nous rights discourse, for instance); and it should be mindful of the fact that globalization simultaneously fosters fragmentation and integration, and that the Internet 'enlarges public sphere and political action through the virtual world that reduces them in the real one' (Ribeiro, 1998, p. 345).

This is to say that despite the importance of cybertools and cultures, a lot of what needs to be changed depends on power relations in the real world. We might give each woman of the world or each ecology group a computer and an Internet account, and the world might remain the same. This means that the relationship between cyberculture and political change – and between cyberactivism and place-based practice – is to be politically constructed. It does not follow from the technologies themselves even if, as I will discuss shortly, the technology fosters certain novel modes of knowing, being and doing. We might learn more about this political construction by drawing from the field of feminist political ecology, which focuses on the relation between gender, environment and development (Rocheleau, Thomas-Slayter and Wangari, eds 1996; Harcourt, ed., 1994).

Feminist political ecology starts by treating gender as a critical variable in shaping access to, and the knowledge and organization of, natural resources. Gendered experiences of the environment are explained in terms of women's situated knowledges, also shaped by class, culture and ethnicity. Feminist political ecology unveils the many kinds and importance of women's local environmental knowledge; further, it attempts to link it to social movements and the defence of local cultural and biophysical ecologies. Similarly, feminist political ecology looks at gendered rights and responsibilities, often skewed against women. It finds that 'women are beginning to redefine their identities, and the meaning of gender, through expressions of human agency and collective action emphasizing struggle, resistance, and cooperation. In doing so, they have also begun to redefine environmental issues to include women's knowledge, experience, and interests' (Rocheleau, Thomas-Slayter and Wangari, eds, 1996, p. 15). Women's ecological activism weaves together issues of environmental policy, resource access and distribution, knowledge and gender, while fostering an alternative view of sustainabililty:

> Feminist political ecology provides a valuable framework for analyzing and comparing the stories of women from around the world. It offers an approach which derives theory from practical experience, avoiding the pitfalls of maintaining a strict separation between theory and practice. It links ecological perspective with analysis of economic and political power and with policies and actions within a local context. Feminist political ecology rejects dualistic constructs of gender and environment in favour of multiplicity and diversity, and emphasizes the interconnectedness of ecological, economic, and cultural dimensions of environmental change. It recognizes the relationship among global, national, and regional policies and local processes and practices (Thomas-Slayter, Wangari and Rocheleau, eds, 1996, p. 289).

The relevance of this view for the analysis of women and cyber-culture is apparent, particularly the following: providing a framework for examining women's experience worldwide; linking theory and practice in women's organizations and movements for social change (the gendered roots of activism); highlighting the importance and gendered character of local knowledge; questioning the presumption of economic development and the domination of nature and women; addressing the different structural positions occupied by women and men; using feminist insights to inform policy debates; and imagining global perspectives from local experience. In feminist political ecology, women struggle simultaneously against the destruction of nature and against the conventional (gender- and culture-blind) policies to restructure nature through sustainable development and management; in feminist cyber-cultural politics, women struggle simultaneously against the control of cyberculture by male-dominant groups and against the restructuring of the world by the same technologies they seek to appropriate. To the extent that women's cybercultural politics is linked to the defence of place, it is possible to suggest that it becomes a manifestation of feminist political ecology. This political ecology would similarly look at gendered knowledge; gendered rights and responsibilities concerning information and technology; and gendered organizations. It would examine, in short, the gendering of technoscience and cyberspace.

Politics of networks

To conclude, there are two aspects that must be discussed. The first is the political character of networks. The progressive character of networks cannot be assured beforehand. As I have suggested, progressive organizations and social movements in the biodiversity conservation arena do not form an autonomous network of their own, but one that is enmeshed in a larger one, with dominant and subaltern sites that are not independent of one another. That it would be hard to construct 'a network of one's own' is also attested by the experience of the pre- and post-Beijing women's movement, as lucidly analyzed by Sonia Alvarez. For Alvarez (1997, 1998), the transnationalization of Latin American feminist advocacy made possible by the proliferation of women's networks has had significant, and not always felicitous, local consequences. To be sure, the growing transnationalization of the women's movement has had many positive effects, such as the incorporation of ethnic and sexual diversity, the strengthening of alliances with transnational NGOs and movements, and the transformation of state policy at many levels. These achievements, however, have had their downside, as Alvarez explains, in terms of the growing professionalization, discursive accommodation, and compromise that women's NGOs have made with male-dominant and often market-driven policies. This accommodation has at times constrained more radical feminist cultural politics. Verónica Schild's analysis (1998) of the professionalization of the Chilean women's movement also suggests that this process has contributed to demobilizing popular women's movements and introducing neoliberal cultural discourses of market and individuality among poor working women.

This is to say that the politics of networks does not necessarily follow from who does the networking. Yet networks have important political effects. Networks elicit a way of looking at the world not so much in terms of fragmentation – as many Marxists tend to do[9] – but of possibilities for coalitions. For some feminist geographers, coalition politics is a feature of networks based on a positive notion of difference. Place-based social practices can lead to articulations across space; 'the form that this global articulation takes, though, is often more a network than a system: a coalition of specific, different groups rather than a universalization of any one political identity' (Chernaik, 1996, p. 257). This thinking about networks resonates with the feminist position of conceptualizing space, place and identity in terms of relations rather than the imposition of boundaries (Massey, 1994).[10] It is clear, in addition, that place-based social movements create spatial effects that go beyond locality. They produce forms of 'glocality' that are not negligible. Witness, for instance, the social movements networks of indigenous peoples in the Americas, and of women and environmentalists in various parts of the world, despite the caveats already mentioned. The indigenous networks of the Americas are perhaps the best example of the effectivity (and limitations) of transnational networks of organizing and identity.

But can these parallel forms of glocality lead to alternative social orders? This last aspect of 'the question of alternatives' remains largely intractable. For Dirlik, the survival of place-based cultures will be ensured when the globalization of the local compensates for the localization of the global – that is, when symmetry between the local and the global is reintroduced in social and conceptual terms. The imagination and realization of different orders demands 'the projection of places into spaces to create new structures of power ... in ways that incorporate places into their very constitution' (Dirlik, 1997, p. 39), the release of noncapitalist imaginaries into the constitution of economies, and the defence of local cultures from their normalization by dominant cultures. For this to happen, places must 'project themselves into the spaces that are presently the domains of capital and modernity' (Dirlik, 1997, p. 40). To the extent that new ICTs are central to the remaking of the domains of capital and modernity, cybercultural politics has an essential role to play in this political project. Cybercultural politics might provide a prime mechanism for 'scaling-up' – in Latour's terms – the networks through which subaltern groups seek to redefine power and defend and construct their identities.

The issue of glocality and scaling-up of place-based coalitions must nevertheless be approached with caution. As Gustavo Esteva and Madhu Suri Prakash say in criticizing the slogan 'think globally, act locally', we have to be wary of all global ways of thinking. In fact, 'what is needed is exactly the opposite: people thinking and acting locally, while forging solidarity with other local forces that share this opposition to the "global thinking" and "global forces" threatening local spaces' (Esteva and Prakash, 1997, p. 282). It is clear that places linking together create supralocal realities. Perhaps the language of networks and glocality is only a provisional way to refer to these realities that are still poorly understood from non-globalist perspectives, while respecting the vitality, size and scale of places. Place-based initiatives offer forms of radical pluralism that oppose globalism; engaging with supralocal forces, as Estava and Prakash say, does not make local people into globalists.

This in no way entails reifying places as 'untouched' or outside of history. To give attention to place is to destabilize 'the surer spaces of power and difference marked by geopolitical or political economy perspectives' (Jacobs, 1996, p. 15). To speak about activating local places, cultures, natures, and knowledge against the imperializing tendencies of capitalism and modernity is not a *deus ex machina* operation, but a way to move beyond the chronic realism fostered by established modes of analysis. Alternative ecological public spheres, for instance, might be opened up against the imperial ecologies of nature and identity of capitalist modernity. Can we think of cyberculture in similar terms? What types of public cyberspheres can be brought into existence through the networks envisioned by women, ecologists and others? And will they foster different ways of interacting and relating, of thinking about life, gender, justice and diversity?

New technologies fostering new knowledge

This brings us to the second, and last, aspect I want to discuss. Is it possible to think that new technologies, by their very character and in the hands of subaltern groups, would foster novel practices of being, knowing and doing? This is a complex question to which I can only give a very partial answer by invoking briefly the work of Katherine Hayles and Donna Haraway. For both authors, the critiques of objectivism made possible by feminism and technoscience point to novel practices of knowing. For Hayles, knowledge can now be thought in terms of interactivity and positionality:

> Interactivity points toward our connection with the world: everything we know about the world we know because we interact with it. Positionality refers to our location as humans living in certain times, cultures and historical traditions: we interact with the world not from a disembodied, generalized framework but from positions marked by the particularities of our circumstances as embodied human creatures. Together, inter-activity and positionality pose a strong challenge to traditional objectivity, which for our purposes can be defined as the belief that we know reality because we are separated from it. What happens if we begin from the opposite premise, that we know the world because we are connected to it? (Hayles, 1995, p. 48)

Surely, many 'premodern' or nonmodern groups have always lived with and from 'the opposite premise' of nonseparability of self and other, body and world, nature and society. The cultural models of nature referred to before attest to that. Interactivity and positionality are thus 'natural attributes' of many people; as Hayles is quick to add, to live by these principles entails not only different epistemologies but different values. New technologies are hailed for their interactivity, but in modern contexts this interactivity is often disembodied and disembedded. Third World social groups might be more prepared culturally to embrace the interactivity and positionality that is facilitated by new information technologies. As Austerlic (1997) says, the periphery's advantage in this arena lies not in the design of hardware but in the contents, and these are culturally defined. Science fiction occasionally plays with the idea of 'downloading' Third World cultures on to global webs. This idea suggests that an entire cultural politics is at stake in the appropriation of new ICTs by non-dominant groups.

New technologies summon a third principle, that of connectivity. Haraway retakes this notion, depoliticized in much techno-celebratory literature, through the image of the hypertext (perhaps more apt for our age than the network metaphor). Hypertexts are about making connec-tions, only that today we are compelled by technoscience to make unprecedented connections – between humans and nonhumans, the organic and the artificial, and with bodies, narratives and machines alike; in Haraway's words, we have to accept becoming 'ontologically dirty' (Haraway, 1997, p. 127). Which connections matter, why, and for whom become crucial questions. Haraway's renewed call to feminists and others is clear: 'I want feminists to be enrolled more tightly in the meaning-making processes of technoscientific world-building.... The figure [hypertext] should likewise incite our lust for just barely possible worlds outside the explicit logic of any Net' (Haraway, 1997, pp. 127, 129). Coalitions need to be built for more livable technoscience. 'My purpose is to argue for a practice of situated knowledges in the worlds of technoscience, worlds whose fibers infiltrate deep and wide throughout the tissues of the planet, including the flesh of our personal bodies' (Haraway, 1997, p. 130).

To be sure, we have to be mindful, as Virilio and Castells warned us, of the misery being brought to billions by transnational capitalism and technoscience. But we must also bear witness, Haraway insists, to the myriad ways in which situated knowledges extract freedoms from those regimes. We have to pay attention to how various groups appropriate the universes of knowledge, practice and power mapped by technoscience, often through unprecedented condensations, fusions and implosions of subjects and objects, the natural and the artificial. Perhaps then we can reweave that net called the global by fostering the production of other forms of life. Today Haraway's call can only be ignored at a high cost. It has to be approached, of course, from culture and place-specific perspectives. Biodiversity advocates of rainforest regions, for instance, are having to engage with technoscientific discourses of biotechnology bent on utilizing diversity for commercial purposes (Escobar, 1998b). Indigenous activists similarly build networks to defend their cultures and ecologies against neoliberalism and depoliticized policies of diversity. The Women on the Net is another reflection of the fact that this challenge is being taken up in many quarters of Asia, Africa, Latin America and elsewhere.

Constructing cyberpolitics

New computer, communication and information technologies offer unprecedented possibilities for alternative social and political practices, actors and identities. Whether these possibilities are realized will depend on many factors, beyond the identity of the networkers themselves, particularly the relationship maintained between activism in cyberspace and place-based social change. Progressive groups wishing to appropriate and utilize these technologies for social transformation must build bridges between place and cyberspace – between activity and interactivity, presence and telepresence, existence and tele-existence, as Virilio would have it. These bridges have to be constructed politically.

The experience of those working at the intersection of gender, environment and development offers lessons for such a political construction in the field of cybercultural politics.

For historical and cultural reasons, women, environmentalists and Third World social movements might be more attuned to the principles of interactivity, positionality and connectivity than the feminist critique of science, and the new technologies themselves, seem to foster. These principles are conducive to new modes of knowing, being and doing; they may ground a cultural politics of technoscience capable of transforming technoscience's current impact on the world. This requires that the interfaces we build among ourselves as users of the new technologies, the new ICTs themselves, and the task of social transformation be grounded in concrete bodies and places. 'Rooting women's communication experiences and ways of communicating in their social and cultural concerns and backgrounds' is a principle of feminist communications (APC, 1997, p. 9). The transformation of gender and ecological relations calls for actions that link together place and cyberspace. It is not impossible to think that the same networks that so many fear will erase places once and for all could enable a defence of places out of which gender and ecological relations might emerge transformed.

NOTES

1 More specifically, Castells speaks of the convergence of microelectronics, computer, optoelectronics, and biological technology such as genetic engineering.
2 Virilio also sees profound ecological consequences from these changes. For him, ecology needs to be concerned with 'the degradation of the physical proximity of beings, of different communities' (p. 58). The new ICTs tend to break down connections to the soil and one's neighbours. Transactions at the speed of the light transform our immediate environment and the horizon and physical dimension of our actions. Urban ecology should be concerned with the pollution created by speed. The sense of the space, of being there, is what is fundamentally polluted.
3 The U'wa Defence Project International is a collaborative effort between Amazon coalition, Amazon Watch, Cabildo Mayor U'wa, Centre for Justice and International Law, Colombian Human Rights Commission, Earth Trust Foundation, FIAN Germany, National Indigenous Organization of Colombia, Project Under Ground, Rainforest Action Network (RAN) and SOL Communications. For further information contact:
http://www.solcommunications.com/uwa.html; uwaproject@aol.com
4 This is a very inadequate explanation of the biodiversity network. See Escobar (1997, 1998a) for a lengthy analysis. It is possible to differentiate among four major positions in the uneven topology of the biodiversity network: resource

management (globalocentric perspective); sovereignty (Third World national perspectives); biodemocracy (progressive Southern NGO perspective); and cultural autonomy (social movements perspective).

5 For an up-to-date statement on cultural models of nature from the perspective of ecological anthropology, and ethnographic cases in many parts of the world, see Descola and Palsson, eds (1996). Guteman and Rivera (1990) have suggested a set of useful principles for thinking about cultural models of land, nature and the economy; see also Escobar (1998b).

6 This is very clearly the case in environmental discourses, for instance, of biodiversity conservation, where women and indigenous people are credited with having the knowledge of 'saving nature'. Massey (1994) has already denounced the feminization of place and the local in theories of space. For a good example of the asymmetry Dirlik talks about, see the quotes from Castells's book above.

7 The June 1998 issue of *Development* (Volume 41, No. 2) is devoted to the question of place and alternative development, with a lead article by Arif Dirlik. See also Massey (1994); Lefebvre (1991); Soja (1996).

8 It is not the point to recapture here the complex debate on space and place of recent years. This debate – which initially brought together Marxist geographers and feminist political economists, and to which anthropologists, philosophers and ecologists have contributed more recently – started with the growing concern of globalization and its impact on space and time (the 'space-time compression' theorized by Harvey, 1989). The debate on place and space also has a source in explanations of modernity, particularly Giddens's analysis of the separation of time and space that makes possible the disembedding of social systems and the differentiation of space from place: 'The advent of modernity' – says Giddens – 'increasingly tears space away from place by fostering relations between absent others, locationally distant from any given situation of face-to-face interaction' (1990, p. 18). Virilio's 'telepresence' of real-time technologies is a new step in this genealogy of the sundering of place from space.

9 For Marxist critics, networks are actually a manifestation of the fragmentation that the world economy imposes on most localities today. Networks, in this view, are incapable of anchoring a significant struggle against capitalism and globalization. Against this capitalocentric view, some feminist Marxists have reacted by insisting on the need to visualize the multiple forms of economic, cultural and ecological difference that still exists in the world today, and the extent to which these differences can anchor alternative economies and ecologies (Gibson-Graham, 1996; Escobar, forthcoming).

10 Chernaik also takes on the notion that home and place are ambiguous categories for women. She advocates a dialectic of place and street – of place and cyberspace, we could say – in women's 'construction of a house of difference.'

3

VIRTUAL VOICES:
REAL LIVES

Gillian Youngs

The Internet opening new spaces

How can feminist ideas be created in a masculinist world? (question from student).

Politics rests on the possibility of a shared world (Haraway, 1991a, p. 4).

Complex systems and virtual worlds are not only important because they open spaces for existing women within an already existing culture, but also because of the extent to which they undermine both the world-view and the material reality of two thousand years of patriarchal control (Plant, 1996, p. 170).

This chapter investigates how the boundaries of women's and feminist potential may be considered as altered by the existence and use of the Internet. It considers how we may be entering a new phase of feminist politics characterized by the possibilities of geographical, social and cultural transcendence. It looks to areas of established feminist thought to assess critically these possibilities and to identify ways in which they should be understood in historical contexts. The author is approaching this essay as an opportunity for thinking through the boundaries that have defined women's experience and contained it in various ways. Thus the Internet and its new communications frameworks are understood as a fresh stimulus for further thought about the history of women's lives and the major structures of familial, social, political and economic patterns that have contributed to shaping them. This is a key starting point: an understanding of the prospects offered particularly for 'sharing' thought in this area among women who would not otherwise have been in contact with one another. Thus the SID/UNESCO

Women on the Net (WoN) project on which this volume is based does not just signify new networks of women and joint projects developed in connection with them, it also represents exciting philosophical openings for revisiting a history of thought about women, some of it already documented and some of it not, in new shared circumstances.

These points indicate the complex of women's communications issues associated with the development and use of the Internet. There are discoveries to be made about the present and the past as well as prospects for the future and all of these are equally influential. The following discussion explores specific ways in which the Net represents the dawning of a new communications age for women, including those who see themselves as feminists or would-be feminists of various kinds. In linking its considerations directly to aspects of feminist thought, it also presents relevant themes of long-established debate in this area and examines how these may be influenced by new exchanges, associations and knowledges generated by women's use of the Net.

Towards a new era of cyberfeminisms?

The use of the term feminism in an international context is highly problematic, as has been consistently underscored by critical debate around and about Western-centric traditions of thought on women's 'emancipation' or 'liberation'. The specificities of historical developments related to these concepts are at issue. They concern state and market formations, and ideological parameters and threats. Recognition of the materiality of feminism – that is, its concrete social and geographical attachments and particularities – is implicit in any critical reflection on Western feminist knowledge and principles. There is an understanding that boundaries of many kinds shape the processes by which knowledges are developed and established, understood and communicated. These boundaries are physical, organizational and symbolic. The socio-historical specificities of knowledges are fundamental to critical understanding of their own bounded nature: the grounds on which they are based, and the associated limitations in the potential for understanding which they offer. Hence my reference to 'threats' above. There are very real senses in which knowledges, especially those that are well-instituted and dominant, can threaten as well as aid understanding because of the limitations they can impose on a sense of inquiry. By establishing frameworks for understanding, knowledges can delineate too strongly a contained world view. Therefore there is an ever-present need for those who engage in and apply them to be open and critical of their predispositions, assumptions and boundaries of perspective. The use of the term 'boundaries' is helpful in relation to knowledges because it automatically encourages us to think in terms of lines of identity and to recognize that knowledges are part of what separates people from one another, particularly in the context of large-scale social groupings defined politically, economically, socially and culturally.

Knowledges are material, and they are material to our understandings of hierarchical and difference-based identities, including those of the male/female variety, however defined. Knowledges are also material because of their centrality to theory–practice dynamics and thus historical transition, change and transformation. Knowledges facilitate the maintenance of the social *status quo*, and, of course, in radical forms, question and challenge it, helping to create conditions for change. It is useful to think in terms of 'battlefields of knowledge' (Long and Long, eds, 1992), especially when addressing international circumstances. The issue of knowledge has become a central part of critical studies of international relations in recent years (Der Derian and Shapiro, eds, 1989; Peterson, 1992; Youngs, forthcoming b). The boundaries of international theory continue to be challenged to reveal their predispositions, assumptions and partialities, notably in veiling the active existence, contribution and potential of women in national and transnational settings. The sphere of international politics has been in significant senses a last bastion of masculinist analytical blindness.

> Perhaps international politics has been impervious to feminist ideas precisely because for so many centuries in so many cultures it has been thought of as a typically 'masculine' sphere of life. Only men, not women or children, have been imagined capable of the sort of public decisiveness international politics is presumed to require. Foreign affairs are written about with a total disregard for feminist revelations about how power depends on sustaining notions about masculinity and femininity (Enloe, 1989, p. 4).

The disruption of what Enloe usefully terms the 'comfortable assumptions' underpinning this situation has been multifaceted. It has continued to expand in its diversity, involving an increasing number of women's voices and contrasting feminist perspectives from differing social and geographical locations. The fundamental question 'Where are the women?' (Enloe, 1989, pp. 1–18) has been and continues to be vital, whether we are thinking about areas of theory, policy or practice. Posing that question and pursuing it places, in very real senses, women in search of women, women's understandings in search of other women's understandings, women's experiences in search of other women's experiences. Analytical challenges also include searching for the bases and characteristics of differences and commonalities, interconnections and distinctions. These will assist increasingly detailed explanation and investigation of global and local patterns of inequality and oppression and their interdependencies. This involves 'resiting the political' (Dean, ed., 1997) to go beyond assumptions about where and how politics and collective identities associated with them are located.

> Questions about the nature of differences, whether they are essential or constructed, have fallen by the wayside before the realization of the relationality and contextuality of attributions of difference. What matters, then, is attention to the multiplicity of possible connections at a particular location, and the political meanings and opportunities these connections might engender. Freed from the constraints of the previous decades' pre-occupations with unidimensional accounts of race, gender or sexuality, current feminist theory has started to look to the uses and effects of particular articulations of race, gender and sexuality (Dean, ed., 1997, p. 2).

Feminist knowledges in such a context rely on open exploration of the problem of difference as a political issue with material bases. This can best be done collectively, because how else is it possible to achieve shared reflective senses of both categories of difference and their material conditions? Difference potentially represents a subject for collective radical thought and action. It offers possibilities for bringing together rather than tearing apart. As Jodi Dean affirms, 'The proliferation of differences, whether as privatized market effects of global capital or the results of rights-based struggles for inclusion and recognition, makes possible a variety of forms of coalition and resistance' (Dean, ed., 1997, p. 2).

The challenge is to uncover such possibilities and build concretely upon them. The sharing of knowledge between women across various boundaries of diversity is clearly essential to such a process. WoN as a project has begun to demonstrate how new communications technologies can be integral to, and perhaps even primary in, this process. It signals the potential of a new era of cyberfeminisms where the priority in collective knowledge building among women is to undertake it first and foremost on a cross-boundary basis, whether we are thinking of geographical, national, social, cultural or racial boundaries. It would be naïve not to recognize that implicit in such endeavours are the threats of 'battlefields of knowledge'. The assumptions which create boundaries are not easily broken down. Politicizing the issue of difference to enable us to work with it towards collective goals, to prioritize it rather than leaving it to one side, is uncomfortable. The WoN participants have experienced this discomfort, as have others who have endeavoured to work in such cross-boundary circumstances. Creation can be a painful act as women definitely know. One of the things I have learned as a member of the project is that to work towards identifying shared global politics requires very deep reflection about the bases for one's own politics, whether these are defined in feminist terms or not. But to do so in the kind of shared environment of WoN offers the potential for 'resiting the political' in meaningful and direct ways. The Net has particular significance for women's politics and the possibilities for women's global politics, and the remainder of this chapter reflects on some of the reasons why this is the case.

The public/private context of women's lives

One of the influential ways in which the era of the Internet can be said to have transformed the conditions for communication among women relates to the complicated area of public/private divides. I use the description 'conditions of communication' here to indicate that the circumstances within which women communicate are an essential part of understanding not only the limitations on how or what they communicate but also their possibilities for imagining alternatives. There is a long history of feminist debate about the social locations of women and the ways in which these shape their power relations and possibilities in the world as well as their own consciousness about their lives, roles and ambitions. The public domain, the major spheres of political and economic influence in society, has not only been dominated by men but also, importantly, by masculinist knowledges and values. The separation of the private and public spheres has been integral to the formation of societies and the complex of patriarchal power across public/private divides. The influence and identity of women has been predominantly located in the context of the so-called private space of the family, the domestic, the sphere of social reproduction and caring. While they may have extensive roles beyond, in the so-called public world of political, economic and social work, these will still largely reflect their overall unequal status in relation to men. This does not mean, of course, that there are not many prominent and successful women, and social opportunities differ in relation to other categories of inequality such as class or social hierarchy and colour or ethnicity. Thus women cannot be considered as one global group in relation to questions of inequality. However, the United Nations Human Development Report (HDR) (UNDP, 1997) illustrates that gender disparities remain a deep structural consideration in global terms.

In developing countries there are still 60 per cent more women than men among illiterate adults, female enrolment even at the primary level is 13 per cent lower than male enrolment, and female wages are only three-quarters of male wages. In industrial countries unemployment is higher among women than men, and women constitute three-quarters of the unpaid family workers (UNDP, 1997, p. 39).

As the HDR states straightforwardly, 'no society treats its women as well as its men'. Furthermore, with increasing numbers of women joining the global workforce, the characteristics of the unequal dual roles that women bear in the private and public spheres is gaining in importance. But as I argue elsewhere (Youngs, forthcoming a) the 'patriarchal prism' through which the world is generally interpreted veils such considerations. This prism obscures the multiple productive roles of women and their social significance.

[It] is based on a prioritization of public sphere activities over the private realm on the basis of a power relationship between the two. The public sphere of states and markets is defined primarily in terms of their major players, governments and transnational corporations as well as the influential international entities involving and/or affecting both, such as the European Union (EU) … and the World Trade Organization (WTO). The statistics which are utilized to describe the power and division of wealth across the world economy reflect this framing of it in terms of these major players but they also reflect associated narrowly-defined interpretations of production and consumption at state and market levels. These are related to the elevation of the public over the private as determinant of international reality, a process which in theory and practice works to obscure various aspects of social reproduction in the private realm, that is the home and the family [see also Peterson, 1992; Whitworth 1994].

The active and diverse involvements of women in producing and reproducing the world in which we live are significantly lost in the mainstream statistical-speak of Gross National Product (GNP) and the dominant representations of states and national and global economies. As Jan Jindy Pettman points out: 'Much state discourse renders women invisible, as if citizens and workers are gender neutral, or assuming they are men' (Pettman, 1996, p. 13). In a feminist critique of political economy J. K. Gibson-Graham (1996, p. 8) depicts capitalism as the 'phallus' or 'master term' (Gibson-Graham, 1996, p. 8). It defines the household as the space of 'consumption' (of capitalist commodities) and of 'reproduction' (of the capitalist workforce) rather than as a space of noncapitalist production and consumption.

Feminist writings have long stressed that constructions of society on the basis of unequal status for women, and partial representations of society which veil their various contributions, have impacted on women's lives, identities and reflexive processes. To the extent that the conditions which shape our lives influence the parameters within which our consciousness operates, the patriarchal prism has interior as well as exterior impact. This is partially concretized and reconcretized through the range of discourses in which we engage on a daily basis. Many of these discourses are institutionalized through state, medical and commercial bodies and practices, and our engagement in them is as much a process of self-definition as it is of social definition. In other words, the discourses through which we live various aspects of our lives at intimate and public levels, in personal and institutional settings, contribute to the ways in which we understand those lives and our specific identities in relation to them.

[I]n every society the production of discourse is at once controlled, selected, organized and redistributed by a certain number of procedures whose role is to ward off its powers and dangers, to gain mastery over its chance events, to evade its ponderous, formidable materiality (Foucault, 1984, p. 109).

Traditions of feminist thought and action have highlighted that such thinking is relevant to resistance as well as conformity.

Transcending silences

The feminist practice of consciousness-raising takes as its object women's experience of our lives. It involves the coming together of women in women-only groups to discuss our lives from the shared perspective that society is patriarchal and oppresses women. Yet this very process of sharing experience with other women leads to a recognition that the terms in which we understand things are not fixed. Experience is not something which language reflects. In so far as it is meaningful experience is constituted in language. Language offers a range of ways of interpreting our lives which imply different versions of experience (Weedon, 1987, p. 85).

The issue of women-to-women interaction in feminist thought and practice has been key. This is a recognition of many things. Perhaps most important among these is the constriction of women's expression under patriarchal, or what would be regarded as 'normal', social conditions. This exposes the pressures on individuals to conform to such conditions, in the recognition that real penalties can result from acts or expressions of non-conformity.

> [A]s history constantly teaches us, discourse is not simply that which translates struggles or systems of domination, but it is the thing for which and by which there is struggle, discourse is the power which is to be seized (Foucault, 1984, p. 110).

But it also stresses the significance of the silencing of such expressions. This silencing has concrete effects, too, not least for female identity and consciousness. Isolated within patriarchal conditions of conformity, a woman's individual thoughts against such conditions, while silenced and not shared with others, have limited potential either for herself or others. Acts of self-expression and communication are understood as intrinsic elements of liberation in feminist practice, hence the importance of creating 'safe' environments such as women's groups of different kinds. These provide usually temporary opportunities for abstraction from normalized patriarchal conditions, from the disciplining which leads to conformity in such circumstances, and from the threat of exclusion which inhibits 'forbidden speech' (Foucault, 1984, p. 113). There is, of course, no suggestion that such abstraction is ideal or complete in any sense, but it offers at least a challenge to dominant conditions which can lead to different, empowering kinds of knowledge sharing.

'Empowering' has multiple meanings here: the strength that shared reactions and circumstances can give to individuals to take their own thinking further, to cope better with their conditions of existence, and to reach out to others in similar circumstances. These are some of the elements relevant to understandings of liberation as it has been mobilized in feminist discourses challenging patriarchal assumptions and practices. This liberation directly links issues of individual consciousness to group (women's) consciousness, including the identity effects of private/public boundaries and the constraints which result in thought and practice. Transcending the embedded assumptions of institutionalized private/public divisions and understanding their importance for negotiation of questions of power in social contexts are central. Fundamental to the collective as well as individual approach to such consciousness-raising is an understanding of the importance of communication among women, of bringing them together and disrupting the patriarchal conditions which separate them under conditions of public/private divides. While such separation is linked in part to the predominant social definition of women and their concerns within private (familial/home/domestic) boundaries, it also relates to other aspects of inequality, as already indicated, for example class or social hierarchy, colour or ethnicity. Increasingly in recent years feminist debates have located these concerns in a number of different areas: international/global settings, addressing critically the hegemony of Western feminist thought; issues of difference, including in relation to public/private constructions and relations in contrasting social and cultural settings; and the possibilities of multiple feminisms with the priority of sharing new knowledges about women, their lives and aims, their strategies and priorities. Jan Jindy Pettman's framework for 'a feminist international politics' involves a process of 'worlding women' which means 'taking women's experiences of the international seriously, while not assuming that any experiences are transparent or politically innocent' (Pettman, 1996, x). The UN World Conferences on Women have been key catalysts in this respect, as have the growing number of organizations, groups and projects focusing on different areas of women and development. The Internet and its use in these and wider contexts by women has contributed to the growth of new possibilities for women through communication.

Virtual space as women's communicative space

So how should we be thinking about 'virtual space' as women's communicative space? One helpful way, I would argue, is to maintain a strong sense of the public/private contexts which shape women's lives and communication, including, importantly, with one another, and to recognize that liberation strategies have long been focused on challenging the discursive boundaries resulting from them. In other words, while virtual space needs to be considered in terms of its distinctions, it should also be related to well-established women's and feminist emphasis on the radical potential of communication. I have indicated that the notion of 'safe' environments in which women can meet and communicate has been fundamental to the transition of feminist theory into practice through, for example, consciousness-raising. The basis for safety has at least in part been the establishment of a collective boundary which, albeit temporarily, for instance in group meetings, offers some protection from the most overt pressures to discipline oneself to speak according to social norms of women's identity. The safety has been a discursive safety among other things. In that sense it represents an openness to provisionality and exploration rather than fixity.

The knowing self is partial in all its guises, never finished, whole, simply there and original; it is always constructed and stitched together imperfectly, and therefore able to join with another, to see together without claiming to be another (Haraway, 1991b, p. 22).

These conditions have been created traditionally in local settings but increasingly these have become national and international, and through the Internet the global possibilities continue to expand. As with most technologies, however, the Internet has brought new risks as well as such possibilities. At the same time as it has expanded the communications links for women, it has expanded opportunities for surveillance of their interactions and harassment of various kinds. As many have pointed out, the Internet is not an ideal but rather a socially produced space, and despite its unique qualities it must be treated as such if the parameters of what it offers are to be usefully understood (Sardar, 1996).

Whatever the difficulties, challenges and threats, a growing number of women are actively using the Internet to expand their communication with one another, and while it may not be appropriate to think of this virtual space as discursively safe in the ways face-to-face meetings and exchanges can be, the openings it offers build on what is being and has been achieved in such contexts. I am emphasizing here the linkages in women's and feminist communications strategies historically as well as contemporaneously. The Internet era may be new but it builds on what has already been achieved by women in overcoming their social segregation to share and talk to one another and to work individually and collectively for social change. It is a new locus of communications among and about women which links to a history of diverse efforts by them and those supportive of work to transform gender inequalities, including through radical forms of communication. This signals the priority of thinking specifically about the nature of the Internet as women's communicative space. This entails a purchase on the linkages between different kinds of social space and virtual space, for few of us need reminding just how much local spaces, including homes and various forms of community and work locations, retain their central importance in women's lives.

The Internet clearly does not float free from other social locations but is directly connected to them in diverse and complex ways. Individuals and groups are socially located in their uses of the Internet. Where we live, the nature of our polities and economies, the availability of communications technologies, and our abilities to use them, are among major factors affecting differentiated access to the Internet, and the knowledge sources and networking possibilities it offers. The WoN project has been addressing the meanings of such issues for women's collective projects and, like other such projects, has highlighted the problems of English-language domination on the Net and the technical barriers to women's active and innovative use of it for their own designated aims. Empowerment in this medium definitely includes technical empowerment, so long an area of disadvantage for women. Some of the most exciting stories from the WoN project have featured the sharing of information and expertise among women internationally to bring about such empowerment. This is symbolic of the productive nature of the Internet era for women's development and strategy and it entails the discovery as well as the overcoming of boundaries.

The radical potential of the Internet

This is an area of significant radical potential for women on the Internet. The new links offer women on an international basis new knowledges about one another and collective communicative openings to share experiences, views and goals and to strategize. The shared characteristics of such endeavours are potentially transcendent in a number of ways. And it can be argued that they represent consciousness-raising possibilities in new transnational settings. Such activities may involve only a limited number of women at present but the possibilities for growth are inspiring. This is a new stage of discovery by women about women. The precise nature of this discovery is worthy of emphasis, as also is the direct nature of the communication facilitated by women as individuals. This returns us to the notion of a safe environment in the sense that such direct communication offers distinctive forms of protection from the disciplinary influences which impact on discursive practices as discussed earlier in this chapter. The growing attention to surveillance issues in relation to the Net, including the involvement of state institutions (Nguyen and Alexander, 1996, pp. 109–10), is undoubtedly part of the politics of the future, and for women seeking a safe cross-border, cross-cultural communications space, an area of concern. The possibilities for safe interaction which virtual space offers present new challenges for communications between women, defined by them and among them, and, importantly, away from wider social gazes (in public and private contexts) in which they may feel more constrained from breaking boundaries and testing norms. In such a sense, I would argue virtual space provides radically new settings for women's communications, and ones which, as has become evident in the WoN project, can work to set fresh agendas about priorities in these areas. Such perspectives do emphasize that it is not only women's access to technology and their knowledge and skills with regard to it that count, but also the circumstances in which they use it and the freedoms they feel to think about and test the opportunities provided by it. In so doing, women are confronting the embedded male domination of technology and its social purposes and working to transcend, at least in some ways, the impact of this domination on their lives and experiences, certainly their identities.

The Net's cross-boundary potential

This discussion has located consideration of women and the Internet in general terms in several key contexts. It has related the boundary-crossing characteristics and future potential of the Net directly to the development of feminist thought about global politics. It has aligned contemporary feminist theoretical trajectories towards 'resiting the political' with the virtual communicative capacities of the Net and its radical potential for women-to-women cross-boundary interaction. The conclusions which can be drawn suggest a number of interesting parallels between the concrete connective qualities of the Net and the present open and self-conscious goals of feminist politics.

The title of the chapter signals the new critical terrain of such politics. Virtual voices are by their very nature disembodied. They help to hinder assumptions about the real lives to which they are connected. They allow space for alternative imaginings and projections and they permit paths of shared discovery to and from the virtual and the real. The virtual space of the Net transgresses traditional public/private frameworks which have contributed in multiple ways to the fixing of gendered identities. Importantly, it also transgresses the national boundaries within which such identities are predominantly shaped.

For women, who traditionally in theory as well as practice have been absent from the realm of global politics, this represents a distinctive development. It identifies the Net as a unique and highly flexible sphere of women-to-women cross-boundary interaction. It offers significant possibilities for new forms of knowledge building by women for women, and, in its cross-sectional capacities, allows theory to be put in touch with practice in new and dynamic ways.

One of the guiding characteristics of the WoN project, for example, is the diversity of its membership and the recognition that many members engage in multiple roles as activists, academics, and institutional and community workers. Many of the exchanges of the group have been focused on the bases of membership and how the identity of the group as a whole should be understood and projected. This process demonstrates the degree to which WoN is symbolic of actual contemporary efforts to resite feminist politics through endeavours of joint investigation, discovery and articulation. Identity issues in such circumstances cannot be avoided, either in collective or individual terms. Neither, crucially, can efforts to make them politically and practically meaningful. This has been one of the prime preoccupations of WoN. It did not have to be identified deliberately as an agenda item; it happened inevitably. It occurred across face-to-face and virtual boundaries and endures as an ongoing issue.

Cyberfeminism and change

Transcending our lived and grounded identities in order to build innovative forms of shared politics which breach traditional boundaries of state, race, class and gender, may be recognized as necessary without a sense of the practical means to achieve it. Throwing away political assumptions is like jumping into the unknown. What is interesting about the Net is its capacity to represent a virtual unknown; to provide the unknown without the actual necessity of open risk. By open I refer here to the 'safe' space which the Net can represent and its particular significance for women as explored above: safe from a public gaze and its disciplining effect, safe for breaking through the publicly asserted boundaries of social and self-imagining; safe also in its local availability, albeit only potentially for most women of the world at present. This reframes at least to some degree the invisibility problem of women in global politics. I have indicated that an aspect of this invisibility is the extent to which public/private frameworks intrude on women-to-women relations and their widest potential. The Net offers the means for women actively to transgress such restrictions on their collective knowledge building and strategizing in circumstances which can connect local and global sites and issues. In this chapter I have deliberately identified this as a question of theory as well as practice and it would be hard to underline the significance of this strongly enough.

Feminist analysis has always stressed the links between knowledge and action, the oppressive dynamics of dominant patterns of theory and social relations, and the importance of critical thought to the potential for social transformation. The arguments presented have located the promise of the Net for women in this theory–practice mode. New forms of practice need new forms of theory. As feminist theory enters a new phase of critical awareness and sensitivity to discovering shared politics in conditions of difference, the Net offers a specific communicative domain for bringing women together for such purposes. Through their virtual voices they can confront and challenge the ideas as well as the conditions and practices that separate and connect them in their real lives. Cyberfeminisms may be the new collective knowledges which result, utilizing the radical potential of virtual space to work towards real change.

4

INTERNET, EMERGENT CULTURE AND DESIGN

Silvia Austerlic

Internet, a new culture of design

The goal of this chapter is to visualize the Internet as a space for cultural production and a novel medium for understanding and organizing collectively constructed knowledge. Internet can be seen as bringing about a new culture of design, originating not in science but in engineering, and yet to fully enter academic discussions. Rather than seeing technology and globalization as neutral instruments, the design perspective suggests they are proposing a new rationality and an ambitious yet concrete opportunity for change resting on a new knowledge economy and on culture-based local identities. We may interpret in this light, for instance, the new international community and decentralized managerial networks through which a 'global' or 'universal' logic find their meaning.

The Chilean Fernando Flores – one of the first people who applied cybernetics on a large scale to problems of social organization in Latin America – maintains that the new information technology poses a radical challenge: how to navigate global spaces in order to design local actions (Flores, 1994). We are in a period of juncture and transition, and the future will depend on the consensus we might be able to generate. We must be able to generate spaces in which we can envision more just worlds, and commit ourselves to creating them. Flores believes that we must find a universal logic of organizations that makes possible long-term strategies. The design of tools and the organization's cognitive capacity are closely linked in this vision, which also suggests ways to transform cognitive and cultural resources into capital. Consequently, we need a theory of the economy that makes visible all these manifold forms of capital as central players. Individual and social transformation occur side by side in this new theory.

According to Colombian anthropologist Arturo Escobar, computer information and biological technologies are bringing about a fundamental transformation in the structure and meaning of modern society, from the vantage points of biology, language, history and culture (Escobar, 1997). The point of departure of this inquiry is the belief that any technology represents a cultural invention, in the sense that it brings forth a world: it emerges out of particular cultural conditions and in turn helps to create new ones. The explosion of new technologies, the formation of geopolitical blocs, and novel forms of digitalized planetary connectivity are fostering novel scenarios and world orders, calling for alternatives approaches. Notions such as globalization, innovation and technology themselves awake unprecedented fears and possibilities, especially since they reflect the tremendous cultural changes we are witnessing. We may thus understand globalization as a dynamic and conflictive period marked by the irruption of processes fuelled by new and original media that alter scales and categories of social life.

Brief ontology of design

In this context, 'design' is understood in a broad sense, as a potentiality which characterizes each human being and which manifests itself in the invention of new social practices, be they products, services or trends. Here 'innovation' means not only material and technical creations, but, more importantly, new forms of living life and facing challenges, resulting in contrasting 'styles'. Hence the need to formulate new conceptual tools that allow us to be sensitive to changes, and to approach them with creativity and a keen sense of their historical specificity. A corollary of these definitions is that each person can be seen as the designer of his/her particular field of knowledge and action, which requires that we specify the 'domain' (the local context) which is the object of design actions. Design actions, in turn, may produce changes in the reality of the user. The core of design process is thus the formulation of specifications in time and space, which makes of design a fundamental activity with ramifications in all areas of human activity.

For the German designer Gui Bonsiepe – who moved to Latin America in 1968 – the epistemology of design can be articulated around seven principles. First, design is a domain that can become manifest in any area of knowledge and human action; second, it is oriented towards the future; third, it introduces something new in the world, and is thus linked to innovation; fourth, it is connected to body and space, particularly cognitive space; fifth, design is oriented towards effective actions; sixth, it is linguistically anchored in a field of values and judgements; and finally, seventh, it establishes an articulation between user and artifact; the user – in his or her perceptual, logical and operational dimensions – is of major concern to the designer (Bonsiepe, 1991). The interface constitutes the designer's central domain of attention; it is through interface design that the designer articulates a space of action for the user. In a sense, design outlines the socio-cultural efficacy of a community of clients, encompassing this community's lifestyle and technological media. Design is the design of something that does not yet exist; its ontological structure is composed of four domains: a user or social agent; a task to be fulfilled; a tool or artifact to carry out the task; and an interface that connects the three former domains to the human body.

A sustainable strategy for developing countries

As a designer working in the field of social communication and infomation since 1995 I have begun to explore the enormous human potential of the Net as a tool for developing countries, where sustainable development does not have to do with owning new technological information, but with solving 'South' communication needs and problems. Therefore, in order to challenge the 'have-nots' situation, we should not only teach this 'profile' of potential computer users the technical aspects of the Net, but also help them to find new creative strategies for community organization and for designing, in cooperation, decentralized 'soft-hearted' communication systems – the kind that have few material resources but are full of good quality information.

From design's perspective, if we could produce 'problems' and 'solutions' in terms of 'information', potential community networks could be articulated in profitable technosocial systems, and the benefits would consist of people using them for encouraging dialogue and providing a forum for voices that too often go unheard. Via computer networking technology, communities can now be connected electronically in order to pursue activities such as community and public health projects, long-distance learning, performances and 'virtual spaces' for creative interchange.

One of the chief advantages of the Internet is the access it gives to a vast amount of information while permitting the exchange of ideas and experiences with a multiplicity of new social actors. Before this potential is realized, however, any organization, enterprise or social actor must define its identity and underlying vision and goals. To this end, it needs to develop a complex management capability in each of the areas in which it acts, with concrete projects and objectives; it must also be capable of continuous self-improvement. Only in this way will information become a powerful tool for decision making and for competing successfully in the global market. In this sense, connectivity is not restricted to the digital aspects but involves the human actors – organizations, the public sector, the community. What is at stake is the transformation of the practices that are engendering new worlds at present.

In this cultural context, when I refer to the Net I am not talking about a terminal. Rather I imagine it as a source; with the possibility to expand traditional limits and to find new possibilities to democratize development, using the vast communication potential of the Net. And when I say communication, I do not refer to the new media only, but to communication as the core of our humanity, as a social commitment to rebuild what global forces have destroyed (Schuler, 1996).

Design as a tool for change in Latin America

It is clear that any country that decides to utilize design as an instrument for competing in international markets must abide by international quality criteria, decided upon by advanced countries on the basis of growing complexity and automation. These criteria are often at odds with the needs of developing societies, given that they tend to produce exclusion, unemployment and a very technologized future. The current technological revolution, however, opens up new avenues and para-meters of access to global possibilities that could channel local action. It is not in the domain of hardware and software, but in education that Latin America might have greater opportunities. Bearing in mind the goal of design with new technologies, the question thus becomes how to weave together the designer's mind, an orientation towards quality, and a set of effective practices within the overall context of a 'modern' project that visualizes and materializes them. What is needed in order to compete in the information society is not so much quantity, but the added value – understood as meaning and context – of what is being said; this in turn requires attention to cultural context, and to the wider dimensions of telecommunications when thinking about content.

So, if it is true that new technologies are transforming modern structure, can the Third World countries reposition themselves creatively in the space of this transformation as relevant and vocal actors in the conversations that are shaping the world, and perhaps as creators of alternative discourses about society, nature and economy? I believe that this innovative attitude is possible; it is in fact validated by recent Latin American literature on design by authors such as Fernando Flores, Gui Bonsiepe, Fernando Flores Morador and Tomás Maldonado. Our dignity as Latin Americans demands from us a critical and creative attitude in facing the challenges of the future, and the future is the space of design. As we navigate among the various currents of design in this chapter, we embark upon a collective task of design ourselves.

An interesting example of identity-driven technological appropriation is the Red de Humanistas Latinoamericanos (Latin American Humanist Network, RHLA), an electronic forum devoted to information production and exchange of issues relevant to Latin America. The Red has a Web page created in January 1996 and a discussion list (August 1996). In March 1997 it embarked on the creation of the Latin American Virtual University (Universidad Virtual Latinoamericana, UVLA), with which I work from the perspective of communicator and designer. For the director of the RHLA, Fernando Flores Morador, 'the secret of cultural identity lies in our difference from known cultural tendencies. To be different is the alternative left us if we want to be ourselves; to this end, we must identify those areas in which we can build our difference. It is a question of exercising a universal culture for our particular realization' (Flores Morador, 1996, p. 30).

ICTs and education for innovation

There is this hope, in some communities worldwide, that information and communication technologies (ICTs) can make a difference that improves the quality of life, especially for the poor living in rural and remote areas. Material requirements are simple: such basic needs as uncomplicated access to safe drinking water, education and good health facilities, to have enough to eat and to have a shelter. The fulfilment of these needs requires the construction and operation of water supply schemes, schools and health facilities; it requires the production of food, expert knowledge and other resources. It is important to realize that education, for it to be meaningful, must be in concert with expert and indigenous knowledge, and with local needs. Knowledge is dependent on time and space, and no amount of 'globalization' can remove these elements if education is to be relevant to people. Therefore, education should be in the domain of the very basic level of human organization and evolve around cultural needs, in tune with local knowledge and the evolution of the community's own knowledge base.

Design shares with education its orientation towards the future. Like language, it is constitutive of human action. Thus we need to talk not just about the design of objects, but about the design of situations in which life unfolds. Situations, not objects, are constitutive of design. How do we educate people capable of innovation, that is, of detecting change and acting from a new paradigm yet to be invented? How can we design our own autonomy? What is at stake is our own identity and the creation of our own peculiar models of technological and cultural change.

For some, new technologies embody a critique of conventional development; in this respect, they afford hopeful opportunities for developing countries. Whereas conventional development demands passivity, homogenization, and unidirectionality towards particular states, new technologies foster interactivity, multiplicity and alterity. Hence the need to question the centrality of markets and production as principles of social life, something that the neoliberal ideology in vogue seems incapable of doing.

If philosophy constituted the pillar of the classical university, and the sciences were the basis of the modern academy, design could well become the foundation of the university of the future to the extent that it purports to integrate cultures and forms of knowledge into a new educational strategy. For Bonsiepe, it is urgent to invent, identify and define the principles of design; this could be a Southern contribution to avoid increasing peripheralization, for 'we are trapped not so much by lack of knowledge, as by the ignorance of our ignorance. In this resides the essence of underdevelopment' (Bonsiepe, 1996, p. 5).

To counteract peripheralization it is thus necessary to constitute critically the mind and identity of Southern peoples as the most suitable field for experiments in a type of modernity centred on a mature cultural emancipation. We might find signposts for this process in various places, from Paulo Freire's notion of education as a practice for freedom (Freire, 1985) to Fernando Flores Morador's theses on Latin American reality (Flores Morador, 1996). What we need now is to outline the contents of new profiles of leadership, belonging, and work based on well-defined politics of solidarity and national identities freed from the shackles of conventional development.

Inventing our future

Within the new agendas, where ICTs can help is, for example, in the planning and design of these activities by providing relevant and useful information, though we also need a social framework for finding what works in terms of adaptive strategies in communities, focusing on the basic elements of a livelihood 'system' (households, families, communities) – instead of solely on the relationship between an individual and work/job – and identifying what technologies and policy interventions can make a real difference to those living in poverty. Central to this process are the indigenous forms of mobilization and organization, and the means of communication. The major concern is to devise new ways to use the electronic media to enhance the effectiveness of the existing forms of communication. Cultural identities are important. New computer networks can be thought of as an important tool, but this is only a partial viewpoint, for it leaves the most critical questions unanswered: who uses the tool and controls its use, what policies guide its use, and what is the purpose of the tool.

An orientation towards information and virtuality is not enough without a new approach to the contents of education. As the Rector of the Latin American Virtual University says, 'each of us can either invent our future with novel and appropriate elements, or insist on the perpetuation of what has become obsolete' (D'Ambrosio, forthcoming). The creativity demanded by this project certainly entails risks, difficult beginnings, and leaving our fears behind. Yet, we have new tools at our disposal with which we can give direction not so much to these tools' future evolution but to our knowledge and to our desire to inaugurate a new era on this old planet, an era capable of generating agreements on how to conceptualize and bring about an authentic Virtual Peace.

5

EXCLUSION AND COMMUNICATION IN THE INFORMATION ERA
From Silences to Global Conversations

Sohail Inayatullah and Ivana Milojevic

A call for authentic conversations

The discourse of the Internet continues the cant of the tale of progress – a story that does not account for excluded ways of knowing. But the Net is a necessary evil. The challenge for women and men desiring an alternative noncapitalist future is to not be seduced by tool-centred approaches, but rather to participate in the creation of authentic global conversations. Far more is required for cultural pluralism than a fast modem.

Many claim that, with the advent of the Web and Internet, the future has arrived. The dream of an interconnected planet where physical labour becomes minimally important and knowledge creation becomes the source of value and wealth appears to be here. Critics point out that perhaps the 'cyber/information era' view of the future is overly linear, exponentially so, forgetful that two-thirds of the world does not have a phone and much of the world lives over two hours away from a phone connection (Hamilton, 1997, p. 31).[1] While new technologies have speeded up time for the elite in the West and the elite in the non-West, for the majority of the world there is no high-tech information era. In the hyperjump to starspace, we have forgotten that while ideas and the spirit can soar, there are cyclical processes, such as the life and death of individuals, nations and civilizations that cannot be so easily transformed.

While certainly there are more people making their living by processing ideas (Halal, 1996, pp. 13–16),[2] perhaps we are engaged in a non-productive financial/information pyramid scheme where we are getting further and further away from food production and manu-facturing, building virtualities on virtualites until there is nothing there, as in *advaita vedanta*[3] wherein the world is *maya*, an illusion.[4] The coming of the information era, ostensibly providing untold riches in bits of freedom for all, in fact limits the futures of others because it robs them of their future alternatives by amplifying the world view of the dominant. Reality has become constructed as the World Wide Web (WWW), but perhaps this web is Max Weber's iron cage – the future with no exit, wherein there is an inverse relationship between data and wisdom, between quick bytes and long-term commitment, between engagement to technology and engagement with humans, plants and animals.

Immediacy and distance

Research on e-mail culture points out that the twin dangers of immediacy and speed do not lead to greater community and friendship, rather, they can lead to bitter misunderstandings (Gwynne and Dickerson, 1997, pp. 64–6; Morse-Houghten, 1997, pp. 65–6).[5] E-mail then is perhaps not the great connector leading to higher levels of information but the great disconnector that gives the mirage of connection and community. E-mail without occasional face-to-face communication can transform friendships into antagonistic relationships. Just as words lose the informational depth of silence, e-mail loses information embedded in silence and face to face gestures. The assimilation and reflection as well as the intuition and the insight needed to make sense of intellectual and emotional data are lost as the urgent need to respond to others quickens. Women's time, slow time, lunar time, spiritual timeless time, cyclical rise-and-fall time and circular seasonal time are among the victims, leading to temporal impoverishment, a loss of temporal diversity where 'twenty-first century' as a temporal demarcation is for all, instead of peculiar to Western civilization.[6]

Cybertechnologies thus create not just rich and poor in terms of information, but a world of quick inattentive time and slow attentive time. One is committed to quick money and quick time, a world where data and information are far more important than knowledge and wisdom. Cybertechnologies not only create an information rich and poor but also an information quick and slow. Time on the screen is different from time spent gazing at sand in the desert or wandering in the Himalayas or playing with loved ones. Screen time does not slow the heart beat down, relaxing one into the superconscious; rather, we become lost in many bits, creating perhaps an era of accelerating information but certainly not a knowledge future or a future where the subtle mysteries of the world, the spiritual – the depth of the ever-present positive silence – are felt.

This quickening of the self was anticipated by McLuhan in 1980. 'Excessive speed of change isolates already fragmented individuals. At the speed [speech] of light man [*sic*] has neither goals, objectives or private identity. He is an item in the data bank – software only, easily forgotten – and deeply resentful' (McLuhan quoted in *New Internationalist*, December 1996, p. 26). Selves lose reflective space, jumping from one object to another, one website to another, one e-mail to another. It is not a communicative world that will transpire but a world of selves downloading their emotional confusion onto each other. Writes Zia Sardar, 'Far from creating a community based on consensus, the information technologies could easily create states of alienated and atomized individuals, glued to their computer terminal, terrorizing and being terrorized by all those whose values conflict with their own' (Sardar, 1996, p. 847). It is as if we have all become psychic with all thoughts interpenetrating, creating a global schizophrenia (Inayatullah, 1993, pp. 95–130).

Social scientist Kevin Robbins is not convinced that our lives will be changed meaningfully by the information revolution; rather, he believes the ICT hype merely replaces the classical opiate of religion and the modernist idea of progress. Indeed, for Robbins, the new technologies impoverish our imagination of alternative futures, particularly our geographic imagination. Focusing on distance, Robbins quoting Heidegger reminds us that the end of distance is not the creation of nearness, of intimacy, of community. 'We are content to live in a world of "uniform distancelessness", that is, in an information space rather than a space of vivacity and experience' (Robbins, 1997, p. 208). There is the illusion of community – in which we can create virtual communities far and away but still treat badly our neighbours, partners and children.

Nonetheless, writes Robbins, more than destroying the beauty of geography, techno-optimists such as Bill Gates, Nicholas Negroponte and others take away space for critical commentary (personalizing the discourse by seeing critics as merely imbued with too much negativity), that is for the creation of futures that are different. Critical commentary, however, is not a matter merely of being pessimistic or optimistic but a matter of survival. As Paul Virilio writes: 'I work in the "resistance" because there are now too many "collaborators" once again telling us about salvation through progress, and emancipation, about man [*sic*] being freed from all constraints' (Virilio, 1996, p. 78, quoted in Robbins, 1997, p. 210).

The great leap forward

For cyberenthusiasts, new technologies give more choice. Bill Gates believes 'it will affect the world seismically, rocking us in the same way the discovery of the scientific method, the invention of printing, and the arrival of the Information Age did' (Gates, 1995, p. 273, quoted in Robbins, 1997, p. 199). Nicholas Negroponte, author of *Being Digital*, writes:

> While the politicians struggle with the baggage of history, a new genera-tion is emerging from the digital landscape free of many of the old prejudices. These kids are released from the limitation of geographic proximity as the sole basis of friendship, collaboration, play, and neigh-borhood. Digital technology can be a natural force drawing people into greater world harmony (Negroponte, 1995, p. 230, quoted in Robbins, 1997, p. 200).

Douglas Rushkoff (1997) believes that computers are creating a generation gap between the 'screenagers' and others, with screenagers having the most important skill of all – multi-tasking, choosing and doing many things at the same time (of course, forgetting that women have always had to do many things at the same time – taking care of the home and children as well as other types of formal and informal work). In any case, ICTs are creating a new world, an interactive, truly democratic world.

For proponents, the new technologies reduce the power of Big Business and Big State, creating a vast frontier for creative individuals to explore. 'Cyberspace has the potential to be egalitarian, to bring every-one into a network arrangement. It has the capacity to create com-munity; to provide untold opportunities for communication, exchange and keeping in touch' (Dale Spender, quoted in Shute, 1996, p. 9). Cyber-technologies will allow more interaction, creating a global ecumene. They create wealth, indeed, a jump in wealth. The new technologies promise a transformational society where the future is always beckoning, a new discovery is yearly (Serageldin, 1996, pp. 100–14).[7] The oppressive dimensions of bounded identity – to nation, village, gender, culture – will all disappear as we move in and out of identities and communities. It is the end of scarcity as an operating myth and the beginning of abundance, of information that wants to be free. The late twentieth century is the demarcation from the industrial to the information/ knowledge era. Progress is occurring now. Forget the cycle of rise and fall and life and death. That was but misinformation.

While the growth data look impressive and the stock of Microsoft continues upward, there are some hidden costs. For example, what of the negative dimensions of the new technologies such as surveillance? Police in Brisbane, Australia use up to a hundred hidden cameras in malls to watch for criminal activities.[8] Hundreds more are anticipated, creating an electronic grid in central Brisbane. While this might be benign in Brisbane (though Aborigines might have different views), imagining a large grid over Milosevic's Yugoslavia or Taliban's Afghanistan (or under Zia-ul Haq's Pakistan where every 'immoral' gaze would have led to arrest) is enough to frighten the most fanatical techno-optimist. Or is it? Many believe that privacy issues will be forgotten dimensions of the debate on cyberfutures once we each have our own self-encryptors so that no one can read or enter us (the twenty-first century chastity belt). Technology will tame technology. Over time, the benefits of the new technologies will become global with poverty, homelessness and anomie all wiped out. All will eventually have access – even the poorest – as the billions of brains that we are, once connected, will solve the many problems of oppression.[9] While we have always imagined such a future, it is only now that technology makes it possible.

The world capitalist system

While cyberenthusiasts rightfully point to the opportunities of the one world created by new technologies, they forget that the one world of globalism remains fundamentally capitalistic with the local (local economy and power over one's future) increasingly under attack. The tiny Pacific Island of Niue recently discovered that 10 per cent of its national revenue was being sucked out through international sex-line services (*Courier-Mail*, 20 February 1997, p. 19). The information era, as P. R. Sarkar points out, is late capitalism, a system in which all other *varnas* – psycho-social classes and ways of knowing (the intellectual, the worker and the warrior) – become the 'boot lickers of the merchants' (Sarkar, 1984, p. 97). And: 'In order to accumulate more and more in their houses, they torture others to starvation ... they suck the very living plasma of others to enrich the capabilities' (Sarkar, 1959, p. 3). While intellectuals invent metaphors of postmodernity and postindustrialism, capital continues to accumulate unevenly, the poor become poorer and the less powerful become even weaker (they can now have a website). The information era still exists in the context of the world capitalist system – it is not an external development of it, and it will not create the contradictions that end it. As Cees Hamelink writes, 'The institutional arrangements within which ICTs functions are largely defined by the rules of the capitalist market economy which is a manipulative system: it thrives on a conception of people as instrumental to each other's objectives. It is difficult to believe that the system can be beneficial to a constructive cultural pluralism' (Hamelink, 1997, p. 42).

The knowledge society or non-material society that many futurists imagine conveniently forgets humans' very real suffering. But for virtual realities, we have virtual theories. The challenge then for those who do not wish to collaborate is to imagine and design alternative institutional arrangements for information and communication technologies. 'The challenge is to propose structures of ownership, funding and public accountability that can accommodate the requirements of cultural pluralism' (Hamelink, 1997, p. 42) – that is, to create a cultural ecology of ICT. To do so, ICTs will need to be taken out of the relatively 'tool-centric' world view which avoids the institutional, cultural, and historical settings in which ICTs exist and develop, and sees technology as culturally and linguistically neutral.

While we imagine such alternative futures, the immediate negative aspects of the new technologies stare directly at us. Child porn videos or the pornography on the Net might be one of the most striking examples. In these cases, new communication technologies not only help to immortalize the product of a distorted view of sexuality within patriarchal societies, but also help predators to find new victims, creating a reverse civil society, a community of the predatory violent. Rapists or paedophiles can connect with their like-minded friends and together they can create a virtual world in which the 'abnormal' becomes 'normal' and the most secret ideas become common property, encouraging people 'on the edge' to proceed with what they might have considered problematic before. The introduction of the 'right to own a PC' in the twenty-first century might even enhance this type of behaviour.

Introducing computer literacy in schools, and having more and more information for everyone, both in the developed and in the undeveloped world, is perhaps a beautiful idea but it cannot solve our many social and cultural problems, let alone all the world's problems as some 'technophiliacs' want us to believe. Again this is partly because these technologies are developing in the context of a world view still fixated on progress which, in the words of Foucault, 'make us an object of information, never a subject of communication' (Foucault, 1979, p. 200).

Earlier it was Comte's positive science that was to solve all the problems of religion, of difference; now, with the end of the Cold War, it is liberal democracy. Michael Tracey, in his essay 'Twilight: Illusion and Decline in the Communication Revolution', writes that it is not an accident that just at the precise moment 'the planet is being constructed within the powerful, pervasive all consuming logic of the market, there is a second order language, a fairy tale ... that suggests in Utopian terms new possibilities, in particular, those presented by the new alchemies of "the Net" ' (Tracey, p. 50). What was once the cant of progress is now the cant of cyberspace: from love to democracy, from evil to poverty, all will be delivered, all will be redeemed – virtuality is 'here'.

Thus, while the Internet helps connect many people (especially those in the North) and supplies much needed information (especially important in the South) it also represents a specific form of cultural violence. While it intends to create a global community of equals, making identification based on age, looks, race, (dis)ability, class or gender become less relevant, it also, by promoting, enhancing and cementing current ways of communicating, silences billions of people.

Exclusion

Some of the excluded are non-English speaking nations, 'irrelevant' nations and peoples, national, religious and ideological minorities, poor in poor countries and poor in rich countries, the majority of women, most old and disabled, and almost all children (although certainly not Western screenagers). In the twenty-first century most of the world's population will still be silenced. Reality will still be that of the strongest and most powerful. The new communication technologies will further enhance differences between the poor and the rich, between women and men, and between the world and the narrow part of it defined as 'the West'. And once poor, if the world and women catch up with the dominating forces, it will be on their terms and it will be in their language.

The language on the Net is even more limited than its English pervasiveness: it is a language of technical rationality which prevents all other forms of knowing and experiencing this world. There is little space for communicative poetry, for feeling what is unsaid, for reading other signs, for weaving with another presence. But the Net does allow us to give and receive information and it enables us to contact people we would otherwise never meet. Thus as individuals we are becoming richer and richer every day, while as a world we are becoming poorer and poorer. Will these culturally rich individuals automatically be able to create a future world consisting of many cultures and many meanings, and endowed with better abilities to understand? Will there be some 'invisible hand' which can help create all this? Or will we all become 'neuromancers', alienated in one way or another?

Women and global conversations

Before crying over our lost battle, we (women, non-English speaking people, not so technically oriented individuals) can start thinking in terms of what exactly is silenced, and what we can do about it. How can we engage in global conversations while not losing our own identities, our own understanding of reality, our ways of speaking, or our own language? How can we use the Net without being used by it?

Women and others do not necessarily have to be disempowered. Women have proved they can speak the language of their 'enemy' (as has the South of the North). After all that is what women learn in schools, gather from books and from all the other print media: someone else's history, someone else's perspective and someone else's knowledge. Most feminists agree that in order to achieve this women had to either became bilingual (some successfully and many through the destructive process of othering their own selves) or to abandon their own traditional language. While it is not so clear what this traditional language might be, obvious differences between women's and men's ways of speaking are found to exist. Research, in general, shows that women ask questions while men make statements, that women talk about people and feelings while men talk about things, that women use more adjectives, more modal forms such as 'perhaps', 'sort of', 'maybe', and more tag questions and attention beginners (Fishman, 1990).

It is often stressed that language not only reflects but also perpetuates and contributes to gender inequality, and that through language hierarchy between genders is 'routinely established and maintained' (Fishman, 1990, p. 225). Feminist researchers find that men are more likely than women to control conversation while women do 'support work' being some sort of 'cooperative conversationalists' who express frequent concern for other participants in talk (Cameron, McAlinden and O'Leary, 1993, p. 424). The main solution for the transformation of the current conversational division of labour between sexes cannot be only in the area of language because even the most 'neutral' terms can always be appropriated by the dominant culture (like the meaning of the word 'no' can be at times constructed to mean 'maybe' or 'wait a while'). Susan Ehrlich and Ruth King write: 'Because linguistic meanings are, to a large extent, determined by the dominant culture's social values and attitudes, terms initially introduced to be non-sexist and neutral may lose their neutrality in the 'mouths' of a sexist speech community and/or culture' (Ehrlich and King, 1993, pp. 410–11). The organization of words and ideas into knowledge was similarly conducted in a context of masculine power where women were made invisible, their existence either denied or distorted and their ways of knowing and issues of interest labelled irrelevant. While many feminist linguists are attempting to reinvent language and support women's emancipation through linguistic interventions, it is clear that this has to be done simultaneously with political, economic and cultural transformations in the areas of knowledge, language and the written word. The question is: can the Net become a site for this reinvention? Can women's and others' ways of knowing and speaking find space and voice on the Net? Can we escape the tool-centric approach of the new information and communication technologies to create a softer, listening future in which we co-evolve with nature, technology, the spirit, and the many civilizations that are humanity? Can the Net be communicative, in the widest sense of the word?

While it is obvious that women can and do use the most dominant language, it is also claimed that women would rather use 'softer', more intuitive and face-to-face approaches. In a future controlled by women, oral tradition, body language, sounds, dreams, intuitive and psychic ways of communicating possibly would be equal with the written text, or at least not so much suppressed. Maybe, in such a society where women would participate at all levels and in all spheres it wouldn't be necessary to introduce 'dressing Barbie' video games in order to make girls more interested in new computer technologies. Maybe new software would be more interactive and more user (women/other) friendly and maybe new communication technologies would look completely different. Maybe they would not be so individualized, and maybe, net-weaving would be done in a context of community or friendly groups and not in a context of alienated individuals. Priorities would probably be somewhere else: where the quality of life of the majority of people would have the highest value.

A real information society

Thus there are progressive dimensions to the new technologies, and these can be developed further. As Fatma Aloo of the Tanzanian Media Women's Association argues, ICTs 'are a necessary evil'.[10] Women and other marginalized groups must use and design them for their own empowerment or they will be further left out and behind. Without being part of the design (the 'knowledge ware') and use process, they will have to other themselves even further when they use the ICTs.

What is needed, then, is the creation of a progressive information society. It would be a world system that was diverse in how it viewed knowledge, appreciating the different ways gender and civilization order the real. It would not just be technical but emotional and spiritual as well, and ultimately one that used knowledge to create better human conditions, to reduce *dhukka* (suffering) and realize *moksa* (spiritual liberation from the bonds of action and reaction). The challenge, then, is not just to increase our ability to produce and understand information but to enhance the capacity of the deeper layers of mind, particularly in developing what in Tantric philosophy is called the *vijinanamaya kosa* (where knowledge of what is eternal and temporal is touched). Certainly, even though the Web is less rigid than a library, it is not the liberating information technology some assume – spiritual energies and shamanistic dissenting spaces (Nandy, 1996, pp. 636–9) cannot enter. Of course, underlying an alternative view of an information society is a commitment to *prama* or a dynamic equilibrium wherein internal/external, 'male/female' and spiritual/material are balanced.

From global conversations to a *gaia* of civilizations

We thus need to imagine and help create social spaces so the new technologies participate in and allow for the coming of a real global civilization, a *prama*, a *gaia* of cultures; one where there is deep multiculturalism; where not just political representation and economic wealth are enhanced but the basis of civilization: the epistemologies of varied cultures, women and men, how they see self and other. To begin to realize that, first we need to critically examine the politics of information. We need to ask if the information we receive is true; if it is important, what its implications are, and who is sending us the information. We also need to determine if we can engage in a conversation with the information sent – to question it, to reveal its cultural/gendered context, to discern if the information allows for dialogue, for communication. We thus need to search for ways to transform information to communication (going far beyond the 'interactivity' the Web promises us), creating not a knowledge economy (which silences differences of wealth) but a communicative economy (where differences are explored, some unveiled, others left to be).

To do so, in addition to engaging critically with the assumptions beyond the information discourse, we also need to expand the limited rationalist discourse in which 'information' resides. What we learn from other cultures such as the indigenous Indian Tantric is that the new electronic technologies are just one of the possible technologies creating world space. Indeed they just act at the most superficial materialistic levels. As important as cyberspace is *microvita* space (Sarkar, 1984; Sheldrake, 1981; Boulding, 1990),[11] or the noosphere being created through our world imaginations, through our increasingly shared collective consciousness.

Certainly while the reality of the information era is one of exclusion, the potential for shared communication futures remains. To realize these will require far more communication – sharing of meaning – than we have ever known and at far greater levels, in the light of the many ways we know and learn from each other. While we have highlighted the structures of power that create colonization, we also need to acknowledge personal agency, we particularly need to be far more sensitive to how we project our individual and civilizational dark sides on others. The information era will further magnify our assumptions of self-innocence and other-as-guilty unless we begin to reveal our complicity in soliloquy posing as conversation. If information can be transformed to communication, then perhaps the Web can participate in the historical decolonization process, giving power to communities and individuals in the overall context of global human, economic, environmental and culturally negotiated universals.

NOTES

1 Anita Hamiliton for *Time* magazine reports that this, at least in Africa, is quickly to change. 'Thanks to a $1.2 billion satellite system to be completed by 2001, the average distance to a phone could go from 35 miles to just two with the installation of about 500,000 solar-powered telephone stations throughout the continent. An added perk: TV and radio reception for all' (p. 31). We shall have to wait to see if the equally important issues of upkeep, community ownership and pride, as well as continuing education – that is, the cultural appropriation of the new technology – have equal levels of financial and organizational investment.

2 Halal writes that in the US 'Blue-collar workers should dwindle from 20 per cent of the US work force in 1995 to 10 per cent or less within a decade or two ... non-professional white-collar workers [will be reduced] from 40 per cent to 20–30 per cent. The remaining 60–70 per cent or so of the work force may then be composed of knowledge workers. ... meanwhile, productivity, living standards and the quality of life will soar to unprecedented levels.' See also, *The Think Tank Directory,* in which it is reported that the number of think tanks have exploded from 62 in 1945 to 1200 in 1996. For more information on this e-mail: grs@cjnetworks.com or write 214 S.W. 6th Avenue, Suite 301, Topeka, KS 66603, USA.

3 One of the six schools of classical Indian philosophy. Only Brahman, the supreme consciousness, is postulated as real. Everything else is an illusion – *maya*.

4 Recent debacles in the world financial system – the crisis of the Tigers – is evidence of this.

5 Gwynne and Dickerson (1997) report on the dangers in businesses when bosses use e-mail to berate employees, creating considerable ill-will and inefficiencies.

E-mail exports the anger of the sender to the receiver. Diane Morse-Houghten writes that 'E-mail leaves a lot of blank spaces in what we say, which the recipient tends to fill with the most negative interpretation' (p. 65). To avoid sending the wrong message, four rules are suggested: '(1) Never discuss bad news, never criticize and never discuss personal issues over e-mail. And if there's a chance that what you say could be taken the wrong way, walk down the hall to discuss it in person or pick up the phone' (p. 66).

6 For more on the temporal hegemony, particularly in the construction of the twenty-first century as neutral universal timing instead of as particular to the West, see Inayatullah (1988).

7 Serageldin (1996) compiles an impressive array of statistics. 'Items in the Library of Congress are doubling every 14 years and, at the rate things are going, will soon be doubling every 7 years.... In the US, there are 55,000 trade books published annually.... The gap of scientists and engineers in north and south is vast with 3,800 per million in the US and 200 per million in the south. ... [Finally], currently a billion e-mail messages pass between 35 million users, and the volume of traffic on the Internet is doubling every 10 months' (pp. 100–1). Of course, why anyone would want to count e-mail messages is the key issue – as ridiculous would be to count the number of words said daily through talking, or perhaps even count the silences between words.

8 Stated on the television show *Sixty Minutes*, Channel 9, Brisbane, Australia, 16 March 1997.

9 While these are optimistic forecasts, Roar Bjonnes reports that, according to *The Nation* magazine, '368 of the world's richest people own as much wealth as 40 per cent of the world's poor'. In other words, 368 billionaires own as much as 2.5 billion poor people. Moreover, the trend is toward greater inequity with the 'share of global income between the world's rich and the world's poor doubling from 30-1 in 1960 to 59 to 1, in 1989. The information revolution will have to be quite dramatic to reverse these figures'. E-mail: Rbjonnes@igc.apc.org, 13 August 1995. Bjonnes is former editor of *Commonfuture* and *Prout Journal*.

10 Comments delivered at the 'Women and Cyberspace Workshop,' Santiago de Compostela, Spain, 20 May 1997.

11 For example, as mystic Sarkar (1984) reminds us, behind our wilful actions is the agency of *microvita* – the basic substance of existence, which is both mental and physical, mind and body. *Microvita* can be used by minds (the image of monks on the Himalayas sending out positive thoughts is the organizing metaphor here, as is the Muslim prayer in unison throughout the world with direction and focus) to change the vibrational levels of humans, making them more sensitive to others, to nature and to the divine. And as Rupert Sheldrake (1981) and Elise Boulding (1990) also remind us, as images and beliefs of one diverse world become more common it will be easier to imagine one world and live as one world, as a blissful universal family.

PART TWO

Women Creating
Global Communication

PART ONE having addressed some of the underlying analytical questions about how women and other groups can open creative spaces that form new cybercultures, Part Two takes up the shift in our understanding of communication policy, knowledge systems and global networking as a result of women's engagement in the cyberworld. Here we move to some examples of how women are navigating the technoscientific world – virtually and in reality. The chapters chart women's engagement with the policy world shaping the new communication age and information technologies.

Alice Mastrangelo Gittler describes how women's groups have taken up new information and communications tools to support their global networking. Highlighting the Fourth World Conference on Women held in Beijing in September 1995 as a catalyst for women's electronic activism, she discusses the successes and shortcomings of the Net in linking the world community of women's NGOs. Linking women's practical experience with an increasing need to influence national and global policy, she shows how the new communication age offers tools to improve, support, protect and enhance women's partnership in creating a more gender-equitable global culture.

Members of the Association for Progressive Communication (APC) Women's Programme, a group referred to by many in the book as a key protagonist in women NGOs' initial connection to the Net, reviews its own work to understand a spectrum of relationships between women and the Net. Based on an extensive survey of nearly 800 women worldwide, the chapter shows how women from different social and cultural settings perceive the new ICTs in their work to promote women's rights. The survey reveals that while the potential is certainly there, the Net and Web are not always the most accessible resources for women to use. It points to the huge differential access separating women in the North and South, the continuing problems of infra-structure, the issue of time for women already massively overburdened, and the need to encourage women to overcome their fear of technology.

In their chapters Sophia Huyer and Nidhi Tandon explore how women are entering into the policy world of the new ICTs. Huyer examines how women were able to use their lobbying and advocacy skills to turn around an important Conference on Global Knowledge held in Toronto in June 1997. Women used their established advocacy and networking powers to convince the global community that the new technologies have to be designed in order to incorporate and build on women's knowledge and understanding of what women daily deliver. Nidhi Tandon, focusing on sub-Saharan Africa, shows how ICTs can be powerful tools for change that cross the borders between enterprise, research and government at the policy level. Tandon gives examples of how women's groups in Africa are already recognizing the possibilities of the new technologies to build on innovations for change as they take up ownership of the Internet.

6

MAPPING WOMEN'S GLOBAL COMMUNICATIONS AND NETWORKING

Alice Mastrangelo Gittler

Women responding to the new electronic communications

The revolutionary promise and potential of electronic communications are capturing the attention, imagination and energy of the world. The global women's movement has been no exception. Worldwide, women are putting information and communications technologies (ICTs) to work for the movement; communicating among dispersed networks, mobilizing action in times of crisis, participating in policy debates and voicing new perspectives. Information and communications have always played a vital role in the global women's movement. Electronic communications are facilitating women's networking and advocacy in ways not previously possible. For many women and women's organizations, taking hold of new technologies was and is no small feat. Facing inadequate telecommunications infrastructure, persistent stereo-types, policies that favour commercial sectors over community net-working and limited resources, women have responded with practical solutions and policy advocacy. They have used e-mail in concert with fax and printed materials, designed and conducted gender-sensitive training and developed new *netiquette* to address regional e-mail cost differentials. Women have also come to recognize the need to address telecommunications and ICT policy makers at national and international levels.

The story of how the international women's community has used and adapted ICTs over the past decade is remarkable. Computers and fax machines found their way into many women's information and communication tool kits by the mid-1980s. Electronic communications, first e-mail and later the Internet and World Wide Web (WWW), came into the spotlight at the same time as women were beginning preparations for the Fourth World Conference on Women and NGO Forum held in 1995 in Beijing. These preparations were to be a major catalyst for women's entry into and establishment of a firm position within the electronic arena. This chapter tells one version of many stories, based on the author's work with women worldwide, about information and communications, computers, science and technology.

Part history, part 'here and now' and part reflection, the chapter attempts to map out the ways women have taken on ICTs over the past decade. Beginning with a brief look at 'life before the Internet', the chapter highlights women's electronic networking for the Fourth World Conference. It documents the practical ways in which electronic communications have facilitated women's advocacy, as well as dis-cussing the barriers women have faced and the strategies they have employed to address them. The chapter will also trace the ICT policy concerns articulated in Beijing and consider new directions in policy initiatives. It concludes with a look at lessons learned and reflections on the questions and challenges that lie ahead for the global women's movement as we continue to shape and take hold of ICTs.

Life before the Internet: communications and networking

Even before the word networking became synonymous with the Internet, women's information-exchange strategies facilitated and, to a large extent, made possible the growth of an international movement working on issues of concern to women. Popular theatre and radio listening groups, wall newspapers and women's wire services, fax trees and newsletters have informed, mobilized and built a global network of women activists. New information tools have joined rather than supplanted this media mix.

In the years immediately before and following the 1985 Nairobi conference that marked the close of the UN Decade for Women, the increasingly available personal computer was being put to use by a better organized, better informed global movement. Yet access to computers and appropriate training remained a major obstacle and concern for women. As a 1983 *Story of a Small International Women's Organization and its Word Processor* reported:

> The decision to purchase a word processor was not easily taken. The reasons were both practical and philosophical. First, the [International Women's] Tribune Centre has made a conscious decision ... to work with systems, techniques, and technologies that were affordable and

replicable by the groups in Third World countries with whom it worked. ... the idea of acquiring a word processor or computer seemed a step in the opposite direction (IWTC, 1983, p. 1).

Seven years later it was doubtful that groups with the resources to do so would choose not to use computers. Desktop publishing was giving women's media-producing organizations more control over their publication production process. Increasingly, flyers, brochures, reports and proposals could be produced in-house and in smaller runs at reasonable cost. Databases were making it easier to maintain mailing and distribution lists. The number of women's newsletters produced and distributed by large and small organizations alike soared. Still, even among those with computers, training remained a missing ingredient impeding full and effective use of the technology. In response to a survey sent to 25 women's information-producing organizations in Africa, Asia, Latin America, the South Pacific, the Caribbean and West Asia, one Pacific respondent remarked, 'I've come across many women with access to computers but without the training to use them to their full potential.... Pacific women are increasingly aware of the need for effective, usable materials. Desktop publishing is a key to addressing this need'.[1] Other respondents raised similar needs but were optimistic about pursuing means to make better and more widespread use of computers (IWTC, 1993, p. 6).

By the late 1980s, the fax machine was becoming an indispensable tool for women's global networking, and one that was considerably more accessible than computers. For groups collaborating across great distances and in countries with slow-moving postal services, fax became a quick and fairly reliable, if expensive, means of communication. For example, when women's media networks came together at a meeting convened by DAWN in 1992, the result was WomeNet. This fax distribution list began with ten women's media networks covering every region of the world (Frankson, 1996, p. 107). WomeNet was instrumental in multiplying messages and mobilizing action in campaigns such as efforts to demand the release of Wangari Maathai, the founder of the Greenbelt Movement arrested by the Kenyan government, and the *Violence Against Women Violates Human Rights* petition drive in 1993 that eventually gathered over one million signatures.[2]

As 1992 approached, electronic mail and conferencing were making their way into the public eye and women's organizations were beginning to experiment with these new technologies. At the Global Forum in Brazil, the NGO meeting paralleling the Earth Summit,[3] special training sessions for women were offered by the APC, an international umbrella network of electronic networks primarily serving NGOs. Women's NGOs were beginning to use electronic mail and conferences as part of their pioneering advocacy efforts at United Nations conferences that continued through Beijing. This strategy involved obtaining early drafts of policy documents under consideration, analyzing them, drafting recommended changes and lobbying government delegations directly at preparatory meetings and the Conference itself. Electronic communications made it feasible for women to obtain and disseminate copies of draft policy documents and participate in shaping the issues from where they were, even if it was not New York or Brazil. The use of electronic communications for UN advocacy was not the whole story by any means. Networks of women's documentation centres and researchers were linking up via electronic mail, while others began to distribute their newsletters electronically. But it would be the preparations in late 1993 for the Fourth World Conference that marked the point where women's use of ICTs really took off.

Discovering new tools to support activism and organizing

The Fourth World Conference in Beijing in 1995 came at an opportune moment. The Internet was being hyped and women's organizations were well prepared for action. The Beijing process differed from previous women's world conferences in both scale and approach. The global women's movement had grown in numbers and influence. It had been ten years since the movement had come together on a global scale. Women's NGOs were determined to make their concerns and demands known to governments and the world, and to facilitate the participation of as many women as possible in the process. In preparation for Beijing,[4] UN meetings were held for Latin America and the Caribbean, Africa, Asia and the Pacific, and Europe and North America to develop regional plans of action which would eventually become part of a global *Platform for Action*. Overlapping these were NGO meetings held at local, national and regional levels where women would articulate their concerns and demands. Preparatory committee meetings held at UN headquarters in New York would be where much of the negotiation of the *Platform* would take place. These meetings, like the Beijing meetings, were opportunities to renew commitments, to share successes and lessons learned over ten years, to foster new collaborations and partnerships and to bring previously invisible issues to the forefront of the development community. Electronic communications helped make this a reality.

Using e-mail, Gopher, conferencing and, to a lesser extent, the WWW, women accessed draft versions of the *Platform for Action*, regional action plans and caucus documents. They downloaded them, disseminated them, analyzed them, drafted additions and deletions, reached consensus on issues, circulated statements and mobilized support. NGOs in some countries found themselves better informed than their national delegations. The public electronic spaces for discussion and information sharing also helped demystify UN proceedings. Discussions previously reserved for a few governmental delegates and observers at the United Nations were now open to anyone able to access the medium. [5]

Electronic communications promoted a feeling of being part of a larger process, As Ana Rivera Lassen said, 'La China parece mas cerca desde la pantalla de mi computadora' (China seems closer from my computer screen). Women who met on-line found an immediate network in Beijing. Electronic conferences and mailing lists sprang up on issues ranging from violence against women to spirituality, gender, science and technology. Newly formed coalitions planned events for the NGO Forum with partners around the world. The Once and Future Pavilion, a women, science and technology event at the NGO Forum, for example, was planned primarily via an electronic conference and mailing list. Electronic spaces became the critical source for timely information about Conference registration procedures, travel and administrative details. The accessibility of the Conference information and discussions made possible the participation of many women previously outside the movement, whether individual women, women in academia or women scientists. It also allowed diverse perspectives and voices to be heard and spaces for ongoing discussions not possible with other communication tools. Electronic communications allowed women to bypass mainstream media and still reach thousands. For example, 100,000 visits were made to the APC Website on the Conference. International Women's Tribune Centre's *Global FaxNet* reached 500 multiplier groups by fax, and upwards of 700 by e-mail. When *Global FaxNet* was posted on the Web, over 80,000 hits were recorded in the week before the Beijing meetings (IWTC, 1997).

As women became excited by the possibilities, they also found serious shortcomings. Much of the information to be found on-line was in English. Groups in developing countries incurred much higher relative costs to send and receive information. Even with equipment in place, inadequate telephone lines and lack of Internet access in countries made linking into electronic forums difficult and at times impossible. The costs associated with filtering and passing on information drained resources and meant that those receiving information relied on others to select information for them. Those without direct e-mail access could often only participate in a one-way fashion.

These challenges, however, did not stop women from finding creative solutions. Groups sought to make the best of what was available and to maintain as inclusive an information-sharing process as possible. In Zambia, copies of the draft *Platform for Action* were downloaded and distributed by diskette, and copies were kept at local libraries. The Agencia Latinoamericana de Información (ALAI) translated documents into Spanish and re-posted them. Groups repackaged and multiplied electronic information into print newsletters and fax briefs, and sent hard copies to partner organizations. The Latin American and Caribbean Regional Meeting on Gender Communications established national liaison points to guarantee redissemination of electronic information. FIRE, the Feminist International Radio Endeavour in Costa Rica, distributed electronic news through its radio programmes (Gittler, 1996a, pp. 90–1). Joining a global community of women working towards a common goal was a powerful incentive for women to get on-line. On the networks of the APC, for example, the number of women's organizations on-line had tripled by 1995.[6]

Training and technical assistance by newly emerging and existing organizations was essential to the ability of groups to tap into the electronic community of women. The Women's Outreach Program of the APC designated women's focal points in each of its member networks to reach out to and assist local women's organizations.[7] Groups such as the Network of East-West Women (NEWW) trained women in their regions. Virtual Sisterhood started an electronic help list and linked women with technical expertise to organizations in need of assistance. Organizations gathered and shared information about women's on-line activities as sources of inspiration and practical ideas for others. Individual women, including many young women, trained their colleagues. Access and training were major concerns, but as women's familiarity with the tools grew, other issues began to emerge as well. At home and in their regions, in real and virtual encounters, practical problems also gave rise to larger questions. Women who found information in English or found their languages impossible to e-mail began to question the seemingly homogenizing effects of ICTs. Groups whose networks included many women without electronic communications, but continued to use new technologies questioned the impact of their compromises. Women in countries without direct Internet access began to look at national telecommunications policy more closely.

Preparing for Beijing: questioning information technologies

The Fourth World Conference on Women would be a major opportunity to articulate women's concerns and demands on information and communications. In the preparatory process, 'women and the media' had been defined as one of twelve critical areas of concern within the *Platform for Action*, the policy document that would be negotiated and adopted at the Conference. In 1994 and 1995, women's media and information groups and gender, science and technology networks each came together, albeit in different gatherings, to discuss and define global and regional perspectives on the gender dimensions of ICT development.

At the Women Empowering Communications Conference in early 1994, 400 women from 80 countries met in Bangkok to share skills and strategies and to help set an agenda for Beijing. Remarkably, it was the first ever global meeting to bring together women working in alternative and mainstream media. The resulting Bangkok Declaration expressed concern over globalization of media and economies and called for the strengthening of all forms of women's media. It also focused on the need for information forms that reaffirmed women's knowledge and wisdom. While information and communications technologies were not mentioned specifically, the issues surrounding knowledge production, and the centralizing and homogenizing effects of mainstream media, would resurface in debates around ICTs.

The Women Empowering Communications Conference was to be followed by other regional and global meetings around media, information and communications. The regional preparatory meeting of Latin America and the Caribbean for Beijing, later that year, identified access to new technologies and communications as a 'fundamental human right.' (ALAI, 1994, p. 269). The Women, Information and the Future (WIF) statement, drafted by women working primarily in documentation and libraries, highlighted the role of technology in facilitating the development of networks and called on governments to assure women's equitable access to new technologies (WIF, 1994). The *Toronto Platform for Action,* drafted at the UNESCO International Symposium on Women and the Media, pointed to the important role of new ICTs, and made reference to the need for 'training in communication methods and technologies' (*Toronto Platform for Action*, 1995, p. 5). Issues around knowledge and information or the need for decentralized information systems were raised with respect to media, but not in direct relation to electronic communications.

The work of the UN Commission on Science and Technology for

Development (UNCSTD) in 1994 and 1995, with substantial input from women's gender, science and technology networks, also informed the policy debate around ICTs for Beijing. The Commission's Gender Working Group was advised by a team of women from NGOs, the UN and academia and was charged with researching and preparing recommendations on gender, science and technology (IDRC, 1995). The findings of the Group noted that 'the information society has remained largely silent on gender issues' (IDRC, 1995, p. 269), raised concerns about the 'policy vacuum' and recommended 'that ICT policies consider gender issues and that women play an active role in their development' (IDRC, 1995, p. 282).

The declarations and statements drafted before Beijing became the basis for women's demands as the negotiations on language in the *Platform for Action* began. The result of these efforts can be found under the Women and Media section of that document, adopted by UN member governments in attendance at the Fourth World Conference. The Platform calls for women's increased participation in and access to new technologies of communication. The recommendations, however, are limited to encouraging and recognizing electronic communications systems (UN, 1995, pp. 133–5). Governments are called upon to integrate gender concerns into policies, but specific recommendations relating to telecommunications policies were not articulated.

Post-Beijing: learning, networking and advocacy

Increasingly in the years following the Beijing process women have taken up their concerns directly with national governments and global telecommunications bodies. Participation in regional and global preparations for the 1995 meetings built a network of women concerned with gender and information technology policy. Women's achievements and difficulties in taking hold of new technologies served to inform and spur on efforts to influence policy makers. Continuing disparities in access and infrastructure, issues relating to knowledge and control of electronic spaces, and the lack of women's input and involvement in information technology development, design and policy making are among these concerns.

In 1997, Global Knowledge 97, a conference hosted by the World Bank and the government of Canada in partnership with a large group of public and private organizations, focused attention on the vital role of knowledge and information in sustainable development. At this meeting a *Canon on Gender, Partnerships and ICT Development* was drafted.[8] The

Canon outlined three basic principles for development and design of ICTs, emphasizing equal participation by women and men, and gender-aware assessments and evaluations of ICT development. It built on previous agreements, strategies and demands, and called for partnerships for a future 'very different from the past' (ICWGK, 1997).

This work will be an important foundation for women's future efforts to influence national and global policies regarding information and communications technology development. A developing collaboration between the United Nations Development Fund for Women (UNIFEM), the United Nations University for New Technologies (UNU/INTECH) and the International Telecommunications Union (ITU) will seek explicitly to include gender in the formation of telecommunications development and policy. A paper by UNIFEM and UNU/INTECH presented at the ITU World Telecommunication Development Conference (Valletta, Malta, 23 March–1 April 1998) identifies effects of urban bias in infrastructure development as well as the high cost of connectivity on women's access and employment. It goes on to recommend key targets, including women's participation in IT policy making and gender-sensitive policy (UNIFEM/UNU/INTECH, 1998).The involvement of women's NGOs in this process will be critical. Their work has been and will be an important factor in prompting action to influence national and global policies regarding ICT development.

Drawing on past experiences and moving ahead

The electronic learning curve for the global women and development community has been steep. As well as continuing to move up it against significant obstacles, women have been forging new paths. Their on-line activities have 'mapped onto established practices of the real world' (Bollier, 1996) and have diverged to take new directions. Since Beijing, new projects and organizations are coming to life and the number of electronic resources, websites and mailing lists are growing daily. For example, the Women Living Under Muslim Laws network has recently connected its 40 regional correspondents around the world via e-mail. Synergie Genre et Developpement (SYNFEV-ENDA) in Senegal is organizing training workshops on electronic networking for women's rights in West Africa. ABANTU for Development has launched a programme to improve electronic communications between African women's organizations, including strengthening connectivity, content and capacity through policy advocacy, regional Internet training and building a network of partners to share experience and knowledge (ABANTU, 1997, p. 13).[9] The list goes on and on.

The lessons learned along the way have been many. One of the outstanding features of women's communications and media, then and now, has been the weaving together of many different media forms and formats in response to very diverse constituencies, organizational forms and working styles. Sharing the daily struggles and victories associated with the practicalities of using electronic networking, whether in training workshops or on-line forums, has been and continues to be a critical part of the learning process. Underlying much of women's electronic networking is the notion that the value of the computer and electronic communications is not in the value of the technologies themselves, but in the ability of the tools to improve, support, protect and enhance women's full and equal participation in all aspects of society.

Just as the stories and experiences of women and information technologies are many and diverse, so will be the challenges ahead. What, for example, will be the effect of the increasing interest on the part of donor agencies in gender and ICTs? Will donors support inclusive information strategies and not just technology solutions? What will be the effect of the increasing commercialization of electronic spaces? Can the Internet be a medium for advocacy and transforming social relations – as well as an entertainment venue and shopping mall? Women's NGOs need to continue to counter stereotypes and media hype about the Internet to make clear that it is a space for activists and promoting social justice. What will be the effects of commercialization on smaller, community-based electronic service providers who have played such a vital role in expanding access and training? What will it take for them to continue as strong, viable entities? How can we use the new technologies to their full potential as interactive spaces and not just document storage?

The electronic revolution is providing an incredible opportunity to rethink some basic assumptions about information and knowledge, about who produces it, how it is valued, where it resides, what it takes for people to use it in meaningful ways, and how we share it. Likewise, it is offering new ways to communicate and work, ways that are more participatory and decentralized. It can also be used to do the same things in the same way, perpetuating inequality, squelching diversity, or fostering exclusivity. Women have always been inventors and innovators, and their electronic networking activities are no exception. Women will continue to make information technologies make a difference.

NOTES

1   Jill Emberson, Pacific Women's Resource Bureau, from survey circulated by IWTC in 1990 (IWTC, 1993).
2   For more details on WomeNet and its growth, see Frankson (1996).
3   The Earth Summit refers to the UN Conference on Environment and Development, in Rio de Janeiro, Brazil in June 1992. The Global Forum was the NGO meeting that paralleled the Conference.
4   Future references to 'Beijing' refer to the Fourth World Conference on Women and NGO Forum on Women. The 'Beijing process' refers to those meetings plus preparatory meetings held by the UN and NGOs.
5   A more detailed account of electronic forums devoted to Beijing can be found in Gittler (1996b).
6   Personal conversation with Susan Mooney at Womensnet, Institute for Global Communications, California.
7   See Farwell *et al* (1998), Chapter 7 in this volume.
8   See Huyer (1998), Chapter 8 in this volume.
9   See Tandon (1998), Chapter 9 in this volume.

GLOBAL NETWORKING FOR CHANGE
Experiences from the APC Women's Programme

Edie Farwell, Peregrine Wood,
Maureen James and Karen Banks

Despite many obstacles, women's networking has made significant progress in the last few years through the adoption and use of electronic communications. The Association for Progressive Communications (APC) has played an important role in this process through initiatives such as the APC Women's Networking Support Programme. Recently, a team of women associated with the APC Women's Programme surveyed over 700 women's groups and individual women to examine more closely the progress made in women's electronic networking. This chapter introduces the APC, outlines the goals and activities of its women's programme, and shares highlights from its survey findings about how computer communications are assisting the women's movement to enhance global networks.[1]

The APC is trying to construct a truly alternative information infrastructure for the challenges of global networking that lie ahead. Through initiatives such as the APC Women's Programme we are providing an appropriate way to address gender disparity on the Net. General findings from the networking survey tell us that electronic communications is an important tool and resource for the women who participated in the study. Moreover, there is an openness on the part of the respondents to explore new tools, build women's resources, and work cooperatively in this area. There remains, however, a need for a coordinated effort to foster mutual approaches and partnerships to confront the barriers women face, particularly in the South, in access and use of computer communication technologies.

The Association for Progressive Communications

The APC is the world's most extensive network of Internet providers dedicated to NGOs and citizen activists working for democracy, environmental sustainability, women's rights and gender equality, peace and human rights. A global network of NGOs, APC's mission is to empower and support organizations, social movements and individuals through the use of ICTs to build strategic communities and initiatives for the purpose of making meaningful contributions to human development, social justice, participatory democracies and sustainable societies.

Through a web of interconnected electronic communications networks, APC is dedicated to the free and balanced flow of information that is critical to the work of global civil society. Since its creation in 1990, APC has been an integral part of the global social justice movement. In 1998, it is a consortium of 25 international member organizations, offering vital communication links to over 50,000 NGOs, activists, educators, policy makers, and community leaders in 133 countries. Every day, thousands of activists and organizations around the world use APC networks to make their voices heard on key issues in their communities, to learn about new ideas and to work collaboratively.

The APC Women's Programme

Started in 1993, the APC Women's Programme is a global initiative aimed at facilitating access to and use of computer communications by women in order to redress gender inequities in the design, implementation and use of ICTs and the policy decisions and frameworks that regulate them. The programme emerged as a response to several convergent needs and demands from women and women's organizations, working within and beyond APC and its network alliances.

Two major factors gave impetus to the programme's beginnings: the 1995 Fourth World Conference on Women and the rapid development of digitalized international communication technologies.

The Women's Programme promotes women's rights and democratic access to new communications technologies, and supports the empowerment of their organizations and networks through the incorporation of computer networking as a tool for coordination, expression and access to information. It also aims to increase women's visibility in the field of information technology. In the North, South, East and West, specialized in areas such as training, information, technical skills or policy issues, many of the Women's Programme members work on a volunteer basis.

The APC Women's Programme offers opportunities to women and women's organizations in all regions. It focuses particularly on redressing inequalities in access to technology related to gender, social or ethnic marginalization, and the North–South technological gap, by providing training and support activities as well as mechanisms to facilitate information exchange, networking and linking of women using information technology as a tool. The programme includes five main components: information facilitation, regional support, policy and advocacy, training, and research.

Putting Beijing on-line

APC served as the primary provider of telecommunications for NGOs and UN delegates during the preparatory process and on-site for the Fourth World Conference on Women in 1995. To ensure that information and communications systems were available before, during and after the conference, APC worked closely with the organizing UN divisions, the NGO planning committee, and many women, NGOs and information providers. APC's support and services ensured that partnerships and progress made at the conference continued on-line long after the event was over. These efforts established computer networking as a powerful mechanism enabling women and women's NGOs to participate in an effective and timely fashion in the initiatives launched at the Beijing Conference.

APC's global Women's Programme intervened as a lobbyist with its own proposals in the 1995 Beijing process. APC, in conjunction with other organizations, made significant input on the theme of new technologies to Section J in the Beijing *Platform for Action*. Section J discusses the importance of new information technology for women and the need to ensure women's access, participation in decision making, training and research in this area. The APC Women's Programme, as part of the communications caucus at the UN World Conference on Women (UNWCW), participated in the elaboration of an 'NGO Communications Strategy Proposal for Follow-up' to the World Conference, in which electronic networking figures as a central element.[2]

Women's networking survey results

In September 1996 the APC Women's Programme surveyed over 700 women's groups and individual women by e-mail to identify women's electronic networking needs and opportunities.

Recipients of the survey were invited to reflect on the work of the

APC Women's Programme and its consequences. Questions were derived
from these general themes:

- What progress had been made in women's global electronic networking?
- What are the success stories and lessons to be learned from our online experiences?
- What are the needs and opportunities for the adoption of computer communication tools and resources by women?
- How can the APC Women's Programme best serve women's global networking needs?

TABLE 7.1
WHO WE HEARD FROM

	Sent	Received	%
Asia/Pacific	52	10	19
Australia	43	12	28
Canada	174	32	18
Eastern Europe/Russia	7	5	71
Latin America	164	41	25
North Africa/Middle East	7	3	43
Sub-Saharan Africa	22	10	45
Western Europe	114	21	18
United States	120	13	11
Total	703	147	21

Respondents (147 responses from 36 countries were received) represent a diversity of groups and individuals including: NGOs, grassroots groups, women's centres, United Nations agencies, funding agencies, solidarity networks, international agencies, freelance workers, volunteers, information technology and media services companies, advocacy groups, and departments responsible for women's programming or studies... working on a wide range of issues of concern for women such as health, justice, violence, communications, youth, peace, environment, development, sexuality, shelter, human rights and labour.

General findings
The general findings reveal that, despite obstacles, women are making great strides in adopting electronic communications, and have benefited from the support and facilitation provided by proactive initiatives like

the APC Women's Networking Support Programme. Increased communication and sharing of knowledge from women in the South and Eastern Europe, as well as in remote communities in the North, has broadened the scope of on-line participation, creating a more equitable global women's forum on-line.

Despite these signs of progress, women everywhere continue to experience barriers to electronic networking: lack of training and the cost of equipment to get connected rank highest. To confront the barriers and harness opportunities, respondents suggested mentoring programmes, plain language support materials, training for and by women, a support network of technical women, and funding to enable access and use. The APC Women's Programme was called on to take a leadership role in facilitating this support.

Electronic tools becoming routine

For many women who knew very little about computer communications before the APC Women's Programme began three years ago, using e-mail has become a routine part of day-to-day communications. More and more women use (or plan to use) conferencing, mailing lists and websites on a regular basis, too. Women in the South and in Eastern Europe primarily use e-mail, conferencing and list serves, while women in the North (and in some instances Latin America) show greater use of Internet tools, such as search engines and the World Wide Web (WWW). These regional differences in tool use are linked to access issues, such as infrastructure limitations or costs to connect, rather than lack of interest or motivation on the part of women to adopt the newer technologies.

Women get their colleagues to adopt electronic communication tools in different ways: humour, 'nagging', making it obligatory to use e-mail instead of fax or phone, demonstrating what the technology can do, or offering training.

Building and sharing women's resources

Many respondents provide websites, databases, mailing lists or conferences, and, by doing so, make a significant contribution to building women's on-line resources. Time and resource constraints, or organizational priorities, keep others from doing so, although some plan to develop resources in the near future. Many 'connected' women (particularly in the South) act as bridges to 'unconnected' groups in their communities by repackaging on-line information and sharing it through other communication channels such as print, fax, telephone, radio and theatre.

Achieving goals

Most respondents feel their use of electronic tools contributes to achieving their goals and cite examples such as: cost effectiveness, ease of communication, reliability, empowerment, increased productivity, balancing information flows, broadening perspectives of the world and streamlining collaborations. Similarly, the APC Women's Programme is identified as playing a key role in facilitating networking and information exchange around the UNWCW, particularly for groups in isolated communities.

Balancing the negative and positive experiences

Although more positive examples of on-line experiences are cited than negative ones, the latter reinforce the many challenges women face in the adoption of communication technologies and help to clarify some of the pitfalls associated with its use. Negative experiences cited by the respondents include: limited accessibility, time consumption, information overload, language constraints, lack of privacy and security, potential fear of backlash or harassment, inappropriate use of information by others, skill deficiencies, and alienation. Women in the South highlight additional challenges: limitations of e-mail only accounts (not having access to remote databases or Internet tools), limited infrastructure (difficulty in getting a phone line), and the high costs of data transmission (networks in the South often charge their users for all messages, both sent and received).

The survey turned up many women who are already on-line 'experts', making innovative use of electronic tools, and inspiring others to do the same. Many individuals and organizations however, still struggle to apply the technology in their work.

Barriers: North and South variations

We have said that lack of training and the cost of equipment to become connected rank highest as barriers to women getting on-line. Regional analysis shows that women in the South and Eastern Europe/Russia, for example, list poor infrastructure as the major barrier, while women in the North list training. Within regions there are variations too: dominance of English, privacy and security issues, high cost of connectivity, and difficulty in getting a phone line or repair personnel are specific barriers for women in Latin America, francophone and sub-Saharan Africa and Russia. Another significant barrier is lack of time and human resources. As one woman wrote: 'in some ways the Internet is a tool for those with lives of leisure'.

Policy: a critical area

Some interesting observations were made which suggest that policy plays a critical role in supporting women's access and use of new technologies: an agency's commitment to information technology and the opinion of women in senior positions within organizations are two factors cited that contribute to a woman's ease and access to electronic networking.

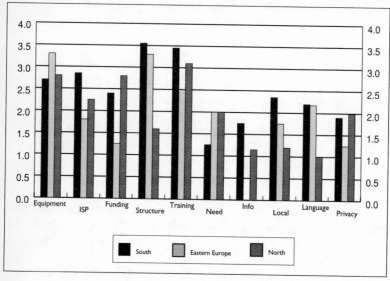

FIGURE 7.1   NORTH–SOUTH BARRIERS

Gender differences

Opinions on the differences between women and men in their ease with and use of electronic communications range from 'women are as capable, eager and effective as men' to 'women have less access to electronic communications and less ownership of equipment ... they need more initial encouragement and training at the beginning and are less active in learning the new technologies'.

Importance of training

The importance of training was repeated over and over again in the responses. Over half the respondents had received some kind of formal training to get up and running on-line. Other women are self-taught, rely on 'computer buddies' to guide them, or learn 'on the job' (mostly in their own time). A number of the computer buddies are involved with the APC Women's Programme.

Cost, time restrictions and lack of gender and/or culturally sensitive approaches are the main reasons women are not receiving training. For women in the Middle East, North and sub-Saharan Africa and Latin America, availability of training is a major factor.

Identified training needs include: basic skills (getting connected, using e-mail, etc.), learning information facilitation techniques, building and maintaining websites or bulletin boards, design and programming skills, setting up and running mailing lists, and exploring other (and new) Internet tools and resources. Technical training for troubleshooting is a priority for many women in the South, too.

Common suggestions for improving training include offering women-specific and free training, and linking that training with ongoing user support and mentoring in the communities where women live. Developing training methodologies and programmes in consultation with the women's movement, as well as using critical thinking skills, 'learning by doing' and action-oriented techniques are also suggested. The APC Women's Programme approach of developing a global network of technical women to serve local needs is repeatedly cited as a training model on which to build.

Gender- and culture-sensitive support materials

Over half the respondents use support materials, such as computer manuals, 'how to' books, or instructional sheets to help them use electronic tools and access resources. Women in sub-Saharan Africa, Asia, Canada, Eastern Europe, Russia and Latin America show the highest rate of use, while women in the United States and Australia show the lowest. Women in North Africa, the Middle East, francophone Africa and some Latin American countries have no access to support materials. Support materials are often not used because they are written for a North American audience, expensive, full of technical jargon, not gender- or culture-sensitive, or out of date by the time they are published.

Funding needs

Canada, Eastern Europe, Russia, Africa, the Middle East, and Western Europe show higher rates of application to funders such as governments, international agencies, foundations and corporations. Examples range from informal requests for equipment to major long-term programming involving several countries, partners or stakeholders. Only a few had been successful in securing funds; many are still waiting to hear from the funder. Lack of knowledge about funding sources and procedures, methodologies to assess local needs and relative country costs, or project ideas are the most common reasons why groups are not applying for funding.

Overall, funding for training, websites and hardware and software to become connected are evenly identified, with support for recurring Internet and e-mail charges following in importance. Specific funding needs identified ranged from appropriate technology (radio modems, solar energy, security, etc.) to long-term support for women's electronic networking programming.

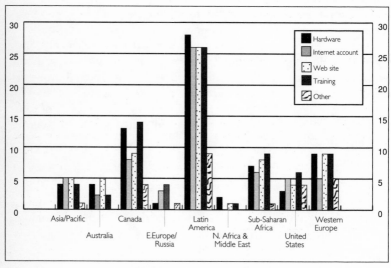

FIGURE 7.2   FUNDING BARRIERS

Reviewing the survey

A working group has been formed with responsibility for reviewing and assessing the findings (within the context of the APC Women's Programme mandate and available resources) and to set forth a plan of action that will guide future programming. Consultations are being organized to discuss the ramifications of the survey findings for women at the regional level. The outcome of these meetings will shape regional programming while informing APC's global women's initiative. A training team is using the lessons learned and success stories from the findings in the development of training curricula and programmes. Finally, selected information from the survey responses has been compiled in a database of women and electronic resources around the world.

This database is available on-line or through e-mail by request, for groups and individuals who do not have Internet access.

Since 1990, APC has pioneered the use of electronic communications in advancing women's issues, and continues its hard work to defend a safe and productive venue for women and women's NGOs on the Internet and within all spheres of computer networking despite a persistent gender gap in the access to and use of information and communication networking technology. The APC Women's Programme will continue to assist social change efforts locally – and globally – by making it possible to save voices, lives, cultures and movements, and, ultimately, by building global cooperation on social justice issues.

Some women's voices from the survey

Argentina

The lack of chances to get connected even by telephone and to send or receive a simple letter are great! I can tell you that a letter to almost any other country in Latin America takes two to three weeks to get there, when a letter to Europe or the US takes only four to five days! That's why e-mail is so important and useful to us, now that telephone lines are more available. I agree that electronic communication has a potential for changes and in our continent it is starting to change the way we communicate with each other, discuss issues, get related to one another, get information, plan lobbying, and work in solidarity with others.

Peru

After six years of being dedicated to administration tasks I was given the opportunity to combine my work with information and communication tasks and this has allowed me to discover within myself unknown areas and a great inclination for the area of information and telecommunications.

India

E-mail is the most reliable and quickest means of communication to Tilonia, Rajastan. Most people find it impossible to fax or phone in. Courier services take two days from the nearest city. So e-mail, for us, is contact with the outside world more than anything else.

Nigeria

So many of our contacts have no access to even e-mail that it requires a lot of work (e.g., downloading, faxing, posting, etc.) to ensure that information does not pass them by and, too often, even this only means that they hear of things after it is too late for them to participate in defining or responding to the issues.

Philippines

It is very frustrating for us who are in Third World countries simply because despite being unable to access the interactive services such as WWW, Gopher, FTP, etc., it is also difficult to enjoy the normal e-mail service due to the existence of the most unreliable phone lines in the world.

Mali

[B]ecause it's a new technology in Mali, the equipment isn't repairable. Our modem is broken right now ... there's no one to repair it.

Switzerland

Women seem more reluctant to use this technology. They need to understand what it can do to support their work before they make the effort to learn. Men seem to be interested in the gadgets and gizmo of the technology and are more exploratory in their approach to learning. Although, once women get on-line and are comfortable with the technology, the exploration starts!

Canada

Women simply have less time to spend hours learning new programmes, how to instal things, what to do when there is a problem, hanging around on the Internet to see what it has to offer. Largely, though not exclusively, women tend to have more and varied responsibilities (work and home) and this simply doesn't allow the time you need to do that kind of exploring that makes you really comfortable with the technology.... I think that what largely has brought the women I know to this technology has been necessity and a willingness to communicate more effectively. What has brought most men I know to the technology has been partly necessity but more a fascination with the technology itself.

Peru

Personally, I believe we can talk about the democratization of communication, but I believe that what is occurring is an increased communication elite, and this is the case with women.... Information is power, and only a small amount of women and organizations have access to this power. We need community centres, where women can send messages, read mail lists, review news and, of course, be able to have a cup of coffee or tea.

NOTES

1 Funding for this research and for the Gender and Information Technology
   (GIT) Project of the APC Women's Programme was carried out with the aid of
   a grant from the International Development Research Centre, Ottawa, Canada.
   We gratefully acknowledge their contribution in support of this work. We would
   also like to thank the many women who participated in the survey research.

   To receive a copy of the survey report, or any other information about the
   APC Women's Programme, please contact: APC Women's Networking Support
   Programme, GreenNet Limited/GreenNet Educational Trust, Bradley Close, 74-
   77 White Lion Street, London, N1 9PF, England. Tel: +44/171-713-1941 Fax:
   +44/171-837-5551   E-mail: apcwomen@laneta.apc.org   URL: http://www.
   apc.org/apcwomen/

2 See Gittler in Chapter 6 of this volume.

8

SHIFTING AGENDAS AT GK97
Women and International Policy on Information and Communication Technologies

Sophia Huyer

Opening space for women's inclusion in GK97

In March 1997, the initial participants' list was released for the Conference on Knowledge for Development in the Information Age – or Global Knowledge 97 (GK97) – and a list of speakers was published in *The Economist*. GK97, held in Toronto, Canada in June 1997, was an invitation-only conference organized by the World Bank and the government of Canada (through the Canadian International Development Agency – CIDA) to 'focus on the challenges facing developing countries and the international community at the end of the twentieth century and the dawn of the information age' (World Bank, 1997b). As the first major international conference to call explicitly for dialogue on bringing the knowledge society to developing countries, GK97 was presented by the organizers as being an important opportunity for representatives of various sectors, including donors, technology decision makers, government representatives, NGOs and the private sector, to explore the implications of information technologies and 'knowledge for development' for the South.

Partly because of the short time period between the decision to hold the Conference and the date it was held – barely six months – and partly also because it was not a typical 'UN-type' conference and therefore not advertised in UN/NGO channels, the civil society groups active around other major international conferences were hardly aware of the existence of GK97. In Canada, as the date drew near, slowly awareness dawned – in NGOs working in information technology, in research groups, and among others engaged with 'knowledge' or 'information' issues – that this was a potentially important conference. It also became apparent to many of us that with little space reserved for NGOs and those not connected with the organizing institutions in some way, it would be very difficult to make a substantive input. What could be done about this was unclear – until the initial participants' list was released. When we saw that the list included only 78 women out of over 600 names, and that the speakers list in *The Economist* included no women at all, several of us in Toronto saw an opportunity to push the conference organizers to bring in new groups.

The members of the network in Toronto which formed to lobby the conference organizers shared several concerns about this event as an important international agenda-setting conference in information technology and development. In our view, the implications for economic, information, social and even environmental systems of the rapid acceleration of information exchange fostered by the new information technologies are far-reaching and profound. If women are not involved in the creation of cyberspace, new technologies and information generation, and information delivery systems which *work for them* – fulfil their particular information and communication needs – they stand to lose much of what they have gained in the past. As noted by the UN Division for the Advancement of Women (DAW), the Beijing *Platform for Action* and other UN conventions, communications are a critical element of women's empowerment and organizing, which ICTs potentially could expand and strengthen. The Women in Global Science and Technology project (WIGSAT), which I coordinate, specifically had three concerns about GK97 (generally shared by the rest of the Committee, although I cannot speak for each member). WIGSAT had had a strong focus from the beginning on international networking around and promoting of women's technological knowledge and creativity for development, and had recently initiated an information technology component. Its concerns were: (1) that women's knowledge and technological capacities would be marginalized from the discussions and policy frameworks that emerged from the conference, as they have been in the past; (2) that very few (in fact, hardly any) women from the South were included on the participants' list; and (3) that this potentially key international agenda-setting conference and the funding, policy and projects which would result from the conference, would not acknowledge or include women's perspectives and abilities. What I can say on behalf of the Committee is that the amount of financial resources for information technology development represented at the conference by the World Bank, major donors, and even more importantly by the major private sector companies made it imperative for us to try to ensure that women benefit from or receive at least some fraction of the billions of dollars which will be spent in this sector in the next few years.

When combined with the catalyst of the initial GK97 invitation list, therefore, these concerns prompted us in Toronto to establish ourselves as the 'Ad Hoc Committee for Women at GK97' in order to initiate an intense campaign of lobbying and mobilizing. We worked for the increased representation of women at GK97 and stronger representation of women's concerns and perspectives in discussions and panels. The sense we had that we could mount such a campaign successfully derived from several additional factors. We owed a great deal to the example of the successful international women's lobby around the UN Fourth World Conference on Women in Beijing in 1995 (IWTC, 1995) and the Cairo UN Conference on Population and Development, among others, at which it was demonstrated that the women's lobby is a powerful force in international policy, and that women are using Internet networking, especially e-mail, to move forward their agendas at the global level. These precedents justified a sense of shock and disbelief – that even after such demonstrations of women's 'clout' in international policy, a major international conference could still be organized with marginal representation of women – that helped to fuel our action. Other favourable contextual factors included the opportunities presented by: (1) ownership of conference panels by some Committee members – ABANTU for Development/Black and White Communications and Web Networks – and by 'friends' of the Committee, including the UN Development Fund for Women (UNIFEM); (2) participation through Anna Melnikoff, of Post Industrial Design, in the parallel NGO event called Local 97; (3) the extensive national and international networks, government and institutional contacts represented in the Committee.

The campaign that resulted, through e-mail and institutional lobbying, was successful enough to achieve three main goals: (1) the participation of women at the conference was substantially increased to one third of total participants; (2) the list of speakers at plenary sessions was expanded until one third were women; and (3) most workshop panels (approximately 75 per cent) included at least one woman. But in the process of the pre-conference lobbying and at the conference itself several difficulties and issues emerged which were a result, in my view, of where the women's lobby finds itself situated, politically and as a movement in the international arena; and of the changing political and economic realities in a world which sees increased global movement and reach of both information and capital.

This chapter is a personal attempt to revisit the experience of the women's lobby before and during GK97, both as a participant at the time and on the basis of interviews, informal discussions with participants, organizers and speakers, and a limited e-mail survey of some

women participants. A formal interview with Diana Rivington, Acting
Director, Policy Branch and Women in Development Division, CIDA,
took place in February 1998. Although she was not an official member
of the CIDA organizing committee, Dr Rivington's position as head of
the WID Division naturally brought her into the conference process.
Several informal discussions and e-mails were exchanged with Nidhi
Tandon, Co-Chair of the Ad Hoc Committee (later the Independent
Committee on Women and Global Knowledge); Shirley Malcolm,
keynote speaker at the ICWGK's women's breakfast event at the conference, member of the Gender Advisory Board of the UNCSTD, and
Director of the Human Resources Division at the American Academy
of the Advancement of Sciences (AAAS); and others who attended or
were involved with the conference in various capacities. I also distributed an informal survey to some women participants (mostly from the
North)[1] to try to get a sense of what those women who were at the
conference thought about their experience, and to obtain their views on
where lobbying and resources should be directed in the future. These
interviews and discussions prompted and complemented a personal
assessment of the GK97 experience, in an attempt to answer some of
the questions it raised. What does the experience of lobbying GK97 have
to say to women's policy advocacy on information and communications
technologies (ICTs)? As an important event in global information
technology for development, what did GK97 achieve for women?
Conversely, were women able to use this conference and the events and
process around it to push forward women's perspectives in information
technology (and knowledge) for development? What has been learned
from this experience, and what paths should we set for advocacy to
promote the creation of an information society and cyberspace which
reflect women's contributions, and which are based on a profound
understanding of women's perspectives, strengths and situation?

Campaigning for women's inclusion

Global Knowledge 97, hosted by the World Bank and the government
of Canada, was held in Toronto on 22–25 June 1997. The intent was to
explore the role of knowledge and information in sustainable development, and how new public and private partnerships around knowledge
and information could 'transform' the development process 'and the
ways in which information and knowledge can serve as tools of
economic and social empowerment'. This conference was planned as
the first in a series of conferences which would be connected by 'on-

going dialogue' among national governments, donors, business, governmental organizations and NGOs (World Bank, 1997b).

Considering that one of the major themes of the conference was to build 'new partnerships that empower the poor with information and knowledge, foster international dialogue on development, and strengthen the knowledge and information resources of developing countries' (World Bank, 1997b),[2] it came as a surprise to those of us working in information technology and networking that the provisional invitation list included such a small number of women.[3] It is true that, despite constituting a fast-growing segment of Internet users, women continue to make up a small proportion of users of information technology and the Internet, and that most women users are in industrialized countries (Division for the Advancement of Women, 1996, p. 4). The initial list, and the mindset it represented, was an example of how difficult it continues to be to ensure that women are equally represented in the policy, project and funding discussions around knowledge and information technology for development. In our view, this list failed to reflect that women's presence on the Internet has increased greatly, while the number of women's initiatives in ICTs at local, national and international levels is growing by leaps and bounds (see for example, APC Women's Programme, 1997; Huyer, 1997; and Marcelle, 1997; and this volume, *passim*) – something which the conference organizers soon learned. The campaigns sparked by the GK97 participants' list not only substantively influenced the organization of the conference, but demonstrated in themselves that women are using the Internet and ICTs in empowered and innovative ways.

Three major initiatives which developed in response to GK97 were: (1) a global e-mail campaign kicked off by the Ad Hoc Committee to advocate women's representation and encourage the nomination of women participants; (2) the establishment of the more formal (formally represented at the conference as an Associate Sponsor) ICWGK out of the Ad Hoc Committee,[4] and (3) the presentation of the 'Canon,' a document calling for the recognition in ICT policy, design, planning and implementation of the gendered differences of use, design and access to ICTs. The goals of the Ad Hoc Committee were to increase the number of women participants; to ensure that there were panels addressing women's concerns and integrating women's perspectives; to ensure that each panel and plenary included at least one woman; to organize a major conference event that focused on women's concerns with respect to knowledge for development; and to present at this event a 'Canon on Gender, Partnership and ICT Development' prepared by the Committee members and intended as a policy agenda for ICT policy and planning.

Our various contacts with sympathizers within both CIDA and the World Bank revealed there was interest in receiving nominations for women participants – the organizers had compiled the original list from nominations received through contacts such as the World Bank and the CIDA/Government of Canada system, embassies, country desks and bilateral partners – none of which would normally be considered cutting-edge institutions in gender and ICTs. Once the campaign was on, members of the Committee circulated notices through their electronic networks: the Canadian node (Web Networks) of the APC circulated a request on its newly established GK97 gender list serve (funded by CIDA); WIGSAT and ABANTU for Development used their international electronic connections and list serves to contribute to the global reach of the campaign; and other members provided names from across North America (and Europe). Of this database of 120 or so names submitted to CIDA and the World Bank, we were proud to say that two thirds consisted of women from the South.[5] At the same time, Diana Rivington had also circulated an e-mail among her networks. A collaborative strategy saw Committee members work their political connections within the Government of Canada and the Liberal Party, local Members of Parliament, CIDA, and Status of Women Canada.

The result of this campaign was a marked improvement in the representation of women on the invitation list (and subsequently at the conference), as I have discussed. Although 'women are waiting patiently' to be involved in such initiatives at 50 per cent levels, as Jennifer Makunike-Sibanda of the Zimbabwe Broadcasting Corporation noted at a closing session of the conference (World Bank, 1997a), this comparative success can be attributed to several factors.

The international women's lobby
The international women's lobby is now well respected and carries a fair amount of clout in international governmental circles, including UN and donor agencies. This stems to a great extent from the instant, effective response the women's movement was able to organize – thanks in large part to the Internet and e-mail – in response to attempts by the Beijing organizers of the Fourth World Conference to restrict access to the NGO Forum. This was a watershed event. The response was so strong that the Director-General of the UN at the time, Boutros Boutros-Ghali, felt it necessary to address the movement's concerns himself – or at least be seen to be doing so – and demonstrated to the world the power of the women's movement (IWTC, 1995, p. 1; Chen, 1995, pp. 477–91). While CIDA has a strong gender stream in its programming, and the World Bank has made some substantive steps in this direction

as well (and undoubtedly there are gender supporters in both agencies), according to informal discussions with several staff within CIDA it was not until an international campaign made itself evident to the conference organizers that enough weight was given to the 'gender' issue for it to be reflected in the conference schedule and participants list.

The size of the e-mail campaign
As soon as the word was out, a barrage of e-mails urging organizers to incorporate a gender perspective and presenting nominations for participants was directed at organizers at CIDA and the World Bank, and many nominations were sent to the Committee for its compiled database of women experts in ICTs. Several CIDA staff commented on the effects of this deluge.

Independent Committee on Women and Global Knowledge
The Committee gained much of its credibility as a visible collaboration of some of the leading organizations and individuals in gender and ICTs locally, nationally and internationally: ABANTU for Development, the APC Women's Programme, the Canadian Committee of UNIFEM, the Metro Action Committee for Women (METRAC), and WIGSAT. It also included women who had founded innovative private sector initiatives such as Post Industrial Design, Devlin Communications (computer software developers) and the Cool Women site.[6] The Committee thus presented a specific, credible entity for organizers to work within addressing the concerns expressed by the larger women's lobby.

What have we achieved, what have we learned?

Several questions, however, also emerged during this process. What negative effects did the e-mail campaign have? Did the conference *substantively* incorporate women's perspectives? What could or should be done differently next time?

Although the Internet and e-mail are increasing the rate at which the international women's lobby can respond to specific events, the impact of this increased speed of response, as well as increased numbers of responses, needs to be recognized and taken into account. The e-mail messages sent out by Diana Rivington and Committee members to their respective networks were meant to generate lists of potential participants which would be forwarded to the meeting organizers. However, as these messages continued to be forwarded around the world, even after the deadline for submission, many chose to send their recommendations directly to CIDA and the World Bank. As a result, both Diana Rivington and the conference organizers were overwhelmed by individual responses which came in over an extended period of time – many too late to be acted on. Some noted that the initial push of the campaign was necessary to call attention to and provide external pressure around the lack of inclusion of women in conference planning; once the genie was out of the bottle, however – once e-mails were being forwarded literally around the world – the campaign continued almost beyond the point of usefulness. In fact, the intensity of the campaign in tone as well as degree unintentionally encouraged a form of backlash within both the World Bank and CIDA. I was told that out of frustration the organizers came close to dropping the issue entirely. That being said, my personal observation was that the organizers I spoke to were not particularly forthcoming about how they were going to respond to the concerns of the lobby. Even stronger than their lack of openness was the sense I had of being brushed off as a nuisance, as someone representing a group that was causing them a great deal of trouble. This, of course, we were doing, but in my view the organizers could have mitigated the intensity of the campaign to a certain extent by being more forthcoming about their actions. Both sides, I felt, would have benefited from consciously trying to find areas of alliance, rather than proceeding from an unmitigated 'us–them' perspective. Some of the more specific problems with the e-mail campaign included the quality of the information received – the organizers wanted enough information on the nominated participant to be able to ensure a high degree of expertise in ICTs, which they did not always receive, according to Rivington – and an unmanageable amount of information which came from a large variety of sources. It was also implied by some that the participants in the e-mail campaign did not understand the bureaucratic realities which the organizers had to live with. These include the problem that, although many were genuinely looking for ways of filling the gender gap, they had little time to do so and did not know where to find women IT experts.

I see a number of issues or lessons coming out of this experience. E-mail campaigns, although useful, can quickly take on a life of their own. Once 'set loose' it can be difficult for any one group to coordinate or lead, or for lobbying targets to know who to interact with in addressing the concerns raised by the campaign. This is not necessarily a bad thing, and often increases the impact of the advocacy immensely. When dealing with policy makers who are located within and restricted by a rigid bureaucratic structure, however, this kind of response can impede the success of the campaign. In future an understanding of the possible *range* of responses, as well as the potential reactions to these strategies and the restrictions or contexts of the targets, will help advocates to strategize more effectively.

Some of the negative or less constructive effects of the e-mail campaign may have come from our failure, in the excitement of the moment and the pressure of impending deadlines for action, to recognize some of the fundamental differences between the Fourth World Conference in 1995, for example, and GK97. The international women's movement has had huge successes at UN conferences over the last six years: the UN Conference on Environment and Development (1992), the UN Conference on Population and Development (1994), the World Summit for Social Development (1995), the Vienna World Conference on Human Rights (1993), the Gender Working Group of the UNCSTD (1995), and the Beijing World Conference on Women (1995) have all recognized the centrality of women to development, human rights and the environment (Chen, 1995, pp. 477–91; UNCSTD, 1995). The UN has seen an unprecedented degree of international activity in networking, lobbying and advocating around women's concerns, and success in getting women's perspectives reflected in international policy. I for one was acting on the legacy of the Beijing e-mail campaign, which, as discussed earlier, was extremely successful. In comparing the two campaigns in retrospect, however, it seems to me that the Beijing success occurred in part because it had specific and limited objectives: to push organizers to alter logistical and visa arrangements put in place to restrict access to the NGO event paralleling the governmental conference, as well as to restrict interaction between the two. The Beijing campaign was more straightforward in that the UN-based organizers – whose ultimate constituency is the public – recognized the need to respond to civil society during the course of a public policy negotiations conference. So, not unnaturally, many of us expected the same patterns of advocacy and success at GK97. GK97, however, was different in many respects. The concerns of the women's lobby in this case had broader and more profound implications for the conference objectives, which therefore posed greater complexities in implementation. Several major built-in barriers to the conference further constrained the ability of the organizers to respond to the lobby, including lack of time and the fact that the agenda was set primarily by donors, international agencies and the private sector as well as governments, whose constituencies do not necessarily directly include the public or civil society. No public policy documents were to emerge from the conference, as is the case with UN intergovernmental forums. Instead, the purpose was much vaguer and less formal: to present one in a series of opportunities to 'engage in dialogue' on knowledge for development. The participants and organizers of GK97 therefore tended to be technocrats, private sector managers, project and technical personnel and donors who were primarily focused on technical, logistical and funding delivery frameworks for developing countries. In other words, they came to make deals, not policy.

This is not to say that it was not important that we advocated for women's participation and perspectives at the conference. But when we were confronted with a new advocacy challenge, we were confused as to how to make an impact. Several of those who responded to my survey felt that women's concerns were not included in GK97 discussions and events to any real extent. The hasty inclusion of women in the last few months before the conference militated against a really strong women's input. The panel and workshop structure did not help, with its traditional conference format of panel presentations followed by audience questions which inhibited substantive discussion or input by anyone, not just women. There was little connection between workshops and presentations, which often ran over their allotted time, further preventing sustained dialogue, or even comments from the audience. For women, the additional problem was that the panels addressing women's concerns tended to be attended mostly by women, with little impact beyond the converted.

When confronted with all of this, many of us were confused as to how we could accomplish anything substantial. For in one sense the success of the initial campaign to increase women's presence at the conference presented us with the next level of achievement. How do we get past the response that yes, women are present, to a point where the deeper gendered implications for policy, planning and implementation are recognized and acted upon? The GK97 women's breakfast was well attended and recognized as a strong conference event, with a well-received keynote address on 'Knowledge, Technology and Development: A Gendered Perspective' and comments from the Presidents of CIDA and the World Bank. In general, however, from the responses and discussions I have seen, many women came away from the conference disappointed with the low profile of women's perspectives overall.

On the other hand, as the conference organizers reiterated, GK97 was more than just the June 1997 event (Dumelie, 1997). It was originally conceived of as an ongoing 'discussion', with the June 1997 conference as the first of a series. Several list serves were funded by the World Bank and CIDA to promote a wider discussion electronically. With participants from around the world and audiences in the thousands (Gilbert, 1997), the electronic conferences carried a large proportion of the global knowledge discussions. Two of the six or so lists saw especially strong women's input. The main Global Knowledge for Development list serve (GKD97), although initially made up mostly of 'non-women', began to see regular interventions by women as it continued. The GK97 gender list, run by Web Networks, was also extremely active, and a summary of discussions was posted regularly on the main GKD97 list. The dialogue around gender on both lists was dynamic and contributed to a great deal of networking, while facilitating discussions among groups of people which might not otherwise have met. From the policy perspective of institutions and policy organizations, however – as a UNDP representative commented on GKD97 – the broad nature of the discussion and the lack of concrete, substantive comments were less helpful. He was looking for concrete proposals, substantive discussion and a narrowing of focus to get information he could use in UNDP policy and programming (Gilbert, 1997). A further problem was the overwhelming North American participation on both lists: input from developing country persons in the GKD97 list was no higher than 25 per cent, the number of women unknown (Gilbert 1997); on the GK97 gender list, predominantly female, 10–15 per cent of subscribers were from the South and 20 per cent of the posted messages originated in the South (Maureen James, e-mail communication, 23 January 1998).

'Local Knowledge 97', an alternative conference held parallel to GK97, provided a venue for alternative approaches to the information society. A consciously 'open' rather than invitation-only event, 'Local Knowledge – Global Wisdom' looked at some of the potential social effects of the dramatic technological changes flowing from international trade agreements and economic globalization. Emphasis was on a variety of communication technologies, including the lower-tech yet still important ICTs such as radio and community networking. Organized in only three weeks over community radio and community networks, the conference saw 120 participants on the first day, including those travelling from Africa, South America, Europe and Asia (including a South African caucus of 20 people) who had come for the official conference. The focus here was on the art of communication and the generation of knowledge aimed at change through conversation and development through a democratic process involving tolerance and diversity. The women's presence at this event was strong, women being represented equally in presentations and participation (Hirsh, 1997).

Women and ICTs – what next for international advocacy?

In view of the enormity and difficulty of the task of 'genderizing' GK97, women's advocates managed to achieve some important goals: many more women attended as presenters, speakers and participants than would have if there had not been a campaign. In addition, many more women from different regions attended, which in my view was partly as a result of the nominations made through the international links and networks of the Committee.[7] The impact and range of the campaign showed the organizing institutions that there actually exists a pool of women who are experts in this area. The women's breakfast event helped to put women on the 'knowledge for development' agenda in a big way. The organizers of the next GK conference will certainly not make the same mistake!

Women were still missing from some of the higher-powered discussions, however, and from the deal making that went on informally throughout the conference. The next challenge for the women and the ICT movement is to develop effective strategies for that next level of advocacy. What have we learned which would help us increase our impact in some of these sectors? In my view, what women's advocates will need to do in any policy forum is recognize the context and constituency of the targeted event or person, and match our strategy according-ly. In a discussion I had with Shirley Malcolm on the last day of the conference, we focused on the idea that influencing policy in non-public policy arenas requires an approach based on solid, convincing data, expert understanding of the issue, and convincing the 'target' (in this case technical and project managers) through low-key, substantive discussions on a personal level. The approach would demonstrate that planning and implementation of ICTs without including the active contributions of women will have adverse effects not only on women themselves but through them on nations and societies as a whole. In other words, the focus would be to convince decision makers in the sector that recognizing gender perspectives is important to the functioning of the system. The difference from the previous efficiency approach, as discussed by Caroline Moser, is that the definition of efficiency here would be expanded to include *women's* well-being and ability to fulfil their responsibilities (Moser, 1993). The difficulty for women's advocates in achieving this can lie in recognizing the limits that policy makers must work within. Geoff Oldham, Chair of the Gender Working Group of UNCSTD in 1993–5, describes a similar policy dilemma when he discusses the tension which developed between external advisers on gender and science and technology and the UNCSTD Working Group members – government representatives – whose mandate was to prouce policy recommendations for the Commission and, subsequently, for the UN Economic and Social Council, based on 'solid' evidence. The concern on the part of the Working Group members was that 'taking a political position could discredit what was supposed to be a scientific report' (Oldham, 1995, pp. xii–xiii), while some advisers called for a more radical approach to assessing and facilitating women's contributions in science and development systems. The Gender Working Group and its advisers were able to overcome these differences to produce a set of recommendations that the Working Group felt it could, within its political, intellectual and gendered boundaries, reasonably expect to have accepted, and which the advisers felt was, although not the ideal document, a big step in the right direction. The challenge for us is to find ways of repeating this success.

This may involve taking the time to identify allies within the structure, or at least to decide if they exist, and coordinate with them as much as is possible or reasonable. As well, for better or worse, if we want to influence decision makers, we will have to accept that the language we use will need to be understood by them, with all the questions of cooption, incremental progress and perceived usefulness this entails (see Staudt, 1990; Häusler, 1994; and Huyer, 1998 for discussions on the pros and cons of attempting to influence policy and institutions). This is especially true in policy for 'hard' or technical activities. That is, in order to impress information technology engineers we will need to talk about gigabytes and bandwidth, on one hand, and on the other demonstrate both that women's perspective is different as a result of their situation or location, and that mobilizing one half of the population to be affected by these systems will improve their efficiency. For this reason we need more experts in gender *and* technology who recognize that women have a great deal to contribute to knowledge for development, can speak the technical language, understand the technology enough to create women-friendly systems, and focus on expertise in ICTs as a key issue for empowerment in the knowledge society and economy (Swasti Mitter, e-mail communication, 12 February 1998; DAW, 1996).

Of course there is still a strong need for 'outside' advocacy which calls decision makers to account for their decisions. Some of the next questions we need to ask explore the relationship between the various approaches to advocacy. When is it useful to lobby from the outside, risking marginalization, and when is it most effective to work with policy makers, recognizing the dangers of slow progress, cooption, or outright failure? How can the two strategies be reconciled, or when is it useful to coordinate them? How does the decentralization of advocacy that the Internet engenders (in all senses of the word) affect our advocacy? How can we use 'outside' processes to develop alternative perspectives and solutions, and when do we present them in mainstream venues, if at all?

There are many important regional and international conferences on telecommunications and ICTs currently being organized, with many more to come, including the regional International Telecommunications Union (ITU) meetings, Beijing 2000, and the next Global Knowledge conference. What should we be doing to prepare for these conferences? What kind of input would be most effective? One important task would be to monitor the organization of the next GK conference, to ensure that the momentum that came out of GK97 continues in GK99. One of the lessons from GK97 seems to be that women need to be involved at the earlier stages of agenda setting. What is the role of the Canon in all of this? We could build on the Women, Environment and Development Organization (WEDO) example here: WEDO developed its focal document for the UNCED conference, Action Agenda 21, through exhaustive discussions with women in various fora around the world in order to come up with a document which could claim credibly to be a global women's document (WEDO, 1991). Pairing this consultative process with strong lobbying of government delegates at Rio produced substantive integration of women's concerns into Chapter 24 and through the UN document produced at the conference. Can the same be done with the Canon? Diana Rivington spoke of it as a 'lost opportunity': can we use the Internet, e-mail and list serves to produce a document which will reflect a global consensus on women's concerns and perspectives on ICTs?

The only GK97 list serve which is still active, the main GK97 list, established a sub-list of 'working groups' in preparation for the May 1998 UN Economic Commission for Africa (UNECA) gender component. The idea of the sub-list in general has been raised as a way of focusing wide-ranging list serve discussions in a way that will be conducive to making a concrete impact on specific events and sectors. The results of the working group would then be made available from a web site, to make key information and best practices, etc., available to the wider international development community (Kerry McNamara, Global Knowledge Partnership Secretariat, e-mail communication, 16 February 1998). One concern voiced about this process is that it risks further marginalization of women from the 'main' list and discussion (Nidhi Tandon, e-mail communication, 25 February 1998).

In discussion and e-mail interaction I heard the following concerns:[8]

- There is a need for women to develop alternative visions for ICTs as well as alternative approaches to sharing information which build on but are not restricted to the Internet, e-mail and the WWW. What roles do radio, street theatre, newsletters and other forms of communication have to play in ensuring that women are not marginalized in the information society?

- The bulk of capital investment in ICTs globally comes from the private sector. In addition, nations are under pressure to privatize their telecommunications systems, while donors focus on systems which will become self-financing. In this situation, how can women ensure that we have a voice in how the private sector sets up ICT systems? Participants at a recent ABANTU for Development ICT training workshop in Nairobi heard from private sector Internet providers who asked for input on how they could ensure women's access, not for philanthropic reasons, but because they recognized how this could improve their profit margins. Not all telecommunications providers are aware of the market that women represent. How should women approach interaction or collaboration with the telecommunications sector, and how can they have a presence in financing and implementation arrangements?

- One of the most important questions concerns the input of women from developing countries. Women from developing countries made up approximately 15 per cent of participation on the GKD97 and GK97 gender list serves, and less than 10 per cent of the total conference participants. This was due partly to the comparative lateness of invitations, and the previous commitments of many of those invited. More importantly, it indicates the scarcity of women in developing countries who have access to ICTs, and the even smaller number who work in ICT technical professions. A key question is how can more women from the South be involved in the designing, planning and implementation of ICTs? How can their creativity be incorporated so that ICTs and 'cyberculture' reflect their desires, perspectives and abilities? This involves issues of technical training and education, literacy for the majority of women in developing countries who are illiterate, financial resources, availability (or lack of) time to engage in these pursuits in light of their triple roles and disinclination to participate in a predominantly male domain (Mitter, 1995; Moser, 1993; United Nations, 1995; Huyer, 1997; DAW, 1996).

As stated by the ITU in its 1994 Buenos Aires Declaration, 'Tele-communications is an essential component of political, economic, social and cultural development. It fuels the global information society and economy which is rapidly transforming local, national and international life' (ITU, 1994). The UN has emphasized the importance of women's access to ICTs for empowerment and to take their place as designers of a major new global system (DAW, 1996). But the strategies we use to make a place for ourselves in the new information society may differ from the past, reflecting a new global context of globalization, de-regulation and privatization, and the rapid pace of technological development. We may need to reconsider our attitudes to and our participation in science and technology, in order to gain the attention of ICT designers and implementers and to develop creative responses to the status quo which are based on a solid understanding of these systems. This is not to say that the basic in-your-face lobbying approach should be discarded: we still need the 'big stick' to gain the attention of decision makers. But what is also important is to have and use a weight of evidence to convince them once they are listening. I hope that by using this kind of analysis we can build from the experience of GK97 to launch the next phase of global advocacy and technological creativity in the ICT sector of the international women's movement.

NOTES

1 It was not possible, unfortunately, to distribute a survey to all women participants. One result of the haste in which the conference was organized was that e-mail addresses of conference participants were not compiled or included in the final participants' list. One World Bank organizer has assured me that such a glaring oversight at an information technology event will not be repeated at the next GK conference!

2 The other two major themes of the conference were: (1) 'understanding the role of knowledge and information in economic and social development, and the profound changes in the development process wrought by new technologies'; and (2) 'sharing strategies, experiences and tools in harnessing knowledge for development'.

3 One conference organizer later stated that more than 78 of the originally listed participants were women, but they were overlooked because they were referred to as 'Mr'! I should add here that it has been pointed out that there were also other 'linguistic' problems with the list, such as translation and spelling.

4 The other members were: Catherine Devlin, Devlin Applied Design; Susan Bazilli, Metro Action Committee for Women (METRAC); Tonya Hancherow, Web Networks; Maureen James, Internet communications and project consultant/Web Networks (APC); Anna Melnikoff, Post Industrial Design; Mark

Surman, Web Networks (APC); Nidhi Tandon, ABANTU for Development; Kathryn White, Canadian Committee for UNIFEM; Peregrine Wood, Womens-Web/Web Networks (APC).

5 The percentage of women from the South who actually attended the conference was not as high. According to my analysis of the most recent official participants' list, one third of the women who attended the conference were from the South.

6 See www.postindustrial.com and www.coolwomen.org. The Cool Women site has received awards for setting up 'the world's largest electronically-connected kitchen table ... for women to share stories about women in Canada and to discuss issues, concerns and our history'.

7 The messages sent out by the Committee members specifically asked respondents to return nominations to them rather than conference organizers.

8 These topics were raised in survey responses and personal communications from conference participants.

9

GLOBAL BUSINESS, NATIONAL POLITICS, COMMUNITY PLANNING
Are Women Building the Linkages?

Nidhi Tandon

From the personal to the political

1996 was a momentous year for me: I moved. I moved from Europe to Canada, from full-time employment to working from home at my own pace, and I moved onto the WWW. Suddenly, as an occupied mother of two young children, my little old Macintosh PowerBook enabled me to open the windows to all that amazing information out there – from the latest on alternative medicine to the details on the side effects of glaucoma medication; from the literacy movements of Dalit women in India to methods of organic coffee growing in South America; from an ongoing international conversation on knowledge for development to an intimate detailed discussion with a colleague in Senegal.

Suddenly, I was more fully employed than I had ever been before.

Following some of my work with ABANTU for Development, an African women's organization, and discussions with its far-seeing Director, Wanjiru Kihoro, I began to explore the full implications of the new knowledge economy and its importance for Africa and for Africa's children. Within a matter of months, I felt convinced that we had to step out of old development paradigms – now and quickly – and take the reins represented by the new technologies into our own hands – without fear or apology, but with expectation and imagination. The following chapter takes the implications of this personal discovery to the policy realm and my work with women's groups in Africa.

In looking at the evolution of information technologies as functional tools for change and the potential implications for civil society, particularly for women in Africa, the chapter looks at how women in Africa are reclaiming their rightful voices in this way. In examining both national and international policy frameworks the chapter draws up the broad implications of the liberalization of the telecommunications sector for sub-Saharan Africa, determines how ICTs might be used to influence policy at the national level, and indicates what some African civil society organizations are trying to accomplish within this evolutionary environment.

Information technologies as tools for change in Africa

At the global level, we are witnessing a triple revolution in technology, information and capital flows. Global telecommunications business is increasingly dictating the rate of change in the development of ICTs. This rate of change has major and critical implications that cut right across all development sectors in Africa.

The processes of liberalization and globalization have introduced forces that are imperfectly understood by policy makers, and by social and political analysts. African policy makers face additional difficulties. Late in the race towards market-driven growth, burdened by a history of racial discrimination, weighed down by heavy debts and decades of civil strife, they are ill-equipped to understand, let alone manage, the new processes of globalization.

When it comes to defending African interests around the negotiation tables at international fora (the World Bank and the IMF, the WTO, UNCED, UNCTAD, etc.), African public policy is for the most part determined in an *ad hoc* manner and is influenced by contingent factors. African governments, and by extension African peoples, are therefore mostly recipients, not makers, of international decisions that affect their lives.[1]

Civil society organizations have to function within government policy frameworks. At the same time, the new tools of information and communication arguably enable them to make governments more accountable and transparent, and to cross communication borders between enterprise, scientific research and government policy.

Trends in international trade

The telecommunications business may be global in nature, but only in so far as its reach transcends national boundaries. The critical decisions around telecommunications trade policy are far from global – they rest in the hands and in the interests of the powerful few. The key players in this game are the US, the EU, Canada and Japan, who between them account for over 77 per cent of the market (see Table 9.1).

TABLE 9.1   KEY TRADING INTERESTS IN THE ICT WORLD

Leading exporters of IT products in 1995 (in US$ billion)

1. Japan	106.60
2. United States	97.99
3. European Union 15 (extra-EU exports)	57.07
4. Singapore (domestic exports)	41.27
5. Korea	33.22
6. Malaysia	32.84
7. Chinese Taipei	28.71
8. China	14.51
9. Mexico	11.67
10. Canada	11.55
Total of above:	$435.43 billion

Leading importers of IT products in 1995 (US$ billion)

1. United States	139.93
2. European Union (extra-EU imports)	104.84
3. Japan	37.68
4. Singapore (retained imports)	24.72
5. Malaysia	22.22
6. Canada	19.81
7. Chinese Taipei	16.53
8. Korea	16.47
9. China	14.35
10. Hong Kong (retained imports)	12.10
Total of above:	$408.65 billion

Source: World Trade Organization, March 1997

Over the last decade, increasing attention has been devoted to trade in telecommunications services, especially in the GATT/WTO context. Traditionally, international telecommunications services were traded under a system of bilateral agreements between nations. Now, virtually the whole sector is covered by the WTO Telecommunications Agreement which opens the way to a multilateral framework for freer trade, market opening and competition. We are entering a new regime of global competition. In a recent report, the ITU quantified the value of cross-border trade in telecommunications and estimated the 1996 figure to exceed US$100 billion. Considered together, the Information Technology Agreement and the Telecommunications Agreement cover international business worth over US$1 trillion – roughly the equivalent of combined world trade in agriculture (US$ 444 billion in 1995), automobiles (US$456 billion) and textiles (US$153 billion). Compare this with the UNDP's puny annual budget of about US$1 billion (UNCTAD, 1997).

These trade agreements are of immediate importance to African countries, since in an increasing number of sectors (education and health, business facilitation and trade efficiency) telecommunications are a key infrastructure, and to date most of the equipment and services are imported.

Trade relations between unequal economies

Information economies have the potential to realize huge profit margins when trading with other economies. By implication, African trading partners become captive markets of information economies. Is it a co-incidence that sub-Saharan Africa has lost its market share in exports while increasing dependence on official financing (aid)?

The answers may lie in the nature and history of African exports. Consider, for instance, the trade relationship between an agricultural, an industrial and an information economy producing respectively coffee, televisions and computer software. Assuming the products are worth US$300 each and tradable with each other, at 15 cents per kilo, an agricultural country requires 2,000 kilos of coffee to earn US$300. An industrial economy need produce just one television to earn US$300. An information economy, however, has only to sell one copy of a software programme to earn the same amount.

In short, an information economy like the US can trade one copy of its WordPerfect software for 2000 kilos of Uganda's coffee. The questions that follow are: how much longer does it take to produce 2000 kilos of coffee compared with one copy of WordPerfect? Over three years? What is the trade relationship between these two economies? Is this relationship sustainable? And who, ultimately, gets to call the shots?

Levelling the playing field

In February 1997, 69 governments agreed to a basic telecommunications liberalization accord, covering about 90 per cent of the world market with an estimated revenue value of US$600 billion – or 2.1 per cent of world GDP in 1995 (ITU, 1995 figures). Seven of the signatory countries were African: Côte d'Ivoire, Ghana, Mauritius, Morocco, Senegal, Tunisia and South Africa (Dean and Opoku-Mensah, 1997). The telecoms accord came into force on 1 January 1998 once governments ratified the agreement and individual country schedules. These schedules committed signatories to varying degrees of market opening – particularly for investments by foreign companies to compete in their domestic markets.

Broadly speaking, all member countries have agreed on applying a competitive framework in domestic regulations, including the establishment of a regulatory authority independent of the operators. The general view is that this will enable the lowering of international calls costs and improve service efficiency of national telecommunications operations.

Countries like Canada and Japan, however, still balk at removing restrictions on foreign ownership – Japan, for instance, has set a 25 per cent limitation on foreigners buying into its two major domestic companies. Continental Europe, for the most part, retains state telecom enterprises which would continue to hold a majority ownership even after being thrown open for competition and privatization.

What is at issue here is the time taken to open one's market. Under the WTO telecoms accord, countries are having to agree to deregulate within a period of five to ten years. Compare this to the history of the British and the American markets which developed over 17 and 26 years respectively before opening their markets. In other words both AT&T and BT have had a good period as 'lean and mean' private enterprises within which to develop their markets and infrastructure, establish their broadband services to customers and thereby retain a significant market share even after markets are opened to outside competition.

In most sub-Saharan African countries, the telecommunications sector is young and is organized as follows:

- The provision of all services is entrusted to a monopoly state-owned operator (SOO);

- The sector Ministry supervises the SOO and formalizes sector policy;

- The sector regulation is shared between the SOO, the sector Ministry and the Cabinet. The SOO often takes on the responsibilities of the government on policy and regulation matters.

A number of countries have begun deregulation/privatization programmes to:

- Separate regulation from operation and to diminish the SOO regulatory authority; and

- Liberalize the sector in the area of value-added services to allow private sector participation in the provision of these services, jointly with the SOO, in competition with the SOO, or independently with no competition from the SOO.

Can state regulation make a difference?

The simple answer is yes, but the real question is, to whom? Will there be a difference to the telecoms operators in terms of profit and leanness? Most probably not. Might there be a difference to the people in rural areas? Quite possibly yes. Might there be a difference in the cost passed down to consumers? Again, quite possibly yes.

What might state regulation effectively do? When developing countries open their markets to foreign investors, there is a tendency for investors to flock to the high value-added end of the market (such as mobile phones) and show little commitment to long-term investment in the expansion of basic telephone and telegraphy services to rural or remote areas.

An important task is the sensitization and education of senior (telecommunication) policy makers in the economic and political gains to be made by deregulating and opening up the market to foreign companies in a controlled manner. They need to understand that steps can be taken to ensure that the national telecoms infrastructure is developed and that telecom giants do not come in simply to target the multinational business companies, the international traffic, and the mobile phone market, thereby reaping all the profits by freeloading on the local operator's infrastructure without deploying their own.[2]

Depending upon their negotiation capacities and bargaining power, some countries have imposed conditions on their commitments to the WTO accord and on their autonomous liberalization policies and foreign investment allowances. Whether these moves will result in expansion of the basic services to areas and people not currently served by the state monopoly remains to be seen. At the same time, these countries risk losing substantial control over their telecommunications development and the economic rewards that go with it, while increasing their dependence on foreign capital, technology and management.

Côte d'Ivoire, for instance, has reserved its voice telephone service over fixed network infrastructure and telex to state monopoly provision for ten years, but will thereafter open these to unrestricted competition. Immediate open market access is offered to all other basic telecom services, including data transmission, all mobile networks and services, video transmission services, and satellite services, links, capacity, and earth stations.

Ghana is committed to maintaining two facilities-based suppliers providing local, long-distance and international public voice telephone services and private leased circuit services. It also offers to license additional suppliers of local voice services to underserved population centres and to undertake a policy review, possibly allowing new entrants to supply voice telephony, once the five-year exclusivity of the duopoly operators expires.

In South Africa, the government has a commitment to end monopoly supply and to introduce a second supplier by the end of 2003 in public-switched, facilities-based services including voice, data transmission, telex, facsimile, private leased circuits and satellite-based services. Foreign investment in telecom suppliers is limited to 30 per cent (WTO, 1997).

Whatever policies governments adopt in the current climate of liberalization, their relative success in this new environment will depend on the quality, effectiveness and transparency of the regulation of their telecoms. Some state regulation is required to ensure that competition between operators is fair; that consumers are protected and get a fair deal from operators; that profit motivation is balanced against social obligations (such as providing services to marginalized peoples and to remote areas); and that levels of contribution to government revenue are established.

A regulatory framework calls for political, economic, social and engineering skills; ideally, it can be crafted through a process of open consultation and the exposure of telecoms issues to wide public debate.

Given that new market entrants tend to target lucrative business customers, African governments need to consider making new market entrants invest at least 10 per cent to 15 per cent of their profits in developing rural telecommunications; ensuring that new market entrants have a restricted period (say 12 months) in which they have free rein to develop their networks in the lucrative areas, after which they are committed to turning their attention to the less lucrative regions or sectors requiring development.

Working with ICTs towards equitable development

The successful application of any development policy ought to be measured in terms of the extent of improvement of the quality of life for the majority of the population, in the case of Africa the 70 to 80 per cent residing in rural areas. If, furthermore, development policies are inimical to women, then those policies are redundant or obsolete even before they are implemented. How do we ensure that national policies address these common interests? Are ICTs one of the tools that could be used to assist the process?

Historically, technological developments have had both positive effects on production, in terms of rate of growth and cost reduction, and negative effects, through excluding whole sections of the population from its benefits. In the case of the new information technologies, it can be argued that the differences between the positive efficiency effects and the effects in terms of social and economic exclusion are likely to be very pronounced unless we take conscious steps to ensure otherwise. This is why it is important to ensure that women have access to ICT development resources.

Participatory politics and developing a shared vision

The new ICTs do open up major opportunities for Africans to access political and social information and data which could influence national thinking on policies. The ICTs allow people to be involved in processes that were otherwise difficult to access, whether it is about acquiring information, commenting on a draft policy document, finding out what the corporate body thinks, or participating in international virtual and real fora.

In the case of national informatics policies and regulatory frameworks, for instance, as these are still at the first stage of formulation in many African countries, women and their organizations have the opportunity to be proactive about finding out and contributing to policy meetings. Women need to find out who is setting telecommunications and networking policy in their countries and make this information available to other civil society groups. ICTs open up opportunities for discussion of democracy issues amongst NGO activists, which simultaneously promotes a flow of information within and from government. It follows, then, that one of the immediate tasks civil society organizations face is to engage with government bodies in a dialogue about how they could use ICTs to promote democratization.

To establish solid foundations for information networks, women and their organizations need to foster and develop partnerships and avenues for close collaboration between the following groups: civil society; the private sector; the ministries responsible for health, education, agriculture, industry and trade; scientists, academia and research bodies; and donor and investor interests.

In rural areas, people's representatives need to coordinate shared rural public access telecentres, kiosks, mobile computing and telecommunications resources which will be established in time. 'Connected' women are already repackaging on-line information and sharing this with the 'unconnected' through other communication channels such as print, telephone, radio, and traditional theatre.

In Tanzania, for instance, a national zonal database and a documentation department is being established by an officer working in the veterinary investigation centre and responsible for data collection and training methods within the integrated tick and tick-borne disease control project in the Ministry of Agriculture and Cooperatives. The project is also responsible for extension training in animal husbandry methods. The officer is aware that the bulk of livestock care in the country is in fact carried out by women, and that if anyone needs this kind of information most, it is the women in rural households. Her mission therefore is twofold, to get information from the women for the national zonal database and to ensure that training and other information is made available directly to the women.[3]

ICTs, if managed well, can assist a consultative process between civil society organizations across sectors and across countries, to develop a code of conduct or framework of principles that addresses national (and liberalization) policies in African countries. The real challenge is not technical or financial, but organizational and political – and, to a very large extent, one of access to information, understanding and foresight.

Building on existing structures

Despite structural problems, there are innumerable innovative and entrepreneurial ventures that flourish right across Africa – ICTs can be perceived as just one of the tools that women can use to grow and sustain these ventures. Three very different examples follow: advocacy at policy level; distribution of information at different levels; and entrepreneurial ventures.

The Forum for African Women Educationalists (FAWE) is a regional NGO that promotes and advocates the education of women and girls in Africa. FAWE's membership includes African women education ministers, vice-chancellors and senior women in the education sector. The regional headquarters in Nairobi coordinates the work of 26 national chapters and provides information to 53 members in 42 African countries. FAWE plans to set up a list serve for its national chapters, members and technical committee providing information on education issues in Africa.[4] Not only will communication between the chapters be made more cost-efficient by electronic mail, but coordination and information sharing will be made much easier.

SYNFEV-ENDA is a Senegal-based NGO which is using electronic communication as a tool in its information clearing house activities. SYNFEV (Synergy Gender and Development) is a unit existing within ENDA (Environment and Development in the Third World), an international NGO working for the promotion of development in respect of the environment with a key focus to date on the issues of 'economic autonomy for women' and 'health for women'. Since preparing for the Fourth World Conference on Women in Beijing, and building on ENDA's track record of promoting electronic communication for the Third World NGOs, SYNFEV has added the 'communication for women' component to its other activities, aiming at the promotion of electronic communication for women's groups as a tool for action, mainly in the field of health and rights. Its main fieldwork has been directed at francophone African women's groups. At the time of writing, SYNFEV-ENDA has links with 30 women's organizations in West Africa, and 35 links with women's organizations within Africa and internationally; it has also conducted technical training programmes in the region for 25 women's groups.[5]

The Association pour le Soutien et l'Appui à la Femme Entrepreneur (Association for the Support of Women Entrepreneurs – ASAFE) is an NGO which promotes and supports women entrepreneurs in all sectors in Cameroon. ASAFE is a network of 3,000 women entrepreneurs, it provides technical support in business management and has set up a financial system to improve access to credit in urban and rural areas. Women not only constitute more than 50 per cent of the Cameroon population, but also represent 53 per cent of the active population. They have a long track record of entrepreneurship and of being good business managers. Unfortunately, joblessness – generated by the economic crisis – is hitting them hard. They are facing stiff competition from those laid off from the public service as well as from public and private companies, even in those sectors that traditionally were reserved for them, such as food production and the informal sector, 90 per cent of which was controlled by women in the past.

Overcrowding, accompanied by the fall in revenue and compounded by the fact that women take care of basic family needs (feeding, health care, clothing, school fees, lodging) makes them the first victims of the present difficult situation (devaluation of the CFA franc in January 1994, inflation, turnover tax, restructuring and/or closing of companies).

ASAFE pursues a development approach adapted to the particular needs of women and emphasizing parameters such as :

- The fundamental role of adapted management training for women, women's groups and their micro-enterprises;

- The necessity to promote alternative financing, notably the establishment of a loan scheme geared toward women who are excluded from the normal financing system. This system has enabled dynamic and competitive business women to raise personal capital contributions in order to qualify for subsequent bank loans;

- The importance of applied research and studies to recognize the value of traditional practices; to improve basic training; and to promote the orientation of women's groups and their enterprises toward new and lucrative opportunities;

- The urgent need to sensitize women to the business opportunities that the environment offers for sustainable ecological development and to the objective of protecting the environment through projects compatible with this approach.

ASAFE members constantly need information (on sources of raw material, or market opportunities) in order to maintain the competitiveness, profitability and sustainability of their businesses; they therefore work collectively and network within the region in order to effect changes in the environment in which they conduct business. Given the increase in the range of commercial transactions via the Internet, and the innovative methods of payment for goods and services being developed, ASAFE could use the Internet marketing and transactions systems to the benefit of its members.

ASAFE is pulling together a comprehensive proposal to meet these needs using ICTs. The main office in Douala is connected to the Internet, so it is just a matter of time before it conducts some of its commercial activities in cyberspace.[6]

Forging new partnerships

At the ITU's June 1997 Council meeting, it was resolved that money from the telecom surplus fund should be set aside for a number of specific projects in developing countries. Given that the African continent has 33 of the world's 48 UN-designated Least Developed Countries, Africa is expected to be the main beneficiary.

A number of initiatives that civil society organizations need to know about include:

- Centres of Excellence for Human Resource Development – conceived with the aim of developing the telecommunications marketplace in Africa, Asia and Latin America, as well as training policy makers and regulators in the development of national priorities and regulations.

- Afritel – to provide seed money to attract other funding partners, in order to strengthen the capabilities of national telecommunications operators to develop and better manage, operate and maintain the African telecommunications networks.

- Industrialization Africa – funding aimed at promoting know-how on the creation and operation of manufacturing at national, subregional and regional levels. Phase 1 will establish the status of equipment manufacturing in Africa, while Phase 2 will implement a work programme for the establishment of manufacturing facilities in Africa.

These are the more obvious channels for ensuring that African people are active beneficiaries of the information revolution and that they can have a presence in it and become information providers.

Global markets have blurred the lines between the worlds of government and business; during the Cold War, national security was tied narrowly to defence and geopolitical issues. Matters of commerce were kept quite separate. Today, national security increasingly depends on commerce and development, and governments and business are working together to promote trade and investment. Civil society organizations need to acknowledge this shift in relations at the national and international level.

The other factor in this equation that is lacking in most African countries is that presented by science and scientific research.

> The inability to merge science, technology and development at the practical level may be attributed to the many complex socio-cultural economic and political factors that have influenced the course of events in the past 20 to 30 years (in Africa) ... countries in Asia and Latin America forge ahead in the use of science and technology [while] many countries in Africa [are still] characterized by a low level of scientific and technological development (Makhubu, 1993).

In July 1995, the Economic and Social Council endorsed three recommendations for national governments which were outlined by the UNCSTD Gender Working Group (GWG) in its report, 'Science and Technology for Sustainable Development: the Gender Dimension'. This report, which focused on the ways in which science and technology can contribute to sustainable human development for the benefit of both men and women, was prepared by a group of eight men and eight women; individuals from a variety of NGOs active in gender, science and technology; and by individual representatives of relevant UN agencies.

The recommendations endorsed by the Economic and Social Council invite national governments to:

- Adopt a 'Declaration of Intent' on Gender, Science and Technology for Sustainable Human Development;

- The establishment of national *ad hoc* committees to make specific recommendations to national governments on the implementation of the Declaration of Intent; and

- Assistance to national governments to obtain access to relevant information and financial support to further these activities (in the case of donor countries).

Indigenous software development is occurring in Africa, if you take the time to look for it. I will cite here two examples which could be adapted for use around the continent. The first is the Uganda Women's Finance Trust's Loan Tracking System, a tailor-made software application to monitor and evaluate the financing activities of UWFT's branches. UWFT has over 10,000 members in the southern part of Uganda, divided over nine branches. In 1995 they began computerizing their savings and loans activities. As standard software was either unsuitable or extremely expensive, UWFT decided to develop their own application.

The software was developed by a Kampala-based consultant, Hans Verkoijen, in Visual Foxpro 3.0A. It is a multi-user programme version that runs at branch computers on Windows 95. The application is linked with a branch planning tool, which is an Excel spreadsheet that incorporates all expectations on a branch level and generates monthly indicators for monitoring and evaluation purposes. These indicators can be copied into the loan tracking system and reporting is done according to these targets.

The application supports four user levels: system operator, branch manager, savings officer (or cashier) and credit officer. The broad functions of the system are:

- Client administration (clients defined as individuals, groups and businesses);

- Loan tracking;

- Savings;

- Accounting;

- Management information.

This software could be adapted and modified easily to suit similar organizations across Africa. The real issue is making this option accessible to as wide an audience as possible – and one of the more efficient tools for marketing it is, of course, the Internet. The WICCE-ISIS office in Kampala approached Hans Verkoijen for his assistance with their resource centre. They told him what they needed, and he concluded that it would be very expensive to create a tailor-made programme for them. So instead he searched the Internet for some shareware and public domain software, and installed about four library programmes and a mailing list programme.

In Nairobi, Kenya, meanwhile, Technology and Interactive Learning Limited (TIL) has developed its own software package of learning materials to enable secondary school students in Form One to Form Four (Grade Eight to Grade Twelve) to study, review and practise subjects using the computer. The packages enable students to use the computer as a tool for learning, while opening their minds and horizons to the various uses of computers. The learning software currently available cover subjects studied for the Kenya Certificate of Secondary Education (KCSE) programme. These include Mathematics, Biology, Physics, Chemistry, English, Geography, Home Science and Christian Religious Education.

The first edition of these packages, which is already in use, has deliberately been made partially interactive to meet the local demands and standards of existing computers. The second edition, which is fully interactive (sound and motion), will be released within the first half of 1998 to address the needs of the fast-growing school and home markets, where high-performing computers are now in use.

Training for women as beneficiaries, contributors and change makers

Women in Africa are already aware of the challenges and opportunities presented by the new information technologies. They are also clamouring for the training and policy changes that will ensure that they benefit from and contribute to the African knowledge economy. Common suggestions for improving training provisions for women include making training women-specific, linking the training with ongoing user support, and mentoring in the communities where women live.

Comprehensive training for women – technical training on designing and managing an Internet node, and business management – is essential right across the board for network engineers who design systems and services and for operators who manage the nodes. End users of the services provided also require training to be able to use the technology with ease, understand the implications of brokering knowledge, build indigenous content and use information resources strategically.

ABANTU for Development was first established as a small group of African women in Britain working to promote issues of gender equality and women's involvement in development policy and implementation. The organization operates as a collective in the development of policy and programmes aimed at empowering African women and promoting change in Africa and in Northern institutions impacting on African development issues. Through the work of the individual women in Africa and Europe, a gap was identified in training to enable women and women's organizations to become more involved in the development of policy and in interaction with policy makers and institutions. ABANTU began to develop its work in three areas to address this gap: training, information and the provision of advice on resource mobilization.

The 1995–7 ABANTU strategic plan was developed in response to the expressed needs of African women's NGOs and African organizations working towards women's empowerment and social and development change in Africa. One of its initiatives was to strengthen the electronic communications capacities of women's organizations that were already requesting this kind of training.

A training programme was designed to provide Internet training within a specific policy context; it was not just about technical training in a vacuum, but attempted to strike a balance between gender analysis, policy training and technical training. The first regional training workshop was held in January 1998 in Kenya and was a direct follow-up of three previous exercises: a training event at the Fourth World Conference on Women in August 1995; a Pan-African seminar on 'African Women's Organizations in Civil Society: Transforming the State and Economy', held in Cape Town, South Africa in November 1995; and a technical Internet training workshop organized in London in March 1996 for African women.

The participatory nature of ABANTU's training methodology allowed for some shift and fluidity in maintaining a balance in response to the participants' needs and interests. The refinement of the initial proposal benefited from the strategic advice and creative criticism over a period of nine months from a number of women, all members of

APC's women's programme who have had training experience with women's organizations in Africa. What is now important is that women should be proactive and avail themselves of this training in order to contribute to African ownership and effective use of the Internet.

NOTES

1 Yash Tandon, personal communication.
2 Observation made by Vivek Tandon, personal communication.
3 Conversation with Christine Bakuname, participant at ABANTU Internet training seminar, January 1998.
4 Conversation with Wacange Kimani, participant at ABANTU Internet training seminar, January 1998.
5 Marie-Hélène Mottin-Sylla, SYNFEV-ENDA, February 1998.
6 Conversation with Giselle Yitamben, participant at ABANTU Internet training seminar, January 1998.

PART THREE

Women's Voices
On the Internet

PART TWO gives examples of women using the new information technologies, the Web and the Net for global networking and for women's rights advocacy and lobbying telecommunications, economic and social policy makers. In Part Three we turn to the stories of the different members of Women on the Net (WoN) in their localities. In these chapters we hear the diverse voices of women working in NGOs and research groups in migrant and indigenous communities in Asia, the Pacific, Latin America and the Arab World. Displayed here is the wealth of experience women have already gained on the Internet as they break traditional barriers to women accessing public spaces and technology. The authors illustrate the very different and creative uses to which the Internet can be put by women – from exchanging information on the latest pattern of traditional cloths in Tanzania to a virtual mapping out of ancestral lands in the Pacific. It is clear from these chapters that the Internet is a potential tool for empowerment for women's groups. Even if snags abound, it seems that there are new cultures being created. Part Three indicates some of the safe spaces being made or envisaged where women can push their personal and political agendas in a cyberworld which impacts on their real world situation.

Laura Agustín opens with a graphic example of how migrant women, domestic workers and sex workers could well benefit from the new communication technologies if we listened to them and adapted ICTs to their needs and lifestyles. In a call to move from comfortable office lives to the harsh world of those struggling on the margins of society, she envisages how the Internet could function as a survival tool for those cut off from social and legal services.

From Zanzibar, Fatma Alloo shows how women's groups and civil society groups are using the Internet as a tool to intervene in local political disputes, to further their community support work and enrich their cultural lives. Like Kekula Bray-Crawford in the chapter which follows, Alloo breaks with the notion that ICTs are only for the elite and rich North. If communities have access they can use the information in ways that can transform their lives. Bray-Crawford, in her work as a technician in support of indigenous groups in the Pacific and as part of the virtual network Netwarriors, shows just how powerful the Internet can be as a tool for global advocacy in support of local battles. Her chapter illustrates how, if used in a politically innovative way, the Internet is a medium where different cultures and knowledges can be married in relationships that construct and create rather than destroy.

Rhona Bautista takes us to the nitty gritty of how women in Asia are entering the cyberworld against the odds of prohibitive costs, gender discrimination and the daily struggles for survival and their rights. She shows how ISIS-Manila has supported women's political efforts through its resource centre, training and electronic networking. Similarly, June Lennie and her colleagues describe how their activist and participatory on-line research project helped to link isolated women in rural Queensland to the urban feminist research and policy world. Their chapter analyzes the language that the women employ, the topics they research and the use they make of the Internet, in a fascinating study of women creating a new culture across geographic, political and social divides. Sally Burch also gives a positive example of how the Internet has supported civil society's political work through information sharing and networking for social justice. She argues that if women's NGOs work together they can usefully occupy the communication spaces the Net offers and release its political potential for their fight for rights and an end to gender discrimination.

Moving to the Middle East, which perceives itself as outside many other global discussions, the last two chapters argue that the Internet offers a virtual openness of dialogue that can help to change the reality of women's lives in that region. Farideh Farhi, working out of Iran, sees the culture of the Internet as opening up the cultural dialogue between the West and Iran's isolation. If allowed to flourish the Internet could enable global discussions to create new spaces for peoples' movements and thus to change their cultural terrain. Lamis Alshejni, originally from Yemen, argues that Arab women cannot afford to ignore the political potential of the new medium to counteract the many discriminations they face by helping to shape the cultural space of the Internet to include their concerns.

10

THEY SPEAK,
BUT WHO LISTENS?

Laura Agustín

A parable of connection

Scene: A small room with a bed and a washbasin.
Characters: A man and a woman.
It is the third time this man has paid to spend time with this woman.
She only speaks a few words of his language, but he seems kind and she
decides to take the risk. She tells him she is being held prisoner and
wants to get out. Will he help her?

The man is sympathetic but he does not want to get too involved,
certainly not to take charge of this woman. So he takes out his cellular
phone and says: 'Make any call you want.'

The woman has not used a telephone in months. The only number
she knows by memory is her sister's, back in the Ukraine (... or Paraguay
... or Burma). She has trouble dialling, does not know any of the codes,
but the man helps her. They have to hurry, because he has only paid for
a short time, and they have to whisper, because there are people in
rooms on both sides of them.

The call goes through! Her sister answers. The woman can only say:
'Help! Get me out of here! I'm being held prisoner!'

'Where are you?' asks her sister.

'In Israel (... or Holland ... or Thailand).'

'But where exactly?'

'I don't know.'

Stories like this have made headlines all over the world. In the usual
version, the faraway recipient of the call begins a long, arduous search
for help through hotlines to embassies and international police. In the
end, there is a raid and the woman who made the call is liberated. The

police, who knew about the brothel all along, are not the heroes of the story. Neither is the client, who took no risks. In fact, the hero of the story is the small cellular phone that enabled the prisoner to connect to the world and be heard. The story does not end perfectly, however, because the woman is deported, and this is not what she wanted.

This story is true.

When I consider the possible uses of new technology for migrant women, I begin with stories like this one. Here, people are enabled to communicate vital pieces of information. Here, there are processes and chains of events and people help each other. Before we can move to the question 'How will the Internet benefit migrant workers?' other questions must be considered, for these are not simple or straightforward situations.

Geographical double-think

Although commercial sex is now recognized as a global, multi-billion dollar industry, its workers – in their millions – are only referred to as 'illegals', as victims of 'trafficking' and as potential 'vectors' of HIV/AIDS – when they are referred to at all. The same London newspaper that runs the story of 'liberated sex slaves' in Malaysia never mentions the problems migrant Chinese women have finding child care (or fish sauce) in London. It is the age-old technique of 'disappearing' people simply by not acknowledging them.

To be deemed worthy of recognition and help, where you are is all-important. The same person identified as 'indigenous' in the Andes and included in projects of traditional aid is viewed, if she migrates to the North, as a job-stealer, welfare bum, ghetto resident, drug dealer and addict, candidate for deportation and firmly outside the scope of traditional development aid. Unless, that is, she puts on some kind of native dress and plays pan pipes, whereupon she may qualify for 'cultural' funding and will probably be left alone by the police – if she plays well enough to gather audiences.

Those who seek to correct this geographical double-think – whether they are involved in battles for fairer immigration laws or for better working conditions for domestics, dancers or prostitutes – often talk about rights: the right to communicate, the right to health care. Similarly, when possible uses of new information and communication technologies are mentioned, we hear about the right to access. But access is a tricky thing with people who are being watched and controlled, do not have much money and are itinerant. Migrant labourers, whether women or men, whatever their labour, have difficulty finding and using the bene-fits of settled society. Migrants who do not enjoy 'legal' status or whose status depends on a certain amount of fraud or deception, must be extremely cautious about requesting and using services. Migrant prosti-tutes have the additional problems of having to navigate a labyrinth of laws concerning their work. The problems here are logistical and the need is for wireless, rapid and discreet connections.

The literacy myth and the new information culture

Beyond questions of access lie dreams of educational growth, spiritual expression, 'liberated voices' that media like the Internet offer. Again, advocates often mention rights: to education, to 'life-long learning', to 'self-expression' or 'self-realization'. The 'rights' argument, however, sets the discussion firmly within First World norms, where citizens not only already have better access and services but also more citizens are pre-pared to take advantage of them. To use the World Wide Web and even the simplest e-mail programme, after all, requires a very high level of literacy.

Classic 'development' projects, whether applied to populations located in the Third World or to migrants who have left it, have assumed that progress happens in stages, of which literacy is the first. According to this theory, everyone must become literate in the same ways that Western societies have come to take for granted. The use of alphabets to store knowledge is said to constitute humankind's most significant step up on the ladder of progress, the step that distinguishes people from animals and cultures that 'succeed' from those that do not. Yet alphabet technology is comparatively recent and has *not* taken hold with all the world's people. In recent years this Eurocentrism has been widely criticized for extinguishing 'indigenous knowledges', but this has not affected assumptions that even indigenous people need to become alphabetized. According to this way of thinking, if poorly educated domestic and sex workers are to participate in new technologies, they must first attend literacy classes in their own languages, then receive some basic education, computer instruction and perhaps English, after which, finally, they can learn about the Internet. Even were access not a question, the proposition would be absurd.

In the classic literacy myth, the centre of everyone's desire is to enter the Golden World of Books. And the way it is now, the Internet mimics books, whose contents are scanned whole onto web 'pages'. But even among those who know how to read, relatively few routinely read more than headlines, cartoon stories, romance novels, product labels, street signs and horoscopes, and many never write at all. When those who hold reading and writing sacred deplore these 'low' uses of literacy, others feel inadequate and ashamed about the ways they know and learn about the world.

Those using the Internet are avid readers and, more important, are oriented to 'acquiring information'. This concept – that 'information' is something to 'acquire' – is also being discussed currently as a right, but, again, assumes acceptance and agreement about crucial values – how to work, how to know things, how to ask questions, where to look for answers and from whom and how to judge information as 'correct' or 'true'. Most of the world does not belong yet to such an 'information culture', and these values ought not to be imposed, even by evangelists who are sure people will be saved or uplifted by them.

Right for whom and for what?

The question should not be whether we can provide egalitarian access points to the Internet for all the world's people. If we construct the conversation on 'rights to access', 'freedom of speech' and visions of progress and development (who has the electricity and telephone infra-structure, who has the money for a computer, who can go to school to learn about technology, who sees information as a 'consumer' item and a right) then we reproduce the same conversation we found oppressive in the first place.

Some of those now excluded from much of mainstream societies *want* to include themselves in this new technology, whatever it turns out to be. They see themselves as protagonists of the revolution. But what about those who are excluded and who see nothing (so far) about this new technology to attract them or who do not know it exists? Should they be forced to be included, if being included could 'help' them (acquire useful information, tell their stories, and educate others)?

In the United Kingdom, travellers (the old word gypsies is not preferred) have lived deliberately on the social margins for centuries, and have consistently been viewed as either perverse or pathetically disadvantaged, to be hounded out of decent places or forced to adopt a 'normal' way of life. Finally accepting travellers' desire to live in mobile houses, planners build them 'sites' with connections to water and electricity. But the sites are organized so that their vans are in straight rows at measured distances, ignoring travellers' needs, such as space to work with scrap metal.

Many conversations about outsiders like travellers and sex workers revolve around questions of free choice. Even people willing to believe that travellers want to move around will not believe that prostitutes might. Instead, they change the subject to what is wrong with prostitution. If the subject always changes to how to abolish prostitution or how to find work alternatives for all current prostitutes (in their many millions) or how to change men so they do not desire prostitutes, we will never address the realities of sex work that lead to exclusion from services and policies that might benefit them. This is why many activists are focusing on ensuring occupational health and safety regulations applied to sex work.

The acceptable face of 'difference'

To understand policies that consistently exclude people, we need to recognize a contradiction: that societies which not only tolerate but desire 'difference' in its proper place will demonize and harry it when out of place. Circus sideshow performers, transgender artists, beggars who stand at church doors and children who breakdance in the street, when found in a 'nice' residential neighbourhood, will be quickly moved along. When the outsiders are sex workers, they will be moved to very particular locations. So while governments currently discuss 'trafficking' and immigration law as if their only concern were the well-being of 'victimized' women, they continue to facilitate the business of commercial sex in all the most obvious ways and punish only the women involved when someone must be punished. Migrant prostitutes' access – or their perception of access – to even the most basic services is still widely in question, even in Europe. Moreover, many services are provided without understanding how migrants live and what they want. It is essential not to assume that all migrant prostitution is forced and all brothel workers are slaves. It is imperative not to project our own desires and assumptions onto others. The only way we can know what others want is to give them room to tell us. Which brings us to the centre of this essay: How do 'we' know what 'they' want?

How to offer opportunities?

How can we provide possibilities to use new information and communication technologies to marginalized and migrant women? If we believe that the chance to tell their stories *could* be liberating, enlightening or useful to them, how can that opportunity be offered? The specific case

I address is that of women from the Third World – and particularly from Latin America – who have migrated to Western Europe to work as domestic and/or sex workers. These women in their many thousands are found from one end of Europe to another, and very commonly continue migrating as opportunities close and open. Those who offer information on new opportunities, those who facilitate journeys and those who take advantage of migrants know how to communicate with them.

Currently, the world of interested and 'helping' agencies, largely ensconced in comfortable offices, bemoans the manipulation of migrant women by criminal networks and wonders where women have gone when they suddenly disappear. The solution to this is evident: move out of those offices. Supporters need to stop producing and giving out ever more excellent written materials and do more following and listening. They should learn from the 'criminals' and start knowing not only where the women are but where they are going to next. The information available to women comes from those who go to them. To influence the empowerment of a migrant sex worker means accepting her reality and going to meet her there.

Visions of a postmodern scribe

So imagine an educator who carries her wares with her. To visit domestic workers isolated in big suburban houses and not allowed visitors, she goes to a local plaza (or laundromat) on Sunday afternoon. There she offers to help with problems, find people, even predict the future. Instead of a crystal ball, she carries a small computer notebook and a cellular phone. From her bag she may also vend envelopes, stamps, postcards and paper. She may carry a telephone book, the latest edition of the classified advertisements and various small dictionaries. Perhaps she gives impromptu lessons in the local language. She might have a recording Walkman and some music tapes. She is a kind of postmodern scribe, also a cultural worker, or maybe a travelling saleswoman.

She will be able to contact some sex workers in nail and hair salons but she will soon feel frustrated by the vast numbers not reached. In possession of a large van, however, and a driver, she can cover a wide territory. Parking near sex-trade zones, she lets workers know when she has arrived and offers them now a wider range of services, from bed, toilet, shower, food, condoms, blood test to fax/telephone and Internet connections. Some women might want to know the weather in a city they are considering going to, others to send e-mail to alert other workers about trends in police harassment, dangerous clients or new wrinkles in immigration law. The scribe can look for and print from the Internet AIDS information in the women's own language; if they do not read she can tell them what is most important to know. The technology, the education, the services are mobile, like the workers. A fleet of such vans in different parts of Europe would form a true network, which women could enter and leave at different points.

Such an approach – technology not isolated in offices, not connected to formal education, not touted as a new religion, not pushed as a 'right', but instead associated with coffee, sandwiches and chat – would not appeal to everyone. Some women might not be able to take seriously a computer in a van, or have time for it. Others might learn to type and send their own e-mail or look for their own information on the Web. The vans themselves would *be* a communications technology connecting travelling women who rarely avail themselves of services located in inhospitable buildings and neighbourhoods.

Does cyberspace have margins? Can gypsies find vestigial spaces to park in? Will those who become bored reading or do not understand 'clicking' find ways to communicate through images and sound? Could the Internet become softer, like holograms, and find itself on walls, be projected on curtains and heard in the shower? Will there be ways to wrench it out of its current place in hard plastic boxes and give it a 'virtual' reality? How would it be to carry an Internet connection on a wristwatch? Alternatively, what if huge screens were set up in marginalized neighbourhoods and websites beamed onto them with the kind of big sensuous sound found in popular movies and discotheques?

The concept of information needs to be reconceived to include not only 'indigenous knowledge' but also 'street smarts'. Just as Western scholarship overlooked Mayan writing and Inca *quipus* for so long because they did not come in the form of books, so current thinking continues to exclude ceremonies, spontaneous 'happenings', oral and musical events, a group of women spending the evening together watching a *telenovela*, conversations on the assembly line and creativity by teenagers on the dance floor.

Those who wish to honour the value of non-written traditions need to accept that the word literacy can extend to include in 'reading and writing' other things besides letters – the forest, the street, the television screen. Instead of condemning the easy access criminals and entrepreneurs have to migrant prostitutes, we need to mimic that access – find out how they do it, what works best, where and when. Let us go out to those in the margins and listen to them. For, with all the rhetoric about the need to liberate 'unheard voices', we miss an essential point: those voices have been talking all along. The question is who is listening.

INFORMATION TECHNOLOGY
AND CYBERCULTURE
The Case of Zanzibar

Fatma Alloo

Tanzania's uneasy marriage with technology

Upon independence, we in Tanzania dived into the experiment of socialism. The new leaders mobilized us with visions of an equal society as the driving force. And in this process we accepted the lack of access to technology as a necessary ingredient on the road to equality. We even adopted an attitude of being better than our neighbours because Tanzanians were not materialist! This was some thirty years ago when we spoke of other African countries as a 'man eating man society' (no acknowledgment of gender then) because they had chosen capitalism.

Today the scenario is different. A 'liberalized' Tanzania means that efficient infrastructure is in demand and information technology is the buzz word for progress in the 'liberalized' world. IMF and World Bank deals are the order of the day. A culture of consumerism is no longer frowned upon. Tanzania once refused television as a cultural imperialist medium with Mwalimu Julius Nyerere arguing that unless and until Tanzanians could produce their own television they should not submit to other cultures' televized images. Times have changed. For the first time in Tanzanian media history there is no government television. Press freedom in Tanzania has ushered in liberalization with eighteen newspapers, multiple FM radio and television stations and Internet. CNN, with its consumer-oriented approach, is among the four private television channels opened five years ago. Information technology has arrived in Tanzania with diverse consequences for men and women.

Women and the new information age in Tanzania

I have been engaged early in Tanzanian forays into information technology as the founder of Tanzania Media Women's Association (TAMWA) in 1987, an organization which emerged along with the opening up of the Tanzanian economy from 1986 onwards. I saw the potential of use of technology as a mobilizing tool for the women's movement. When we found funding to launch our first women's magazine *Sauti ya Siti* in 1988, we immediately asked the supporting development agency to provide fully fledged desktop publishing with training for TAMWA members.

They did. Around that time, in the late 1980s and early 1990s, the UN was eagerly mobilizing around women's issues. We too joined the bandwagon. The APC women's programme was the first of our support systems to empower us with the technical tools to be part of a global women's movement. TAMWA had one of the first e-mail nodes in Tanzania at a time when technology was treated with great mistrust as a type of monster. In using this new information technology TAMWA challenged the prevailing view that technology is only something for the haves, and therefore to be shunned. The challenge was more provocative because TAMWA was an NGO working in media and in addition one that focused on women.

Within TAMWA, however, it was still a struggle to encourage members to use information technology. Taking TAMWA as an example, it seems that women are particularly shy, even scared, of technology, and it takes quite some time before they will dare to try and use it. And here I include myself. We persevered, however, and the experiment in TAMWA bore fruit. The information technology enabled us to link with the broader women's movement. The local and the international could be connected and could work together on various issues such as violence against women, reproductive health, and empowerment in many fields.

To take one example, TAMWA was fully mobilized through the UN Conference on Human Rights, held in Vienna, to support the global women's campaign under the slogan 'women's rights are human rights'. For the first time, however, it was not only members of TAMWA in Vienna who were directly involved, but also those women receiving information from TAMWA as it was beamed directly to Tanzania. Such was the awareness created during the Vienna meeting that when we came back home we were able to make use of the conducive environment and launch a network made up of women and men artists, intellectuals and decision makers, and campaign in our own country to support human rights efforts.

This was just the beginning of the story.

Zanzibari communications

In mystic Zanzibar, in the popular media image, we find a romantic little sleepy island where *dhows* frequent the coast, a thriving trading community of the Indian Ocean flourishes, and time stands still. This is just not so.

In the late 1990s liberalization is in full swing. The yuppie youth culture sees the consumer economy and accompanying information technology as passports to a dignified job. The young, both men and women, are testing the ground for individual success and wealth. But there are also progressive forces. A thriving civil society is gaining momentum. In both cases information technology is seen as a force for change. It is no longer seen as the preserve of others or a monster, but as a tool that must be moulded to cater to people's self-defined needs.

As one founder of an NGO Resource Centre (NGORC) on the island of Zanzibar, a project of the Aga Khan Foundation, I am repeating the TAMWA experience as people organize and voice their concern through community-based groups and NGOs. As with the women in the 1980s, these new movements have learned that policy makers chart their lives. Now people fight back with the information they can gain through the Internet and other networking tools.

Consider the vigorous debate over tourism and development. Civil society groups resent the fact that policy makers decide to make Zanzibar a paradise for tourism and do not involve the community in development tourism – a course of action that results in environmental degradation and displacement of people's livelihoods. In a well-documented case a British businessman flew into Zanzibar in November 1994 ready to mastermind a development tourism project of US$4 billion. This project was to take place at Nungwi (northern tip of Zanzibar), which was to be developed as the Hong Kong of Africa. Instead of information about such a plan taking six months to filter into the community, with no time to respond, Internet access provided the information which eventually led to the arrest of this businessman as a fraudster who was in fact on the run from Interpol. The Nungwi community was able, through an expedient use of the Internet, to prevent a development project fiasco set up without their knowledge or approval.

Entering the cyber age

Internet access and the fast and relatively cheaper communication channels have raised the curiosity of the NGO community and its willingness to adopt information technology. My organization, NGORC, has carried out several workshops to demystify information technology and to enhance its use as an empowering tool. This training is particularly crucial in Africa, where the popular international misconception presents a 'dark continent' struggling to have access to basic needs. The attitude affects African people, too, who tend to say that before we invest time and resources in information technology we need first to have the basics. This is a spurious argument – one that holds as much danger as arguing that you need economic stability before democracy or – as in the days of the liberation movements in South Africa – that fighters need to wait until liberation before raising women's issues!

In Zanzibar, we are trying to create a cyberculture which takes information technology as a tool to work in our interest. We have now developed an ongoing process so that information technology is an integral tool of community movements. The environment movement, working with NGORC, has successfully used information on the Net to access, translate and disseminate campaigns to their constituency. For example, sea turtles are an endangered species globally. In Zanzibar committed youths run a sea turtle farm and educate local people on the need to preserve the turtles. Through access to information on the Net this group has been able to blend scientific with indigenous knowledge and become a viable, sustainable, community-based group with enough income to run their farm. With the Centre as a facilitating channel they have become part of a cyberculture which gives access to and feeds information into the global ecologist movement.

Another innovative creation of cyberculture by the Zanzibari is the adaption of the medium to a traditional form of communication – the *kanga*. *Kanga* is the traditional cloth worn by women, where women are able to express their sentiments in a culture of silence. Every *kanga* has a philosophical saying drawn from part of the Swahili culture along the East Coast of Africa.

The sayings depicted on the cloth are punchy, suggestive, sharp or reflective, depending on the mood of the woman who is wearing the *kanga*. A *kanga* stating '*Karibu wangu muhibu*', 'Welcome my love', communicates a strong morale boost to anyone, let alone to the man for whom it is being worn. Or a man may give a *kanga* to his wife at the birth of a child, saying '*titi la mama ni tamu*', 'Mother's milk is the best', and so portray his feeling that he would like her to breastfeed – but he can only express a feeling and not a demand.

But messages can also be quite sharp, such as '*Nyuki mkali kwa asali yake*', 'The bee fiercely guards its honey', a strong warning message from the woman wearing the *kanga* to another woman who she suspects is running around with her husband. A *kanga*-displayed response by the girl friend (perhaps at a wedding reception) could be *'Na tule asali tumwache nyuki na ukali wake'*, 'Let us enjoy the honey and leave the bee with its sting!' Both women have spoken their minds yet not verbally, and neither will be guilty of making a direct accusation at a wedding reception! Another *kanga* message can be chosen by newly-weds: *'Nitunze nipendeze waigao wasiweze'*, meaning 'Cherish me so that I nourish you and remain yours!'

The Internet is used to exchange new sayings, maintaining the flow of information about the latest *kanga* patterns both in Zanzibar and among the Zanzabari community globally. Cyberspace has provided the opportunity for a vibrant cultural community to build its creative wealth of sayings and debates in Kiswahili. The Zanzibar community log onto the Internet in order to join the debate, wherever they are globally.

Zanzabari NGOs take the lead in cyberculture

In Zanzibar a viable cyberculture is emerging for civil society as the Internet becomes a meaningful cultural and political tool in our lives. Members of the NGO community have been using the Internet to speak out against overly bureaucratic registration processes for NGOs. They have recommended that the mechanism of the Internet be adapted so that in all the 25 regions of Tanzania there are nodes and training for NGOs, which could then register at a regional level and yet be linked through the Internet to a central node. They propose this linkage to encourage information sharing and awareness building about the various activities of the civil society community.

This step by the NGOs indicates that once people realize the potential of this technology they are willing to embrace its possibilities fully. This is not to deny another equally vibrant side of cyberculture – the yuppie culture where consumerism, the buying and selling of commodities including women's bodies – is also thriving on the Net.

The cyberworld and shifting meanings of community

Even if these examples, taken as a whole, point to a promising use of the Internet, we have a paradox growing up around how the Internet or cyberculture is serving the Zanzibari 'community'. The question here is, who is the community? Community is another buzz word for the developing world and development agencies. It appears to be a positive word but in reality it is a vague concept. Does the Zanzibari global cultural identity form a community? Or do participants in the NGO/ CBO movement form a community? Where do the yuppies, living in Zanzibar but striving to be part of a global modern world of business, fit in? Is a Zanzibar community linked to its historical roots or to its contemporary abode? Does it just describe a sense of belonging? Can such a sense of community enable people to unite and resolve conflicting social struggles, or should communities be negotiating internal political compromises more self-consciously in the pursuit of development, democracy or environmental conservation?

My years of working in media and civil society in Zanzibar and Tanzania, and also internationally, have shown me that communities need to be seen as contemporary forces of social change that unsettle the status quo. For me the interesting question is how we can use the Internet and the spaces being created as different cybercultures to produce an enabling environment where information is used as a tool to better people's lives. What is crucial is that the participation of different people in communities should feed into a creative system of change which improves the livelihoods of all, and not only of the 'haves'. This is the challenge we face not only in Zanzibar but also in the global realm of cyberculture which we are trying to build.

12

THE HO'OKELE NETWARRIORS
IN THE LIQUID CONTINENT

Kekula P. Bray-Crawford

Access and integration

Access to information and facilitation of communication provide new
and enhanced opportunities for expression and perpetuation of the
cultural life of communities and peoples, with the potential to accelerate
political, economic, social, educational and cultural advancement beyond
the scope of traditional institutions and forms of communication.
Regional and global information networks expand the voices of cultures
and peoples via electronic fora to raise awareness and focus international
attention and support on specific cultural issues and efforts. The ability
to transcend present boundaries and create what would be an even finer
web of information systems is the key to taking cyberculture to its next
level.

This chapter assesses the current trends and resources in the area of
communications infrastructure and content during a crisis of culture,
with examples of successful utilization of communications models and
technologies for direct peaceful empowerment of cultures, particularly
indigenous peoples.

Envisioning alternative systems through indigenous wisdom and
cyberculture

My work as a human rights activist focuses on self-determination for
indigenous peoples and the ability to transcend the typical boundaries of
political conflict through a cyberculture. I envisage this cyberculture as
one in which creativity and intellect could challenge neocolonial
initiatives of the twenty-first century and reduce the sufferings endured
by indigenous peoples living with Fourth World aggressions.

The course of my own culture in this information age was set by the evolution of an ancient Hawaiian heritage, on one hand, and a deep desire for the integration of knowledge within the expanding field of computer technology, on the other. This is the edge that I use to navigate and develop what I call 'the Netwarriors' and 'indiginal mapping' (see below). This creativity is now finding an empowering future as it continues to define and establish culturally sensitive uses of technology within the framework of traditional intellectual cultural knowledge and political alternatives. The work has begun to build a bridge of culture, environment and technology for global change.

My path supports a grassroots alternative development agenda, in which indigenous wisdom once again might achieve a greater recognition through articulate technological architecture. Indigenous wisdom could be a vehicle enabling communities to merge together and move towards a restorative system away from a predatory industrial system.

Working for indigenous groups

As an indigenous woman in cyberculture I have had the incredible opportunity to assist in the pioneering stages of establishing a foundation for indigenous rights to be explored and experienced on-line.

This began with the native Hawaiian independence movement in 1992. We were taking greater strides by 1995, when along with my husband Scott Paul Crawford I delivered the first paper on indigenous rights through technology at the Internet Society 1995 International Networking Conference entitled 'Self-Determination in the Information Age', focusing on indigenous initiatives in on-line communications technologies for self-determination.

That summer I received an invitation from Andree Nicola McLaughlin, of the Medgar Evers City University, Brooklyn, New York, to present the first on-line empowerment workshop to the Seventh Annual World Conference of the International Cross-Cultural Black Women's Studies Institute (ICCBWSI), attended by women from over 40 countries and focusing on women's development in Third World countries and Third World conditions in Fourth World circumstances. The presentation received a high degree of resistance, which is indicative of the oppressed conditions experienced by women in Third World countries and mirrors the responses in other fora.

We organized another workshop for the Eighth Annual World Conference for the ICCBWSI in Johannesburg, South Africa in August, 1998. This time we are setting up a computer communications centre, where women in attendance and delegates will have the opportunity daily to sit at a computer, experience the Internet, explore the potentials and possibly create their own web pages for their communities as an economic development initiative, focusing on women of the region, their current situations, needs and solutions. Our goal is to leave at least one community empowered with computers, access, and the ability and commitment to assist others.

In the autumn/winter of 1996, while working as a communications consultant for the International Indian Treaty Council, an indigenous ECOSOC NGO (Category 2), I took a United Nations formal session to the world in real time. This benchmark of opening new space on the Internet set in motion the work of integrating political action with on-line networking in a mobilizing manner, and we founded the Net-warriors.

The Netwarriors movement focuses on UN dynamics and agendas in respect to indigenous peoples' rights. It also reaches beyond this arena for crisis calls affecting indigenous peoples. This particular formal session was the second UN Commission on Human Rights Inter-sessional Working Group on the draft Declaration on the Rights of Indigenous Peoples at Geneva, Switzerland – and we are very proud to say that we completed a successful second year at the UNCHR-IWG in 1997.[1]

In 1998 the Netwarriors have focused on assisting the National Commission for Democracy in Mexico and the EZLN to mobilize world public opinion throughout the holidays. We have become an International On-line Political Observer through this initiative and are receiving when in direct action over 20,000 hits per day. We also took the Netwarriors to the CBD8 (j) in Madrid on 24–29 November 1997 to report on another international standard-setting forum, and the network keeps building.

Indiginal mapping

My professional work also involves the creation of a multimedia, multi-relational database system set within a framework of indigenous cultural knowledge, time and its relationship to land. This is indiginal mapping. SeaSeer, a local software development company, proposes to support the initiative through their expertise in the integration of tools and applications. Artistic creativity, Geographic Information Systems (GIS) and Global Positioning Systems (GPS) provide the other general elements necessary to produce my first indiginal map.

This particular project aims directly at the cultural restoration of traditional knowledge and indigenous wisdom as it relates to site-specific land bases. The core objective is to ensure that indigenous culture survives its transition into a new millennium with a restorative call to the world community.

My regional 1997/8 focus on the Internet is aimed at enabling and access in remote and rural areas of the Pacific. I spent one month in French Polynesia earlier this year training the women of Tuahine (whose members were from Tahiti, Moorea, Huahine, Marqueses and Tahaa) in e-mail communications. They have established a women's cooperative and are working to develop export and trade industries based on traditional goods.

While there I was able to work with the French-owned telephone company to configure Hiti Tau's laptop computers which were donated to them by other networks. Owing to the challenges of language differences, the tools used in my training were paper and a digital camera: pointing and making clicking sounds with my mouth, I attempted to translate between French, English, Maohi, and 'Olelo Hawai'i. Through this intimidating bridging experience, I found comprehension, amazement and a strong desire to learn more. The Maohi (indigenous people of French Polynesia) can only afford a few hours of Internet access per month – an unlimited account in French Polynesia is US$2,000 per month, provided by the government-owned phone company. In December 1996 there were only 10 Internet accounts in the region of French Polynesia; in March 1997 there were 150.

Infrastructure, content and a crisis of culture

As I and other writers on the subject have shown, the swiftly evolving information and communication technologies and networking infrastructures play an expanding role in supporting the cultural expression and perpetuation of the rights and knowledge of indigenous peoples. There are those who feel that the technologies are a detriment to indigenous peoples' rights, but I counter that position, proposing instead that indigenous people are not only fully capable of utilizing this resource but must empower ourselves by it in order to preserve our culture for the next seven generations.

In her paper 'Cultural and Intellectual Property Rights of Indigenous Peoples of the Pacific', Aroha Te Pareake Mead explains:

> It is important to note that Western law distinguishes cultural property from that of intellectual property, in that it regards cultural property as

being tangible physical expressions of culture, such as music, dance and art forms, whereas intellectual property is seen as the outcomes, both tangible and intangible of ideas or processes that have been the result of human intervention....

But there is a *terra nullius* – a Latin legal term meaning 'territory belonging to no one'. The general rule of English common law system was that ownership could not be acquired by occupying land already occupied by another, hence settler governments evoked *terra nullius* in the new colonies thereby refusing to acknowledge existent indigenous habitants....

Intellectual property rights laws do not acknowledge existent customary indigenous knowledge or indigenous ownership. Nor do they agree that indigenous knowledge processes are scientific and technological. Nor do they accommodate a connection between indigenous peoples and their lands and heritage. In short, they do not regard existent indigenous knowledge as being an intellectual property and deserving of protection ... (Suva, Fiji 4 September 1996).

In order to counter the logic of *terra nullius* and to restore indigenous wisdom as a source of cultural and intellectual knowledge, indiginal mapping can be used. Indiginal mapping provides a system of information on different localities that ensures that indigenous children remain in touch with ancestral knowledge and ways through cyberculture.

The politics of cyberculture

As indiginal mapping shows, cyberculture has to be useful for indigenous and other marginalized peoples, and has to be part of a conscious political strategy for change. The information age is so fully upon us that those of us who work within the world of cyberculture speak what is almost another language. As we begin to converse with people from every possible point on the planet to discuss the role of information technologies in our lives and the lives of our people, we must keep central in our minds the purpose and reason for their use.

Interactive media such as the World Wide Web (WWW) are so engaging as to seem almost worthwhile just for their own sake. Almost, but not really. The technology is only a tool, and only as useful as the information it carries. Thus we must continually be aware of the need for content. We cannot become so entranced by the magic of how we put information into cyberspace as to forget that what we put there is actually delivering an impact. The medium is not the message.

While it is possible to dwell on the potential benefits of electronic communications for cultural protection and expression, we must also temper enthusiasm for these technologies with a realistic view of their limitations, particularly regarding access in less developed regions of the world.

David Ronfeldt, in *Cyberocracy is Coming,* warns of the need for equitable distribution of these technologies and freedom of access.

> A new distinction is emerging between the information haves and have-nots. Some actors may become global information powers, but others, notably in the Third World, fear 'electronic colonization' and 'information imperialism' (Ronfeldt, 1992).

If this is true of Third World countries in relation to the First World, then Fourth World nations are at an even greater disadvantage, and in greater need of assistance to gain access to and make positive use of the technologies, which give rise to another main focus of Ho'okele Netwarriors.

Reversing the hierarchy of knowledge

Indigenous peoples of the Fourth World are seeking to assert and perpetuate their cultural identities, along with the integrity of their political voices and rightful political status, as well as their economic and social development. As the world increasingly recognizes that these voices must be heard, for them to be heard in the electronic realm is essential. The voices of the indigenous peoples of the world can help provide the content that makes the use of the technology meaningful in a real way.

A hierarchy of information exists, which runs as follows, from bottom to top: data, information, knowledge, intelligence, wisdom. The indigenous people of the world already hold the ancient wisdom. The question is: can wisdom be translated into data and information in a way that preserves its essence, while allowing us to take advantage of the modern technologies that are available to distribute and share this wisdom in the form of data and information, in an effort to make really knowledgeable and intelligent choices for the future of humanity?

Virtual cultures

Cultures and peoples may benefit from the ability to form 'virtual communities' and to share forms of cultural expression unique to the virtual world. Indigenous peoples who are involved with struggles for cultural survival are very often dispersed, displaced and relocated, having been forced away from their homeland by military, political or economic foreign interests, and those of First World countries.

Communications technologies make possible new kinds of communities, or at least provides possibilities of a certain level of cohesion among a dispersed community which may aid in the expression and perpetuation of cultural identities. Dispersed communities can form and remain cohesive much more easily with the advent of telephones, faxes, e-mail, the Internet and WWW, communications satellites, etc. Territoriality, in one sense, is no longer essentially important in the creation of feelings of community. Thus the body of people capable of participating in the cultural life of the community may be expanded through access to communications technology.

As a direct illustration of this, in 1995 a participant in the creation of the Free Tibet Home Page reported that:

> There is an effort under way now to improve the on-line services in Dharamsala, the home of the Tibetan Government-in-Exile. This will enable a more direct link between Tibet supporters and the officials and organizations where the bulk of Tibetans reside. Tibetan writers are grouping together to inform and educate people on modern Tibetan culture and are looking to disseminate information across countries and oceans. There is a lot of work under way to preserve Tibetan religious texts in electronic form and on CD-ROMs. Most of that is being done in monasteries transplanted to India (Delisio, 1995).

Tibet is a clear example of a situation where both political and technical access from within the territory itself is extremely limited, yet a government-in-exile, working in partnership with its people and various supporters around the world, is establishing a vital cyberspace community to further the purposes of the people and culture of Tibet. Today you will find 19 references on Yahoo of information and sites related to Free Tibet. Progress?

Resources for integration and solutions

Each indigenous people and Fourth World nation has its own distinct history and current political situation, yet all have much in common in their struggles for cultural and political identity, voice and recognition, and sovereignty over their land and natural resources. Each group may feel isolated and disempowered if unable to see itself in the larger picture. But the establishment of relations between various Fourth

World peoples can provide benefits in a number of ways, by sharing experiences, resources and insights so that those who have learned in one way or another can share their knowledge and coordinate actions for solidarity, enhanced effectiveness and the prevention of (or, as in Peng Wan-Ru's case, mourning for) the loss of life.

The electronic media provide vast opportunities for such networking. As new organizational networks are built, cutting across national borders and interests, influential sub- and supranational actors increasingly compete for influence with national actors. As political and economic interests grow in protecting and expanding the networks, the networks themselves may increasingly take precedence over nation-states as the driving factor in domestic and foreign affairs. The setting of standards in the virtual world is paramount in our collective technical manifestations.

Native communities have been actively engaged in creating and utilizing such networks with increasing participation and sophistication.[2] A prime example of indigenous on-line resources can be found at NativeWeb[3] which contains extensive information about a range of native subjects, geographic regions and cultural groups, along with material on native literature, languages, newsletters and journals, organizations and bibliographies. NativeWeb also provides pointers to other native information resources, including WWW sites, Gopher and FTP Sites, UseNet newsgroups, and list serves. There are scores of newsgroups and list serve lists related to indigenous issues, including education, health, language, law, spirituality and ecology.

As indigenous peoples seek to protect and perpetuate their cultural rights and assert control over their land and natural resources, access to international legal tools is essential, and being able to access relevant documents instantaneously can provide significant advantages. For example, advocates can access the United Nations directly for related resolutions[4] – though information in certain areas, such as decolonization, is noticeably unobtainable from the United Nations' website, as pointed out by the Special Committee on Decolonization at the 1997 annual seminar in Antigua–Barbuda.

Numerous other sources also exist for accessing valuable international information. Microstate Resources is a virtual library on the WWW developed by Microstate Ltd.,

> for the purpose of fostering public and private sector development in very small states, autonomous territories, colonies, islands and similar domains where problems of scale, isolation and dependence impede balanced development. Utilizing the most advanced information tech-

nologies, particularly the Internet and the WWW, Microstate Ltd. has developed linkages to the most critical resources needed by small countries and others interested in their affairs (Leventhal, n.d.).

Documents specifically related to indigenous issues can be found at the Fourth World Documentation Project, organized by John Burrows at the Center for World Indigenous Studies (CWIS) Washington State, in 1992. Its goal is to

present the on-line community with the greatest possible access to Fourth World documents and resources. The Fourth World Documentation Project is an on-line library of texts which record and preserve our peoples' struggles to regain their rightful place in the international community (Burrows, n.d.).

Human rights information is available electronically from a wide range of sources to help people understand their rights and combat abuses of those rights by having the proper information. The Human Rights Web provides a good starting place for research in this area, with links to Web sites with a bearing on human rights, Gopher sites, e-mail lists, list serves, and newsgroups.[5]

A vast range of resources regarding sustainable development can be accessed electronically, to assist cultural groups at the tangible level of providing sustenance to the people in a sustainable manner. One outstanding resource is EnviroLink.[6]

Finally, resources which can be accessed via the Net include not only the files which reside in cyberspace, but also the contacts with the people who put them there, and the growing number of experts, scholars, attorneys, and others who also have access to cyberspace.

Partnerships for access

One solution to the issue of access, which depends more on personal relations and less on institutional actions by First World entities, is to develop effective partnerships between those with the technical ability and the access, and those with the issues and the content. Karen Strom, for instance, has provided Web presences for a wide range of Native American tribes, organizations, museums, and projects, which are hosted on her server at the University of Massachusetts.[7]

Partnerships are a good first step in obtaining access to information remotely. A range of services could be provided, in various combinations, depending on the resources and needs, including providing the physical site and/or the HTML design work or other systems design.

The long-term goal is to provide assistance aimed at each entity having its own server or at least access to a local server. Seeing the material on-line, receiving the positive feedback and experiencing the direct results of this presence can provide the incentive to move into a more active participation with the Internet. Further technical and financial support systems can then be employed, utilizing and expanding on the partnerships that are already in place.

Bridging indigenous culture, the environment and technology

Self-determination in the information age of technology has proved successful on several counts but still not enough. Networking is key to the survival of indigenous culture and indigenous peoples' rights under Fourth World conditions. The ability to support others who continue to be deprived of access is crucial. As Kristin Nauth and Laurie Timmerman point out,

> the gap between information haves and have-nots is perilously wide. Connectivity is no simple feat in countries that lack reliable telephone and electrical systems. There are also political hurdles.... In the rear guard are nations like Mozambique, which is just emerging from a two decade civil war and has only three telephone lines per 1,000 citizens (Nauth and Timmermann, 1997).

Protecting and securing an identity through the explosive electronic age is a responsibility indigenous peoples are now embracing. Traditionally removed from the cutting edge of progress, they can join international initiatives to recognize that culture is the basis of knowledge and intellect, and so ensure their identity and achievements in the twenty-first century.

On-line resources provide one level of access to information that may be helpful in mobilizing world public opinion and knowledge to oppose war and crimes against nature and humankind. We need network facilitation, however, to support those incapable either financially or technically of developing or accessing communication infrastructures. Globally, we must act by sharing information in more lucrative and meaningful ways within the new communication infrastructures.

The objectives of military technology are reaching far beyond our imaginations. The satellite pollution surrounding our planet is devastating. The solution to mitigating the disastrous effects of nuclear contamination and waste is not within our grasp or understanding. The compounded waste dump beneath our islands in the South Pacific is far greater than Chernobyl, contained only by 'lava-bubbles' which rest upon an ever-shifting Pacific plate. The ice caps, the ozone, the mass loss of life due to pestilence and the continued genocidal activities of governments – all these shock the mind through the heart if ever truly looked at in the face. Yet we hope, we envision and we struggle in the integrity of our truths to explore and creatively experience a virtual world where these things can be resolved. And, as an indigenous woman, the protection of cultural and intellectual property rights are paramount to my own survival and my work.

NOTES

1 http://hookele.com/netwarriors
2 This includes both the valuable efforts to perpetuate native languages electronically through special fonts, sound files, software applications, etc., as demonstrated by the Hawaiian Language Programme at the University of Hawaii at Hilo on the island of Hawai'i (http://www.olelo.hawaii.edu) and the mirroring of sites in different languages (parts of NativeWeb, for example, are also provided in Spanish).
3 http://www.maxwell.syr.edu/native
4 http://www.un.org
5 http://www.hrweb.org/
6 http://www.envirolink.org
7 http://hanksville.phast.umass.edu/misc/NAresources.html

13

STAKING THEIR CLAIM
Women, Electronic Networking and Training in Asia

Rhona O. Bautista

Do women have access?

The new information technology industry is one of the fastest growing industries in Asia. Information technologies do indeed pave the way for people to exchange everything from recipes to summaries of the Human Development Report swiftly and without the use of intermediaries. The crucial question for us here, however, is how women are benefiting from such a revolutionary technology as the Internet. In this chapter we ask what are women's experiences with this technology, and what are the impediments to women's access and training in Asia?

Women, poverty and access to the Internet in Asia

In the last quarter of 1997 and the beginning of 1998, the tide of growth and economic aggression in Asia completely ebbed away, resulting in a deep financial crisis in the region extending to the 'tiger' economies of Singapore, Hong Kong, Taiwan, South Korea and Japan. This has led to a general worsening of living conditions for women in the region.

Most people in South Asia are affected by human poverty. The Asian region has the largest number of people in economic poverty: 515 million. Together, South Asia, East Asia, South-East Asia and the Pacific have more than 950 million of the 1.3 billion economic poor worldwide, of which 70 per cent are women. According to the UNDP, in Asia 'poverty has a woman's face'. Women are too often disempowered and burdened by the strains of productive work, the birth and care of children and other household and community responsibilities (UNDP, 1997). In the last 20 years, the number of rural women living in absolute poverty has risen by nearly 50 per cent.

Despite this, or precisely because of this, women in Asia continue to work for social reforms and for the promotion of women's economic, political and cultural status. Women's groups are organized around issues of resource access, property rights, inheritance laws and expansion of public and private rights – particularly reproductive rights. For women in Asia, recognizing the value of new access to resources also means access to new information technology.

The economic and social potentials of IT are also now being recognized by governments across Asia. In Singapore, during the Fourth ASEAN Forum in 1996, government ministers responsible for information agreed that ASEAN should seize the opportunities presented by the new media, the Internet in particular.

This enthusiasm, however, has not led to access for the greater part of the population. Usage of IT in Asia is limited to private individuals from the higher income bracket working in colleges and universities, government agencies, telecommunication companies, banks or financial institutions, and business firms (*Philippine Daily Inquirer*, 15 May 1996).

Access to the Internet is particularly difficult for women. Potentially the Internet may be the most powerful tool for accessing and communicating information, but it can also be alienating for women who have neither equipment nor proper training. As it is, the majority of Asia's women still do not have the resources to connect with other women using the old technology such as the telephone. The gap in access to IT is even wider between countries with infrastructural deficiencies. The problem is not only access to technology but also involves factors related to widespread poverty, organization, training in different aspects of information, financial support, and language accessibility.

Fighting for space on the Internet

In 1996, only 3.4 per cent of the worldwide number of computers connected to the Internet were in Asia. It has been estimated that there are approximately 45 million users worldwide but most of these are in developed countries where communication infrastructure makes new types of communication readily available even in the household. In contrast, 80 per cent of the world still lacks basic telecommunications facilities, and two-thirds of the world's population have never made a phone call. Internet access is twelve times more expensive in Indonesia than it is in Italy, and 95 per cent of all Internet users are in Europe and North America (Sandhya and Natesan, 1996).

When women enter cyberspace, their participation and articulation are also hindered by the dominant form of interaction and debate used on the Internet and in e-mail. On the Internet, male perspectives and voices dominate over women's, who have neither been taught nor trained to use this medium (Paterson, 1996; Spender, 1995).

Even in a rich and technologically advanced Asian country like Japan, women are far behind when it comes to Internet access. According to the Asia–Japan Network (AJN), an e-mail network founded by women activists who were inspired by the success of the women's electronic networking initiatives during the Fourth UN World Conference on Women, very few women's groups and NGOs in Japan have e-mail, much less Internet connection. Lack of computers, high cost of hook-up and maintenance, the predominant use of English on e-mail, and the lack of resources and a workforce for translation were cited as the primary reasons for this situation. According to AJN, Internet hook-up in Japan costs US$3,000 and the monthly fee is US$2,000. Lack of training and know-how for the use of electronic mail and the Internet also contributes to their problems.[1]

In Pakistan, computers are being used for desktop publishing in the worlds of high finance, advertising and education. Former Prime Minister Benazir Bhutto, as part of her literacy programme, opened computer learning centres in the country and many private urban schools have computer classes from the primary levels. Access to data-bases is rapidly increasing and the electronic newspaper has made its appearance, but Internet and e-mail are still very much a tool for the elite, and very few women's groups have access to it.

In India all electronic media, ranging from satellite television to e-mail and the Internet, are accessible only to the privileged classes and cater almost exclusively to their predominantly male information and entertainment needs and desires. In Bangladesh, the cost of hooking up to the Internet could feed a family for a year.

In the Philippines, despite the much-touted economic gains in the last five years, access to a telephone line is still prohibitively expensive. Given a mandated minimum daily wage of US$6.36, a telephone line costing US$200 or an Internet hook-up amounting to US$200 is beyond the reach of even the middle class. For the average two-income Filipino household, the computer is still too expensive. It is a luxury item for most families and access to it is work-related. The Philippine computer density is one computer for every 50 individuals (1:50) while other economically developed Asian countries have a ratio of one computer for every 10 persons (1:10).

What all these figures and statistics reveal is that: the 'Infobahn's' traffic flow is heavier on its North-to-South lane. In the South, access to the Internet is primarily available to the traditional elite who are educated, urban-based and largely male.

The Isis IT experience

Even given these difficulties, information plays a vital role in the struggle to promote and enhance women's status in society (Villanueva, 1997). Such a role will become even more important as Asia faces the reality of new computer technologies and their impact on people's lives. But how have women in the region actually utilized these technological advancements in their work?

The experiences and examples of women's engagement in new technologies in the region are steadily increasing (Bautista, 1996). For women globally, new technologies have become an important element in the women's movement. Our own experience in Isis International[2] mirrors most women's organizations' experience in using these new technologies. Isis was introduced to e-mail in 1992. Then, our use of this potentially dynamic and powerful tool was mainly as electronic 'postwoman'. After six years, we have developed projects and campaigns around new technologies (Bautista, 1995).[3]

Isis further strengthened its electronic communication capability in 1993 in its effort to provide service for the various programmes and women's groups with more efficiency and speed. Since then we have participated in training and workshops on e-mail, the first of these organized by the South-East Asia Forum for Development Alternatives (SEAFDA) in Kuala Lumpur. This was followed by the Asian Women's Policy and Technical Workshop, organized by the APC's Women's Networking Support Program (WNSP) in January 1994 in New Delhi.[4]

The training in Malaysia enabled Isis to provide an electronic communication service to the organizers of the Asian regional conference on 'Trafficking in Asian Women' held in April 1993. Isis was responsible for sending news about the conference, the plenary proceedings and workshop results to the various networks around the world, and for fielding inquiries about the meeting. Isis also co-organized the setting up of on-site access to e-mail at the first Asia–Pacific Regional Preparatory Meeting for the Fourth World Conference on Women, held in Manila in November 1993. At that symposium a caucus of six regional women's media and communications networks, led by Isis International–Manila, combined forces and pooled their resources to form the Standing Committee on Information, Documentation and Communication (IDC).

These groups provided news and update on the Symposium to the international community through the production of daily electronic newsletters accessible in 132 countries through the APC and partner networks.

The second major engagement of Isis in the technology was the APC team of 40 women from 25 countries around the world providing the user and training support for electronic communication in Huairou in 1995 during the NGO Forum for the Fourth World Conference. These women brought their unique experiences in women's networking from countries such as Sri Lanka, Ukraine, Senegal, Uruguay, Japan, the Philippines and Canada. We were able to support the women participants in 18 languages. Beside the official conference languages we offered other languages such as Spanish, Scintilla, Hindi, French, Japanese, Russian, Portuguese and Czech.

At the NGO site, there were two host computers that handled Gopher, WWW, e-mail, news and conferences. These host computers acted as a full APC network; connecting the worldwide progressive community, including women who have no Internet connection beyond dial-up access in regions such as Africa and Asia. Apart from the on-site training, the team also went to different groups to share our experiences in promoting women's access to computer communications. We had an opportunity to meet with the lesbian group, the differently-abled group, the peace group and others. The groups focused on demonstrating how this technology can be an effective tool for information sharing and coordination.

After Huairou, Isis served as the regional focal point of APC's WNSP, and has spearheaded several Asia–Pacific projects such as the research on women's involvement in computer networking activities (APC Women's Programme, 1997).

Women's views on the Internet

The following are direct quotes from some of the women who participated in the survey of the APC's Women's Networking Support Programme (WNSP).[5]

> The only negative point is being afraid to start a list serve or chatroom or conference or newsgroup because I do not want to deal with people who are hostile to feminism, and my work is absolutely feminist. It will take so much energy to respond appropriately. I can only spend a certain amount of time on-line each day, and do not want to be swamped by difficult types.

The amount of time it takes to learn to use the technology in the beginning, including getting the communications software to work without conflict ... it costs so much time, energy and phone bills to find resources I want to learn about and the newsgroups that are useful to me ... the amount of time wasted by playing on computers and surfing the WWW.

Because there has been no real research for communication in Indian scripts, usage of this facility is still restricted to the English speakers in our organization.

It is very frustrating for us who are in Third World countries simply because despite being unable to access the Interactive services such as WWW, Gopher, FTP, etc., it is also difficult to enjoy the normal e-mail service due to the existence of the most unreliable phone lines in the world.

The Internet is still very exclusionary and inaccessible and this is consistently the thing that turns me off the most about it. Sometimes I don't even want to be on-line anymore because I wonder what the point is if only a small fraction of the world can use and contribute to this amazing (potential) tool.

Electronic conferencing and resourcing

According to the APC survey reports, despite the obstacles and short-comings, women are increasingly getting on-line – a development that has led to greater empowerment for women. Electronic tools such as e-mail have become a standard part of a growing number of women's day-to-day communications. More and more women are providing websites, databases, mailing lists and on-line conferences.

A woman from Malaysia wrote: 'Learning to use e-mail was a major factor that helped me overcome a lot of my fears in technology'. Another woman from India reported that 'the Beijing Conference suddenly became alive for us as we received daily messages about what was happening, who was doing what and got live perspectives that were not locked in newsprint'.

In Isis International–Manila, together with the E-mail Centre, a communication service provider in Manila and a member of the APC, we established the Asia–Women list serve in February 1996. Asia–Women is used for disseminating information on current issues affecting women in Asia and the Pacific region. It has about 60 subscribers to date, mostly women's organizations and documentation centres in Asia and the

Pacific region. It also features the Isis monthly bulletin, *Women Envision*.

We also facilitate an electronic forum called Asia-gendermedia, set up as a virtual link to the Gender and Media Policy Conference held in Antipolo, Philippines in July 1997.[6] Asia-gendermedia now provides about 65 other media, information and communication organizations worldwide, the majority coming from the region, with a summary of the conference discussions and subsequent resolutions and actions. Using this experience as a model, we are opening other electronic conferences along our advocacy themes of food security, globalization, and violence against women.

Our website, opened in January 1998, contains original feature articles by women; news of issues, campaigns, action alerts, post-Beijing updates and announcements; a listing of books published by Isis; and links to women's resources on the Internet with an Asia and Pacific focus.

Isis is also active in advocating the use of electronic technology and training women's groups in the Philippines. In 1997 we organized three forums and a training workshop with the support of WomanHealth Philippines, E-mail Centre and the APC's WNSP. The forums focused on Emerging Information Economies and Women's Responses, while the training was on e-mail, surfing the Internet, and basic webpage construction.

In April 1998, Isis organized a workshop in Manila, Philippines on Electronic Networking and Resourcing: Strategies for Women's Information Centres. The exchange is geared towards developing the capacity of women's information centres for electronic resource sharing and networking using new information and communication technologies such as e-mail and the Internet. At the end of the workshop, the participants agreed to set up a pilot website project called 'Asian Women's Resource Exchange' (AWORC).

AWORC will be a collaborative project geared towards building sustainable electronic resource sharing among women's information centres in Asia and promoting Internet literacy and activism among individual women and women's organizations. It will be a source of information on women's issues and the women's movements in Asia. AWORC will highlight contemporary and critical issues for women in the region and pay special attention to areas where there is a dearth of information about women. It will be proactive, providing information that may be valuable for women in the future. It will also serve as a communication channel among women's organizations in this region and support their advocacies. The group identified some key contemporary issues for women in Asia:

- Violence against women;

- Status of women;

- Globalization;

- Women's access to information, focusing on gaps among different sectors;

- Women's health and reproductive rights;

- Issues related to the Council of the Status of Women (CSW);

- Female children;

- Elderly women;

- Women and the environment;

- Vision of the women's movement in Asia.

AWORC's main feature will be a multilingual search system of databases and other resources which are housed in individual centres. Other features include: a description of participating women's information centres and agencies; a bulletin board where activities, conferences and other announcements can be posted; electronic hosting of campaigns by Asian women's organizations; and networks and links to sites, list serves and other resources relevant to women in Asia. Another feature that may be developed in the future is a directory of women's organizations in the region.

The six organizations from Japan, Korea, Malaysia, and the Philippines that participated in the Manila workshop will collaborate during the initial stage of website development. They comprise two Women's Regional Information Centres (WRICs), two national WRICs, one academic library and one on-line communications NGO that volunteered the host site. The number of participating organizations will be expanded in accordance with stages of development agreed on at the workshop.

Other activities envisaged around the development of the AWORC website include a skill-sharing workshop for on-line information access by women's groups; information experts in women's groups; and technical support by women.

Asian women staking their claim

Recognizing the potential of the new information technologies, Asian NGOs and women's organizations in particular continue to explore ways to tap these technologies to enhance their organizing, information and advocacy work. Moreover, across the development of these technologies 'cyberfeminist' theorists are emerging, speaking, and gathering. They reshape, redefine and reclaim the new electronic technologies for women.

In Thailand, a group of NGOs – including women's organizations – formed a cooperative to share an e-mail box with assistance from Computer Communication Access. This cooperative is now using a bulletin board system that supports Thai and English for communication.

In Japan, the group Women's On-line Media (WOM)[7] has a home page which provides information not typically available in official publications and government announcements on the current status of Japanese women, as well as assisting in creating a network among different women's groups scattered throughout Japan.[8] WOM also provided information on the Fourth World Conference on Women, and publicized its activities on the NetNews and via its WWW home page.

In Singapore there is Women-Connect-Asia, an electronic network created by four women's organizations to help businesswomen living and working in Asia. Women-Connect-Asia's website features a directory through which women in the region and beyond can offer their products and services to one another.[9]

Most women's groups in Asia enjoy the services provided by the networks of the APC. APC disseminates substantial information through their conferences and Gopher relating to development, environment, women's rights, violence against women and other issues. APC's networks are venues for women's groups and individuals, spaces for sharing information, activities related to UN conferences, and activities and their work in general.

The way forward

The way forward for women in the region is to address the lack of access and training. Access to information, and to the tools to define and broadcast information, are critical issues for women in Asia. Some of the ways being proposed to help women gain wider access to information and information technologies include increasing support for local training initiatives that are gender-sensitive and 'hands-on'; developing user-friendly motivational training and educational manuals in appropriate languages; and providing local user support for women. This approach is based on the fact that only a minority of women are on-line, and these are mostly middle-class, educated, and city-based women. Providing adequate information and public access to the Internet (through personal mailboxes, for example) will help to bridge the gap between women who have access and those who do not.

The Isis Resource Centre can play a crucial role in providing individuals, women's groups and other organizations with access to electronic and print information globally and regionally. We are working to make our resource accessible by Internet with e-mail boxes available for resource centre members and users. In response to the diverse ways in which women in the region access and move information, in the next three years Isis is expanding its use of ICTs. We see this as complementary to our main communication medium of print and our advocacy of women's issues. As well as offering public access, Isis will continue a programme for developing the capacity of women to organize in the field of electronic communication through training and research.

Despite the many obstacles and unfavourable conditions that restrict their access to electronic media, women have shown themselves to be excellent networkers, extending solidarity across national and global boundaries via electronic mail, print, and real face-to-face encounters. One can only imagine the unleashing of the creative energies of women in the service of communication and progress when the barriers to women's full participation in the new information technologies are dismantled.

NOTES

1 These were cited by participants in a forum organized by the Asia–Japan Network and the Asia–Japan Women's Resource Centre on 27 October 1996, to which two Isis staff were invited as speakers.
2 A feminist organization that promotes communication, cooperation and networking among women and groups working with women, and has a vision of developing information and resourcing among women in our region.
3 Isis International–Manila is an international non-governmental women's organization founded in 1974 to promote the empowerment of women through information sharing communication and networking. Isis's network includes individuals and organizations in 150 countries.
4 Thirty-one representatives of women's NGOs and several other organizations representing eight countries passed a resolution for the Beijing conference in September 1995. The participants agreed to promote e-mail as a tool in intervention during the conference. The group also recommended the need for technical resources, including service providers that will organize training programmes. This will enable more women to use e-mail technology.
5 See Edie Farwell *et al.* (1998), Chapter 7 in this volume.
6 Twenty-five media practitioners and activists gathered in Antipolo, Philippines from 30 July to 2 August 1997 to discuss policy recommendations at the Regional Conference on Gender and Communication Policy. The conference coordinators,

World Association for Christian Communication (WACC) and Isis International–Manila, extended their welcome to delegates from Australia, Canada, China, India, Indonesia, Japan, Korea, Malaysia, Philippines, Sri Lanka and Thailand. Each country presented an overview of their women and media situation.

7   WOM is a non-profit, independent organization founded in August 1995 by seven creative Japanese women. It counts among its diverse membership company employees, homemakers, and students.

8   http://www.suehiro.nakano,tokyo.ip/WOM/English/WOM/index.html

9   http://www.women-connect-asia

14

EMPOWERING ON-LINE CONVERSATIONS
A Pioneering Australian Project to link Rural and Urban Women

June Lennie, Margaret Grace,
Leonie Daws and Lyn Simpson

Pioneers in communication technology

As a group of feminist academics, we feel very fortunate to have been involved in an action research project, based in Queensland, Australia, which has had a substantial impact on the lives of many rural women. Of all our project's activities, its unique on-line discussion groups have made the greatest impact.

Our chapter outlines the geographical and socio-economic context of our research, including the roles and identities of rural women. We conduct a critical analysis of a discussion group, taking both its empowering aspects and its limitations into account. Our preliminary analysis suggests that while the on-line conversations and linkages are clearly empowering for many women, some self- or group-imposed constraints were identified which seem necessary to maintain the friendly and supportive atmosphere of the group.

The Queensland and Australian rural context

The state of Queensland is a vast territory in the north-east of the Australian continent. Its population is just under three and a half million people, with over 44 per cent living in the Brisbane capital city area in the south-east corner of the state. Our project was therefore based in a state which has many of the characteristics of a frontier society with its rural areas characterized by sparse population, vast distances and isolation.

Rural Queensland has been affected severely by the economic crises being experienced in Australia's rural sector generally (Cribb, 1994;

Lawrence, 1995; Sher and Sher, 1994). This has been due to many factors, particularly long-term droughts and low commodity prices. According to Lawrence (1995), 'rurality' can now be equated with social disadvantage in an Australian context. Poor telecommunications infrastructure in rural areas, particularly in the more remote areas of Queensland, compounds these disadvantages. In searching for solutions to the current decline in rural areas, rural women have formed successful networking groups around Australia which have received recognition and support from governments (Grace, 1994).

Queensland rural women are concerned about a complex range of social, economic, cultural, political and environmental issues and they bring a holistic and future-oriented perspective to these issues (Grace *et al.*, forthcoming; Lennie, 1996). Australian rural women are beginning to take important leadership roles in community development and in the uptake of new communication technologies such as e-mail and the Internet (Grace, Lundin and Daws, 1996; Grace and Lennie, 1997; Grace *et al.*, forthcoming).

The role of rural women as change agents is a significant factor in the high level of government and industry interest in the advancement of rural women through projects such as ours.

A feminist action research project

Our action research project was undertaken from January 1996 to December 1997 by an interdisciplinary research team based at Queensland University of Technology in Brisbane.[1] To our knowledge, the project is the only one of its kind conducted in Australia. Key aims of the project were the empowerment of rural women and the participation of diverse women. Enabling the voices of rural women to be heard by those in policy-making positions was seen as vitally important to the empowerment of women and to the ongoing sustainability of rural communities.

Access to adequate telecommunications infrastructure to use new communication technologies effectively, and training and support during their uptake, remain significant barriers for rural women. The pioneering aspect of the project was the use of e-mail by the rural participants. While the infrastructure was often inadequate, many women persisted and, often on their own, with very limited support or formal training, were able to use it effectively. Some of these women were the first in their communities to take up this technology.

The project used a participative feminist action research methodology which required close collaboration with rural women around Queensland and with representatives of eight government and industry partners.[2] This strong partnership and sharing of knowledge and information between rural women, academics, and government and industry representatives was one of the unique features of the project and the on-line discussion groups.

An important outcome of the project was the development of a new community development model. Developing good relationships, providing hands-on experience with e-mail and the Internet which took women's needs and the local context into account, and establishing high-quality on-line communication were important elements of this 'friendship' model of community development (Grace *et al.*, forthcoming).

We were aware of the need to consider the often antagonistic attitude towards feminism expressed by rural women and the urban bias of many feminist theorists (Alston, 1995; Hogan, 1994). Shortall (1994, p. 284) suggests that the identity 'feminist' may suggest too narrow a range of concerns, owing to the 'multi-faceted nature' of a farming woman's life. The approach each of us adopted (but not in a highly premeditated way) was not to emphasize our feminism too much in our communication and interaction with participants, so as to build mutual understanding and trust.

The on-line discussion groups

Three different discussion groups were established during the project:

- 'wechat' (short for 'women's electronic chat'), a small informal list;

- 'wechat-l', a short-lived list set up for a 'virtual conference' in conjunction with the Queensland Rural Women's Network conference held in October 1996; and

- 'welink', a larger discussion list which links women in rural and urban areas, across state and national boundaries.[3]

The welink group is the main topic of this chapter and is the only one of our discussion groups which has continued.

The wechat group

This group was established in August 1996 and continued until the end of May 1997. It was made up of 14 women who lived in various parts of rural and remote Queensland, six research team members (five women and one man), and six women representing our industry partners. Nine of the rural women lived on farms or properties and five lived in rural towns, working in areas such as local government. Industry partner representatives included a public servant working on an innovative Community Information Network project in a regional area, an Information Coordinator with the Office of Women's Affairs and the Womenznet manager of Pegasus Networks.

Wechat was an important and successful forerunner to the much larger welink list. It provided a non-threatening environment for building participants' confidence in using e-mail (often for the first time). Wechat also established the friendly atmosphere and the personal and open communication style which has characterized the welink list. Some of the rural women who took part in wechat were provided with modems, assistance with Internet charges and support with getting on-line.

The initial motivation for the rural women to take part in wechat was to enable on-going contact and networking with the researchers and the project's government and industry partners. They subsequently found that wechat allowed them to share valuable information and provided intellectual stimulation and social support through the daily conversations with a diverse group of women. This social support was particularly important to women living on properties who were suffering emotionally and financially during the ongoing drought.

The welink list

Welink was established in March 1997 and was open to a wider range of women and some men, as well as all the wechat participants. By October 1997 there were 115 welink members of whom just over half were active members.[4] Of the active members, most were living in rural areas. There were five active men on the list at that time.[5]

Members of welink have a wide diversity of occupations. The group includes farmers and graziers, community development officers, teachers, health professionals, public servants, voluntary workers, students and academics. Members live in most states of Australia and several overseas countries. The people who participate are a relatively privileged group. No Aboriginal women have taken part and few are from a low socio-economic group. Nearly all the women were from English-speaking backgrounds. The ages of welink members who supplied data ranged from 20 to 59 years.[6] The majority of these members were in the 40–49 age group while lowest numbers were in the 20–29 age range.

Welink participants were encouraged to use the group for whatever purposes they chose. While no formal communication guidelines were laid down, members were asked to write a short self-introduction when they joined, and many did so. These introductions were very important in establishing the friendly, informal and trusting atmosphere. From the start we were surprised by the number of daily postings, the wide variety of topics, and the personal nature of much of the communication.

The following is a sample of topics discussed or raised during September 1997:

Health	Stress, breast cancer, menopause;
Education	Adult learning, distance education;
Agriculture and business	Marketing on the web, mustering;
Weather	Drought, rain, dust storms;
Social issues	Cultural imperialism, debutante balls;
Rural leadership	Queensland Rural Women's Network, funding community development;
Gender	Titles (Ms or Mrs), stereotyping, feminism;
Leisure and entertainment	Travel, poetry, books, genealogy, television;
Family	Bread making, mothers, husbands, parenting;
Communication	Websites, Internet service providers, phone lines, e-mail good and bad.

Empowering aspects of welink

Our analysis of welink is preliminary as this work is still in progress. Some of this analysis draws on interviews and audioconferences conducted by June Lennie as part of her critical evaluation of the project methodology.[7] We also draw on informal feedback from participants and our own observations.

The concept of empowerment has been problematized in continuing academic debates involving critical theorists, feminists and post-structuralists (Bowes, 1996; Gore, 1992; Sanger, 1994). Much of this debate has been useful in that it has highlighted the contradictions and hidden paternalism in some uses of the concept. Nevertheless, we think that the term is one which can be applied in the context of welink, not least because rural women themselves have used the term to describe their experience.

The majority of women who took part in the evaluation of the on-line discussion groups agreed that the groups had met our aim of empowering women very well. They readily provided definitions of the concept of empowerment. Preliminary analysis of interviews with 16 women who took part in welink[8] suggests that, for these women, empowerment constitutes the following elements:

- Gaining increased confidence, including the confidence to express yourself with freedom, to use computers and e-mail with less fear, and later to assist others with getting on-line, and to talk about this form of communication with local groups. Confidence was seen as the key element from which other changes flow.

- Obtaining confidence often comes through access to information which increases knowledge and awareness, provides new insights and broadens your horizons and ideas. As one rural woman said, 'it breaks you out of the cocoon'. Another woman described empowerment as 'having the information and knowing where to get it, then using it'.

- Having your voice heard, feeling that your views are valued and that you are valued. One rural woman said it was about being 'respected for my opinion and it not being seen as my husband's point of view'. Gaining support and encouragement are related aspects.

- Taking control and having the ability to change your life.

A high level of participation in welink did not seem to be necessary for women to feel empowered or for substantial impacts to occur. For example, the following feedback was given by a woman living in a rural town who had not sent messages to the list regularly. It illustrates the multifaceted nature of empowerment and the powerful effects welink has had on women, including herself:

The most interesting thing for me has been the wechat and the welink, the feeling of confidence and comfort and safety that the women, that we've all had to discuss so many issues, to tell jokes, to complain, to share the good and bad experiences, that acceptance of people's opinions. So I think to me the empowerment that that's given … to ask for explanations, to ask, knowing that no one will judge your lack of knowledge. Information is given freely, without judgement. I think that's been fantastic, the way that's grown, from the start to now, it's been wonderful to watch. I know I've been a lurker, watching … it has been fantastic, the way people have changed from the start of welink and the subjects that have been discussed … and I think that's the empowerment that women have given to each other, I think it's not something that one's gained, it's given freely to each other, that's been the most incredible thing (Audio-conference, November, 1997).

Another testimony about the powerful impacts of welink was given by a woman who is a grazier. This woman took an active part in the project and the on-line discussion groups:

> It's been the most extraordinary experience, you've brought us all together, we've seen our diversity and we've seen our sameness at the same time, and for some reason this is working perfectly. People are accepting and giving and I don't know if you've said it but we're empowering one another, it's not something that you're just taking, people are giving it to you and that's making it extraordinary. It's become a source of information and support and friendship and learning experience all in one and it's, you know I don't want it to ever stop because it's added a whole new dimension to my life that I'm enjoying so much more, especially as I'm going through a period now when I really need something to take me out of it. It's truly amazing … (Audioconference, November, 1997).

Having your voice heard

One of the most empowering aspects of welink is the connection which has been created between rural women and urban women (and a few men) who are in strategic positions, such as academics and senior public servants. This gives the isolated rural women in particular ready access to a range of information and a quality of networking they would not otherwise have had. For example, welink facilitated access to government funding opportunities for several rural communities to enhance their access to the Internet services and training.

In the informal, 'virtual' corridors of power, rural women's voices could be 'heard' in ways which had not occurred before. This enabled urban women to enhance their understandings of rural women's lives in ways which often challenged prevailing stereotypes of farming women as adopting very traditional submissive roles or being strongly 'anti-feminist'. As a result, the urban women were much better able to take on the perspective of 'the Other'. This direct feedback from a cross-section of rural women was seen to 'ground the bureaucrats'.

The following message from a city woman working in an Australian government department illustrates this aspect of welink:

> From my point of view, it has opened my own horizons about the lives and thoughts of today's rural women. I am sometimes called upon to think about rural issues, to analyze them, and to interpret them. I love doing this, try to keep up with the issues and would think that I

understand as well as most who live in suburbia. However, the hard statistics can never be as rich as the voices of welink women. I have experienced these voices as intelligent, caring, hardworking, strong, inclusive and with a horizon that is even bigger than the one that stretches out in front of them....

Networking and sharing cultural experiences

Welink has enabled women to network and communicate with others in rural and urban settings throughout Australia and internationally. Horizons have been widened as members have learnt about other places and cultures. A farm woman in Canada has sent vivid stories about ice storms and her experiences as a part-time teacher in a class of rebellious students. The meaning of Australian expressions such as 'smoko' has been discussed and recipes for damper and other local dishes have been shared. An English woman living in Ireland who is interested in alternative healing has shared her knowledge of homoeopathy and meditation; and an American community development worker has passed on valuable ideas about building community which have been used by women in Australia.

The conversations in welink have been taken further through the regular exchange of personal e-mail messages between women who have made contact through welink. On-line friendships have developed and existing ones have been renewed or strengthened through the list.

Enhanced personal and social development and support

Welink seems to have increased the confidence of many of the women in the ways described above; it has provided mental stimulation and broadened participants' thinking. The quality of life of many women has been enhanced through reduced isolation, support and encouragement from other women, increased enjoyment, and the ability to talk more easily about some personal and sensitive topics such as menopause and the often difficult situation of daughters-in-law on farms. The participation of a few men does not seem to have deterred talk about these personal issues.

Gendered discourses of care and connection are common features of the communication. Such discourses are evident in messages which welcome new members or encourage 'lurkers' to join in, in congratulations extended for women's achievements, and in expressions of sympathy or support on the deaths of loved ones, or during serious illnesses or other traumatic events.

The following welink message from a woman on an isolated grazing property is an example of the way in which the group provided invaluable social support following a dramatic change in her social situation:

> Welink and e-mail are really what helped me to survive during the last six months. My baby is now six months old.... I got my computer, connected to the Internet and joined welink two days after I arrived home from hospital with him. As I have said before, I never felt so isolated until I had a baby. I had worked part-time, socialized, played sport, worked outside with my husband, etc. Then, all of a sudden, I was restricted to home. Barely even leaving the house – only to hang washing and push a pram across the downs trying to console an ever-screaming baby.
>
> The subscribers to welink have witnessed me during these last six months and have often been very supportive and helpful. I think they know when things are not going so great, as my messages are few and far between then. As you may have noticed, things are really improving lately, and I now have a baby that sleeps and rarely ever cries!

Breaking down differences

McCulley and Patterson (1996, p. 5) found that, for feminist students, cyberspace 'provides a place to exchange ideas from many points of view, across boundaries of gender, race and culture'. In addition to the less stereotyped perceptions of rural women by urban women, cultural and other differences between participants often became less relevant aspects of the on-line communication as both rural and urban women shared topics of common interest. These topics include children leaving home, books or movies members have enjoyed, postnatal depression, fear of the dentist and experiences of grief.

Commonality of interests and open sharing of stories and information seem important to the sense of 'family', 'community' and 'sisterhood' which has emerged in welink and is often commented on by welink members. This has been identified by others as important to the formation of virtual communities (Jones, 1995).

Differences in perspectives on feminism were clearly evident in the group at times and this topic was openly discussed both on wechat and welink. These groups provided a valuable means for the rural women in particular to talk about this contentious issue and to formulate new insights into feminism in a supportive, friendly and non-threatening environment.[9] Differences between women who strongly identified as feminist and women who were more ambivalent about the identity were therefore broken down to some extent. One farming woman who had clearly associated the term 'feminist' with negative images disclosed in an interview that, following the welink discussion on this topic, she had a 'revelation ... that I am a feminist'.

Some contradictory or problematic aspects of welink

While many of the women who took part in welink clearly experienced various degrees and kinds of empowerment, discourses of exclusion and disempowerment were also evident in a few welink messages and interviews. Analysis of these discourses is important: it can suggest strategies for change and greater empowerment. Issues raised included the difficulty of talking about certain contentious topics and the restrictions on full participation experienced by some women in government and professional positions.

Although one of the aims of welink was to connect rural and urban women, some urban women and town-based rural women felt unsure if they 'belonged' to the group. This was due largely to the high level of participation in the group by women on farms and grazing properties and their strong sense of 'ownership' of the list. Conversations and information were regularly centred on topics of relevance to the farming women such as the drought, agribusiness, Internet connection problems and rural women's networking activities.

The sense of caring and respect for others' feelings, and a desire to maintain and protect the friendly atmosphere of the group, meant that some limitations and constraints on what could be freely and openly talked about on welink were imposed on participants, in varying degrees, both by themselves and by the group. Highly contentious topics have usually been avoided, and this was especially evident in the first few months of welink's existence. The following welink message from a professional woman living in an Australian rural town illustrates this:

> Rural, urban, different countries – we can all learn and share. What about the racial issue? No one has brought that up yet. What about our disadvantaged youth? Aboriginal women? Does anyone really mind as long as we stick to being kind and supportive of each other and sharing knowledge?

This message was part of a discussion which indicated that some members were interested in talking about more controversial issues.

Shortly afterwards one of the researchers forwarded a message relating to the High Court decision which recognized Aboriginal land rights over pastoral leases. This legislation was dramatically affecting graziers around Australia. The message sparked some (at times very guarded) discussion about this highly divisive native title issue.

In an interview, one grazier explained that while it was easy for urban women who were sympathetic to Aboriginal land rights to express their opinion openly about the issue, it was much less easy for women like herself. Farming women risked being seen as racist when they talked about this issue. This woman said she would have been happier if the topic had never been raised as it created such a high level of emotion and anxiety.

An analysis of the messages on this topic, and the related issue of Aboriginal reconciliation, showed that of the 19 messages on these issues, three came from women on Queensland grazing properties and two came from farming women in a Southern state, while twelve messages came from urban academics and highly educated women living in Queensland rural towns. An additional two messages came from a pro-native title grazier (not on e-mail) which were forwarded by one of the researchers.

Although attitudes to feminism, status of women and gender-based issues have been topics of discussion, neither strongly feminist nor strongly 'anti-feminist' messages are often sent. One feminist rural woman who was interviewed expressed the frustration about this she felt at times:

> I like women's company but I hate it when they go back to their old traditional roles … like it's an enormous frustration, because the chat about the daughters-in-law [on properties] at the moment, it's interesting but shit, I listen and think, this group of women need a huge dose of feminist theory ... I have to zip my lip up a few billion times.... I'm very select about what I'd say.

When pressed on how she felt about raising contentious issues, she responded that it was 'not my place to have my say about things', indicating that, to some extent, she regarded welink as a group which was more for other less passionately feminist women than for her.

Some women working in government and other professional roles identified another limitation. While other women could chat about very personal topics they found this much harder to do since they often felt restricted to feeding relevant information to the group and learning more about current rural issues. Also, their e-mail access was at work so they were less able to spend time in conversation each day compared with many of the rural women. Some of the rural women accessed the list several times during the day, often early in the morning or late in the evening when children had gone to bed.

On-line conversation as a vehicle for women's empowerment

At a time of rapidly increasing use of e-mail and the Internet for global communication, the inclusion of often marginalized voices is an important issue of political and social justice. The type and quality of on-line communication which took place in this project appear to have had significant personal, social and political benefits for many of the women who took part. These benefits were experienced not just by the more isolated rural women but also by the urban women, including ourselves, who took part in the vibrant welink community.

We have seen welink as a unique phenomenon which can clearly be constructed as a 'virtual community,' as described by Jones (1995). The group developed a life of its own and had impacts which went far beyond any we had envisaged. Starting this on-line communication with a much smaller group seems to have been important to the success of welink.

Welink is providing a significant means of giving voice to rural women; it gives much needed social support, helps to break down differences and stereotypes and to broaden perspectives. Both commonalities and differences have been acknowledged and celebrated by the group. One of the most empowering aspects of welink is the connection which has been established between rural women and women (and some men) in strategic positions in cities. Welink has also been invaluable in women's networking and leadership activities[10] and in their community development work. While clearly welink has been highly successful, however, some self- and group-imposed restrictions seem to be necessary to maintain the safe and friendly atmosphere, the personal sharing and the strong sense of trust and connectedness.

NOTES

1   Project team members were Dr Margaret Grace, June Lennie, Jo Previte and Associate Professor Tony Stevenson (The Communication Centre, Faculty of Business, Queensland University of Technology), Lyn Simpson (School of Communication, Faculty of Business, QUT), Dr Leonie Daws (Centre for Policy and Leadership Studies, Faculty of Education, QUT), and Dr Roy Lundin (School of Professional Studies, Faculty of Education, QUT). The project built

on an earlier study by Grace, Lundin and Daws (1996) and other research undertaken by the staff and associates of the Communication Centre.

2 Government and industry partners which collaborated in the project are Telstra Corporation, the Department of Public Works and Housing (Queensland), Pegasus Networks, Queensland Health, Office of Women's Affairs (Queensland), Department of Primary Industries (Queensland), the Office of Rural Communities and the Department of Social Security. For a full description of this project see Grace *et al.* (forthcoming). Other information can be obtained on-line at: http://www.fbs.qut.edu.au/rwp/

3 Two of these discussion lists (wechat-l and welink) were established through Pegasus Networks, one of the project's industry partners.

4 A person must have contributed at least five messages to be considered active.

5 Although welink is a women's list, a few men were allowed to join. The participation of men was a source of discussion in the group at one point. While a few women argued that the group be exclusively female, the majority who sent messages about this issue were happy for men to remain in the group.

6 Data on age was provided by 60 welink members. This data was collected up until 17 October 1997.

7 This evaluation is being conducted by June Lennie as part of a PhD she is undertaking at Queensland University of Technology.

8 The 16 women involved in the research comprised eight who took part in one-to-one interviews and another eight who took part in two audioconferences. They included women living on properties and in rural towns; women who were active and less active members of welink; young and older women; and women experienced in using e-mail and those new to its use. One urban woman's comments were also included in this preliminary analysis of the feedback.

9 For analysis of this discussion see Grace and Lennie (1997).

10 For an analysis of the role of welink in supporting rural women's leadership initiatives see Daws (1997).

ALAI

A Latin American Experience
in Social Networking

Sally Burch

Networking and information sharing for social justice

Anyone who is active in the field of social advocacy is aware that networking and information sharing are increasingly vital for effective action in the present-day world. In recent years, the shifting international scenarios are pushing civil society organizations to build bridges, seek connections and contacts, coordinate actions or establish joint work programmes in response to increasingly globalized problems. Networking, as a horizontal and decentralized form of social articulation that facilitates joint action and exchange while respecting the autonomy of the respective components, has been widely adopted for this kind of action. The women's movement in particular has been built around networks. This form of organization has received a great boost in the last decade with the advent of the Internet. Many organizations around the world are adopting this technology eagerly, precisely because of the facilities it offers for sharing information and communicating in networks.

We should keep in mind, of course, that this is much more than a happy coincidence. The growth of networking is not only, nor primarily, a phenomenon of civic movements, but is a global tendency directly related to the technological and scientific revolution and its impact on society and production.

In productive processes human work has given way to technology, strategically based on information and knowledge, as the dominant factor. This, in turn, has unleashed a new organizational logic, not only in the realm of production but of society as a whole (as it is recognized sociologically, societies are organized according to the models of how they organize for production), in the context of globalization. Consequently, today almost any organizational dynamic refers to decentralization, networks, participation, interaction, transparency, redefinition of hierarchies, etc., where what counts is information flow (León, 1997).

Understanding the role of information is crucial to successful networking. Unlike rigid structures, true networks are essentially flexible. They generate multiple channels of communication in which, as in the functioning of the brain, connections are made as needed and then suspended until a new need arises. In this way, information flows through the channel of least resistance, rapidly making its way to the most dynamic points of the network, on any given issue. Physically, this is very similar to the way the Internet works, and that is precisely one of the reasons why it is so appropriate for any initiative based on networking.

Building an information network

Networking has been at the centre of the work of the *Agencia Latinoamericana de Información* (ALAI – Latin American Information Agency), since it was founded 21 years ago. In pursuance of its mission to promote the democratic participation of social movements in Latin American development, ALAI provides communication support for their coordination dynamics. This involves both disseminating information on these movements and the broader context,[1] and offering counselling and training so they can strengthen their own communicational know-how and skills.

Moreover, ALAI's own development as an organization has focused on building an information network. Founded on a respect for pluralism and diversity, it has become a collective endeavour incorporating the active involvement of a wide variety of social actors. In addition to alternative media organizations and journalists, many grassroots organizations, women's groups, researchers, and others regularly contribute their information, which is processed at the central office in Quito, Ecuador. This has enabled ALAI to be present throughout the continent, without requiring a cumbersome international bureaucracy.

As a result, over the years, ALAI has become well known as an authorized source of information on social movements in Latin America, and is also recognized by many organizations as a tribune for their political expression. In the present decade, ALAI has helped to focus the campaigns and concerns of the women's movement, rural and indigenous organizations, human rights groups and ethnic minorities.

Following a commitment to furthering gender equality, in 1989 ALAI created its Area Mujeres (Women's Programme), as a permanent area of work. The Area produces information and analysis presenting the diversity of positions, proposals and issues of the women's and feminist movements of the continent; it also provides training and counselling in communication, including support for women's electronic networking.

For example, it is supporting the Network of Afro-Latin American and Afro-Caribbean Women in devising their own internal communications programme, including a quarterly news bulletin (shortly to be disseminated on the Internet – see ALAI's website) and training sessions in communication for the network's coordinators. In the future, this may also include support for setting up an internal electronic network, although this is complicated by the fact that many of their member groups do not own computers.

Similarly, the Area Mujeres has advised several regional women's coordinating structures, including rural women, communicators and NGO coalitions, in setting up and facilitating their own electronic mailing lists. In its support for rural and indigenous women, ethnic minority groups, women's human rights groups and other bodies, many of which are also part of mixed organizations, the Area Mujeres works in close collaboration with other ALAI programmes. In this sense, one of its strengths is that it also facilitates linkage between these different movements by, for example, channelling information on the women's movement to rural or indigenous organizations and vice versa. A further realm of activity relates to advocacy on the right to communicate and communication with a gender focus, a topic to which I return below.

Promoting electronic networking

Two decades ago, ALAI's goal of developing a democratic communication network in Latin America faced serious limitations, given the precarious communications infrastructure in the region. Mail would often take up to two months to arrive; telephone or telex was prohibitively expensive. When computerized communication became potentially accessible in the late 1980s, the proposal gained new horizons. Logically, at ALAI we were eager to take advantage of this new resource to communicate with our counterparts around the region. Moreover, we recognized that it would provide an incomparable tool for building the very networks and coordinations we were supporting. So we took on the task of promoting access to and use of ICTs among social movements in Latin America.

A first major problem to tackle was that Ecuador, at that time, was one of the few countries in Latin America with no kind of e-mail access. ALAI therefore led the search for solutions, and by 1991 had proposed the creation of an association of NGOs and academic institutions that subsequently set up the first electronic mail network in Ecuador (Ecuanex, a member of the APC).[2]

The news conference on Latin America, – alai.amlatina – initiated that year, was one of the early on-line Spanish-language information services to circulate in the region. Subsequently, ALAI instigated the creation of several regional exchange forums on the APC networks, such as the on-line conferences dh.amlatina (human rights) and amlat.mujeres (women), to which it continues to be a regular contributor.

Electronic networking is now a central element of ALAI's communication training programme for social movements, which emphasizes the development of strategies for using ICTs. The *Area Mujeres* also participates in the APC Women's Networking Support Programme and has been actively involved in promoting its activities in the region. ALAI has thus been closely identified with the spread of electronic networking for social coordination and advocacy in Latin America, and more specifically women's networking. The following pages include some observations that arise from this experience, as well as reflections on the challenges.

The growth of electronic networking in Latin America

Well before the Internet boom took off in Latin America in the mid-1990s, a number of organizations – mainly academic or NGOs – were using electronic networks as a basic means of intercommunication. In numbers, of course, connectivity levels have consistently been lower than in the North, but while for Northern institutions the Internet was often seen as an extra (complementary to telephone, fax, mail and other forms of communication), for many Latin American organizations it was seized on as the only means of having ready access to international communication.

Indeed in several countries e-mail was being used regularly by NGOs even before most commercial companies had access. And it is not unusual to find Northern development cooperation organizations that are only just getting connected to the Internet, in response to the demand from their Southern partners to be able to communicate with them via e-mail.

Secondly, until very recently, the cost of using the Internet was high enough to make it inaccessible to most individuals, so that use was mainly of an institutional nature. This has influenced the forms of use and the kind of common spaces and discussion groups that emerged in the region, generally characterized by information exchange and news on political and social issues, rather than chat or personal comment. For example, among the earliest uses of electronic conferences and mailing lists in the region were the prolific endeavours of Central American organizations, in the late 1980s and early 1990s, to reach out to peace and solidarity groups in the US. More recently, the Chiapas solidarity movement is generating a constant flow of information.

Obviously, the region faces serious obstacles to being able to make full use of the potential offered by the Internet. The first relates to access issues such as cost and basic infrastructure (electricity, telephones), illiteracy, insufficient computer training in schools and other factors. A second is the predominance of English on the Internet (90 per cent of the available information), which most of the population does not understand.

Other obstacles include the relatively recent emergence of a written culture in certain countries and communities in the region, and the fact that information sharing has not been a widely implanted institutional practice. This, in turn, has affected local and regional content development on the World Wide Web (WWW), which on the whole has been fairly slow to take off. And while the information base in Spanish and Portuguese – the region's two main languages – is on the increase, there is still very little available in indigenous and other minority languages.

Women's networking

As in other parts of the world, women and women's organizations in Latin America were initially slower, and sometimes more reluctant than their male counterparts or mixed organizations, to take the plunge in using the Internet. But once they did so, they have not looked back.

Women's electronic networking in Latin America took off in the months prior to and following the Fourth UN World Conference on Women in 1995, largely thanks to the initiative led by the APC's WNSP. During the months before the Conference in Beijing, the APC programme organizers raised awareness about the potential of the technology for women's networking and advocacy, offered training and orientation, facilitated the flow of information concerning the Conference and NGO Forum, and supported organizations in setting up online/off-line information networks so the information could reach non-connected groups.

Similar initiatives were being undertaken around the world, but Latin

America offered particular advantages in that, compared with many other parts of the South, it was becoming fairly easy to get Internet (or at least e-mail) access in the region; it also has relative unity of language (predominance of Spanish and Portuguese) and a particularly active women's movement.

ALAI's *Area Mujeres* actively participated in this process. It regularly disseminated information on-line about the issues relating to the World Conference, and in April 1994 co-convened a Regional Meeting on Gender and Communication,[3] at which 20 media groups agreed, among other things, on a plan for concerted information coverage leading up to the Conference. This led to setting up an information pool during the regional preparatory meeting, held later that year in Argentina, through which several media groups and journalists coordinated their coverage and agreed to put the information they were producing for their own media into a joint on-line space so that it could circulate quickly to women who were unable to attend the event.

This became a pilot experience for the following year's Beijing information pool. During the ensuing months, in a number of countries, women organized networks so that information would not only be able to flow directly from the NGO delegations in Beijing to their home organizations, but could also reach a much wider audience. In Mexico, for example, the local organizations channelled the information received on the Internet through fax trees or printed paper, disseminating it to women around the country. In Nicaragua, it was used as a basis to produce daily radio programmes. ALAI itself produced a daily information service from Beijing that circulated around the region, and in Ecuador was sent out to national and provincial media. This initiative, involving not only Latin America but many other countries and regions, was one of the most significant successes of the APC Women's Programme, constituting one of the first major worldwide cyberspace events.

Challenges for women

The present race between transnational communications companies to corner the future market of digital goods and services via mergers between different branches of the industry threatens to make the Internet a more passive medium where, in the extreme case, interactivity could be reduced to personalized selection of products, programmes and services, leaving little space for information sharing, networking or access to knowledge. One of the dangers this change implies is that access to the Net will be determined largely by profitability factors, leaving a large proportion of the world population outside.

Advertisers exploring possibilities for marketing through the Internet have identified women as their prime target (70 per cent of all publicity is already directed at them), so they are seeking innovative ways of attracting women to use the Internet. As a result, women may rapidly overcome the gender gap in access (at present they are an estimated 30 per cent of users), but mainly through their role as consumers. Presumably these efforts will be directed only at those with buying power.

Increasingly, the challenge for women is not only, nor mainly, a problem of access – although this is still the case for a large sector of women – but of how to harness this technology for their own goals and how to stake out the spaces that will enable them to make an impact on this new medium. Women already have an uphill struggle to overcome the discrimination that affects them in media in general, as well as disadvantages in terms of access to technology and training. The only way they can hope to make an impact in this new space is through collective initiatives.

One of the significant aspects that differentiates electronic networks from other communications systems is that they lend themselves to forming *communicational spaces*. Unlike physical space, cyberspace is not limited by geographical or political borders, nor by distance or time constraints. Like physical space, virtual space can be occupied. Given the huge volume of information flow on the Internet, isolated initiatives are almost certainly doomed to failure. And this is particularly true of the WWW, as a wide-open space that has to compete for audiences.

ALAI's own response to these challenges is to build Internet spaces in collaboration with organizations that share its goals, in a framework of respect for diversity and with priority given to spaces of expression and networking of social movements. Its website, for example, as yet at a pilot stage of development, has compiled documents from different events and organizations on the issues of gender and communication;[4] and, for the last two years, has offered a joint space for disseminating information on the Latin American initiatives of the 16 Days Campaign Against Violence Against Women (held each year from 25 November to 10 December).

Policy proposals and advocacy

One of the basic premises on which our work at ALAI is founded is that democracy and social justice require democratic communication structures, mechanisms and practices. We are convinced, moreover, that real progress in democratizing communication will only be possible once the issues are placed squarely on the agenda of social movements.[5]

For this reason, in addition to being a practitioner in the field, ALAI actively engages in advocacy around the right to communicate and the democratization of communication with a gender perspective. This involves, on one hand, drawing up policy proposals and lobbying international institutions, and, on the other hand, raising awareness and mobilizing on these issues. Networking is obviously an important element of these endeavours, and ALAI is an active member of several networks working towards these goals. In the case of the *Area Mujeres*, these include the APC Women's Programme, the Women on the Net (WoN) project and the WomMed/FemMed Network. ALAI has also set up a Latin American discussion mailing list on gender and communication, <com-genero-l> that is open to all interested.

One example of this work was evident during the run-up to the Fourth World Conference. ALAI presented a proposal to the UN focusing on issues such as: empowerment of women through access to new communications technologies; media content that projects a positive and non-discriminatory image of women; gender equality in media employment; and greater presence of women in decision-making positions.[6] In a joint effort with UNESCO and other NGOs and governmental delegations, the *Area Mujeres* was able to contribute to the inclusion of these issues as a new priority area in the Beijing *Platform for Action*.

Putting proposals on an international platform is only a beginning. Until there exists a broad movement pushing for their rights as citizens and as women in areas such as access to information, to the means of expression and to technology, the field of communication will no doubt continue to be dominated by private corporate interests rather than fundamental social and democratic goals.[7]

NOTES

1 ALAI produces a fortnightly publication on the social and political context in Latin America, entitled *Servicio Informativo ALAI*; an electronic news conference alai.amlatina; a series of mono-thematic publications, *Serie Debates*; and other occasional publications. It also publishes a Web page: http://www.ecuanex.apc.org/alai/

2 The APC is a worldwide network dedicated to serving the Internet needs of NGOs. See Edie Farwell *et al.* (1998), Chapter 7 in this volume.

3 *Encuentro Regional de Comunicación de Género*, Quito, April 1994. The documents are available on ALAI's web-site:
   http://www.ecuanex.apc.org/alai/comgenen.html

4 By agreement with UNESCO, this site contains the documents of the 1995 Toronto Symposium on Women and the Media and the website of the Wom-Med/FemMed Network created at that event, among others.

5 In Beijing, ALAI, APC and others convened an NGO communications caucus during the official Conference, and drew up an 'NGO Communications Strategy Proposal' for follow-up, which emphasized production of media materials and programmes on issues relating to women's daily lives and on the content of the Beijing Platform for Action; monitoring the portrayal and employment of women in the media; networking through diverse communications circuits and systems; and developing media literacy programmes and gender-sensitive training. The full document is available on ALAI's website.

6 See the document 'Global Communications and Access to New Technologies: A Democratic Right for Women', ALAI, September 1994 (available on ALAI's website).

7 This concern has been the basis for convening an International Forum on Communication and Citizenship (to be held in El Salvador, in September 1998), which ALAI is organizing jointly with a number of other Latin American and international organizations. The Forum aims to launch a debate, with the participation of social movements, on the implications for democracy of the present tendencies in communication. New technologies and gender will be among the central themes of this event. For further information see the Forum website at: http://www.ecuanex.org/foro_comunicacion

INFORMATION AND COMMUNICATION TECHNOLOGIES AND IDENTITY POLITICS IN IRAN

Farideh Farhi

Information and communication technology in post-revolutionary Iran

Is it possible to use new information technologies to build communication and knowledge networks which respect cultural diversity? Is there something fundamentally different in the nature of these technologies that makes them different from other media that have also been 'alien' to the cultures in which they have been introduced? To pose these questions within the context of Iran's post-revolutionary cultural politics may be a bit premature since, given the kind of isolation global powers have attempted to impose on this country, the nature and impact of information technology – a force that is refashioning the world and apparently the way people 'connect' to each other these days – have yet to become a source of reflection. In other words, unlike China, Iran is yet to be declared 'wired', even if the technology is there and a limited number of people have access to it. But perhaps it is because Iran has been so isolated and in many ways completely misrepresented in a context where, as Gore Vidal suggested years ago, the real capital of world power is more and more Hollywood than Washington, that speculation about the way these powerful technologies are and will be shaping its cultural terrain is made interesting.

It is well known that one of the themes, if not the only theme, of the Iranian revolution, as well as of the conflicts generally present in the Islamic world over the past century, has been the struggle over the terms of global integration; that is, over the means and forms of local autonomy and of local connectedness. For a variety of reasons that still have not been laid bare, and probably had as much to do with the internal dynamics of Iranian society as with the shock experienced by at least a part of the international community in witnessing the unfolding of the revolution and its aftermath, the terms of local autonomy and local connectedness in Iran were set in an austere and severe manner. Initially they could survive only as a negation of a cultural – read national – loss and not as affirmation of a process through which people generate narratives of individual and social meaning and purpose. Of course, let us not forget that all this occurred in the midst of a physical war – the Iran–Iraq war, a rather solemn and grim war, but also one transposed to the realm of unreal war or 'unwar' in the globalized cultural space, as the world literally looked the other way. Even when all the powers knew that with the aid of their technology, including chemical weapons, the Iranian landscape and 'human waves' were being devastated. Solemnity, therefore, was not uncalled for, at least at the time.

Iran in the era of globalization

During this era of solemnity and severity, the terms of reference for the so-called 'West' were defined, codified, and officially stamped in very clear terms, mostly drawn from notions prevalent during the age of high imperialism of the late nineteenth century. The era of globalization is the era of far less coherent and culturally directed processes, less intended to spread a social system from one centre of power across the globe but nevertheless involved in creating interconnection, interdependency, and homogeneity of all global areas. In such an era, the contours of Iran's global engagement were set, some would say in stone, in terms of conflict, confrontation, war, invasion and the required discipline, martyrdom and presumed selflessness that the society had to reproduce in order to defend and concurrently recreate itself.

Iran having defined itself in these terms, the end of war simply afforded a rather easy shift from the focus on physical invasion and physical survival to the 'real' and more 'authentic' battle against cultural invasion. The Iranian revolution, it was said, was not about bread and butter issues or even mere political reform, but about the souls of men and women who were being led adrift in this soulless and immoral world. Within this context, while information and communication technologies themselves were not biased, their content was considered invasive. Of course, this conceptualization could only make sense or be strictly coherent if a unified national cultural identity of the supposedly 'invaded' culture was assumed. Culture was defined as the repository of national – read Islamic – habits, customs and ultimately souls, while the Iranian people, unified and determined, were represented as upholders of structures that generally were deemed fixed, but nevertheless in desperate need of stern guardianship. There was thus a tendency to elide cultural and national identity as 'the nation', in this case an Islamic nation, appeared to be a more concrete, 'identifiable' entity than 'culture'. The visual media, particularly, have been deemed in need of control. Apparently, images represent the most threatening of all that can come from the West. The strict control of television (as opposed to the printed media, which have been given much more leeway), literal prohibition of movies coming from the West, and visual censorship of the Internet (as opposed to relayed words both through websites and e-mail, which are somewhat irregularly checked for profanity) are all manifestation of the fear of images that are deemed anti-Islamic, especially in their representation of women.

I know that all this sounds like an often-told story of austere ideologies engaged in the writing of their national identities. The only twist in the case of Iran's ideologized Islam is that while it draws its energy from the highest ideals of modernity – that is, social justice, development, and stability – its sustenance, life and blood comes from reinvented tradition. Yet the smallest invention involves a contest. The contest among official voices is of course always loud but unexpectedly diverse and shifting. The interesting thing about these official voices, though, is that they are mostly reactive. In other words, they generally try to reinvent tradition through setting limits, of course not always successfully. For instance, they deliberate on the kind of musical instruments that are permitted to be used in the reinvented tradition of martyrdom festivals (*Ashura*). They are understandably weary of out of control 'tradition'. Operating as a 'rogue' state within a rather hostile global environment, and obsessed with the maintenance of hard-fought state power, often these official voices have been necessarily didactic and stern. A reinvented tradition must immediately be understood as well-preserved and inviolable.

Reinventing traditions

But two points need to be made here. The first is that these reinvented traditions, unlike tradition itself, no longer belong to the arena of the inevitable. They are now decided upon as an act of choice and also have a rationale attached to them. What Peter Berger aptly has called 'the modernizing shift from givenness to choice' has already taken place (Berger, 1974, p. 198). Second, as is well known, successful (that is, lasting) reinventions of tradition are generally the business of popular voices. Official voices feed reinvented traditions but ultimately live in uneasy tension with them. Being only too eager to get involved in these reinventions, the popular forces constantly appropriate, mutilate, and reassemble the narratives produced by the official voices. The narrative on veiling, female domesticity and segregation, for instance, gradually turns into a licence for women to enter and navigate the public space as the veil itself becomes reconstituted as a physical boundary that makes the spatial separation of men and women in the public arena redundant. It also gradually becomes a mechanism through which a democratic voice opposing patriarchal interventions against popular participation is raised. The official voices debate, argue, offer different versions of how Quranic traditions can be reinterpreted, sometimes grudgingly acknowledging the innovations of popular voices and other times simply ignoring them, at least for the time being. But this fluidity and open-endedness of the cultural terrain within which traditions are being re-invented is a point generally missed by outsiders dazed by the hardness of Iranian revolutionary leaders.

Redefining the Iranian political and cultural space

I am probably spending too much time explaining the cultural terrain within which I operate, telling you very little about the possibility of technologies that can build communication and knowledge networks which respect cultural diversity. But my point is precisely that it is because the Western world, in spite of the era of globalization, has refused to acknowledge the fluidity and open-endedness of the Iranian cultural space, and has instead chosen the patronizing tool of sanctions, reprimand, or 'critical dialogue', at least until very recently, that the building of communication and knowledge networks has been so difficult. Of course, as I suggested before, at least part of the difficulty stems from the fact that the contours of Iran's global engagement were set in terms of confrontation and war against cultural invasion and the desire for cultural autonomy. But can this be an excuse for lack of knowledge and communication networks that can see through the official narrative and acknowledge the fluidity of Iran's political and cultural space? As Clifford Geertz rightly pointed out a long time ago, 'culture is not a power, something to which social events can be casually attributed; it is a context, something within which they [social events] can be intelligibly ... described' (Geertz, 1973, p. 14). In other words, the influential or determining character of a culture is not a function of any deliberate aim or intention by which we could describe it as 'acting'. In modern societies at least, whether in the West or the East, people oscillate among cultural communities, and cultural commodities are imported and consumed, constantly shifting the balance of what people do as collectivities. Cultures are therefore protean entities; their boundaries are shifting and permeable. They do not have the characteristics of permanence, integrity or selfhood that are ascribed to agents. Hence the attempt to portray them as such, especially in a very hostile global arena, has serious consequences.

Having become identified as a 'pariah', 'rogue', or 'backlash' state (and at times nation), Iranian citizens are also treated as if they were either agents or bearers of Islamic zeal, and therefore opponents of modernity itself, or a part of an oppositional cultural agency which secretly breeds on global networking and support. The possibility of alive and kicking individual and civic groups doing politics within a contested and Islamic context is denied. You are either a zealot or a silenced or exiled 'liberal' voice.

Needless to say, this kind of explicit or implicit dichotomization has not been very useful in the establishment of communication and knowledge networks which respect cultural diversity. To be sure, networks are being built – but very few, if any, unsettle the rigid divisions outlined above. The so-called Islamists are busily engaged in networking based on the idea that 'we will benefit from their useful technologies but dispense with their harmful values', while networks with the so-called liberals are built based on the desire to give support to the forces of 'moderation', whatever that means. Meanwhile, the Islamic state's yearning to be accepted as a 'responsible' member of the international community has meant that it has very little knowledge of the non-official and progressive voices within the Western or Eastern worlds.

The result has been a very odd combination of national policies that thrive on the denunciation of cultural – read Western liberal – invasion but wholeheartedly rely on the latest fads in the development discourse, be it liberalization, privatization, environmentalism, regionalism or even globalization. To put it more simply, the hostile global environment in which the citizens of Iran navigate has not only prevented or made rather difficult the spread of new technologies into that country, but has also assured the representation of cultures in either direction – be it representations of Iran in the West or the West in Iran – as unitary and rigid agents when borders are crossed. And here it has been that old technology of the modern era, that is, television, that has maintained its hold over our imaginations, making dialogue difficult, if not impossible.

Engaging in the communication medium

It was perhaps his understanding of the power that television holds over the global imagination that made Iran's new President go directly to that medium, not to change mind-sets over night but to create a hole in the wall of misrepresentations. Speaking to an international audience, made possible by the first truly globalized network and its 'star' reporter of Iranian lineage, Mohammad Khatami had nothing more or less in mind than exploding a stereotype from within. Here there was a man of the cloth, impeccably dressed, crossing lines and borders, back and forth, and unsettling them. This was not a mere representation of Iran's 'true' contemporary leadership to the outside world. The world must know that Khatami's 'television diplomacy' was intensely watched inside Iran in the same way the whole population was glued to television for two days to watch a parliamentary hearing over the confirmation of the new President's cabinet. In fact, in the span of a few months Iranian society seemed upside down, with discussions of previously taboo issues abounding. Not only have caution and circumspection been put aside, there is even a sense that things are different 'this time around'. A cursory look at Iranian society's struggle for constitutionalism and against arbitrary rule suggests that all sorts of tactics, from outright force to foreign intervention, have been used to push back gains made by democratic forces. Each time an opening was made, and there have been many, aspirations were duly subdued. But this time, in this connected world and with so many aspiring people, it is not easy to turn the clock back; only patience is required.

This time around there are televisions in more than 80 per cent of the country, almost all villages above 20 people have electricity and at least one telephone line, and there are over eight million students (in a population of close to 70 million). Besides, there are close to 2.5 million Iranians now residing outside the country with ties to an estimated five million inside the country. The youth, with all the restrictions imposed on them inside and outside the home, are asking questions unheard before and even the older generation is refusing to bite its tongue.

When, after the President's interview with CNN, the discussion of Iran–US relations (a previously taboo topic) assumed national dimensions, there was of course no dearth of frantic voices. Islamic alarmists, like a broken record, warned again of cultural invasion, spy dens and appeasement. Others from the other side of the spectrum, demanding moderation overnight and on the spot, decried the 'power struggle' in Iran and the loss of the 'one and only' opportunity to engage with the

US in more meaningful ways. Fortunately, however, between these two extremes there are not merely a few that can be easily brushed aside, but millions whose mere existence has given the government – which has to be responsive to them – the nerve to go 'global' and demand its proper place within the international community.

Going global in cyberspace

Can cyberspace help in this process of going global? Perhaps, but this is unlikely in the near future. The first and foremost problem, as in the case with other countries, is the problem of language. Of course, all users of the available networks know enough English to read the massive amount of information available these days. But the key word here is 'use'. Becoming consumers of the information available does not mean communication. Also prohibitive is the context within which communication occurs. Even if the language barrier is overcome through language skills, the conversation with the outside world essentially involves some sort of explanatory dynamic in which the outsider asks questions and the Iranian protagonist responds by giving different versions of 'We are not as bad as you think!'

A good example of how this process works can be seen in a project coordinated from Columbia University and named Gulf 2000. Focused on the Middle East in general, and the Persian Gulf countries in particular, all events in the Gulf are monitored daily; analysis is offered, and members exchange ideas and information. Members come from the whole area but also include Middle East specialists from all over the world. Indeed, a cursory look at the daily exchanges reveals that comments and analysis by area specialists, Middle Easterners or otherwise, who live in the US and perhaps Europe, definitely outweigh the words and thoughts of those who live in the area. The analyst outsider keeps analyzing various forces that exist in the Persian Gulf countries, keeping score, with as much energy as an avid soccer fan, of daily tussles that can be monitored easily through the multitude of local newspapers that are now on the Internet or daily reportage from on-the-spot and native analysts. When occasionally a local voice is raised about important issues at hand (the possible bombing into oblivion of Iraq by the US, for example, and the reason why most of the people who hate Saddam are not keen on the move, or suggestions for alternative security arrangements), the arguments are carefully read (I assume), but one does not sense an engagement, only polite acknowledgement that the ideas are great but current circumstances and limits do not allow their serious consideration.

Engagement with non-official and peripheral voices, of course, is even more difficult. And here the story is an often-told one, applicable to literally all non-Western countries. Hardware is too expensive, software is in English, and the hierarchical structure of the societies involved makes non-official access very difficult, unless means are found to use the system, so to speak, to go around the system. And this is always a very insecure path as the wires can be unplugged so easily.

New questions, new readings

The problem of communication among diverse peripheral voices is further complicated by the shifting discursive divides created by globalization. For instance, as the events in the Beijing women's conference showed, no longer were North and South the antagonists in the struggle over the heart and soul of feminism; rather, the so-called traditional perspectives from all over the world were siding with each other in opposition to organizations that had non-traditional perspectives, and this was new. The question posed for many organizations now is how women's rights can be pursued in societies that have religious governments or powerful and effective religious institutions. In other words, this is no longer a question that can be ignored in the hope that the forces of modernization will make religion irrelevant to these societies. All over the world, many women and men are actively engaged in new readings of religious texts in the light of new social realities in which women are living. Clearly, an important point of entry into conversation among women in various societies (East or West) facing reactionary interpretations of how women should behave in the public space is the exchange of information about the means and arguments being used to reinterpret religious texts and traditions.

Such a conversation, however, via Internet or otherwise, requires the shedding of misconceptions first. It also requires an understanding that the struggle to reinterpret religious texts and traditions is based not only on the firm belief about the unbreakable link between faith and freedom, but also on the conviction that conversation among diverse cultures is only made possible when there is confidence that the points put forth in the conversation represent earnest efforts, in all their cultural variations, to reflect upon common problems of humankind. To put it more bluntly, the point of conversation is not to report on miseries so that some others – who are considered less miserable – can feel better about being in a more favourable position; but rather to initiate a process or begin a journey that acknowledges the interconnectedness of it all.

17

UNVEILING THE ARAB WOMAN'S VOICE THROUGH THE NET

Lamis Alshejni

Freeing the voice of Arab women

The voice of Arab women has been silenced historically and was considered shameful in public; a reality still in some communities. Today many Arab women speak out regardless of social, political or religious constraints; nevertheless, the Arab women's voice tends to remain silent on the Net, owing not so much to extraneous influence as to Arab women themselves too often failing to see the Net as a space where they can express their opinions.

Arab women – as an organized movement – have recently started the struggle for their rights. The status of women varies from country to country: Saudi women cannot drive a car; Kuwaiti women cannot vote; most Arab women are unable to be divorced without the husband's consent even if they pursue legal procedures; and all Arab women are only entitled to half the inheritance of a man. The focus of the Arab women's movement today is to challenge discriminatory laws through legal, theological, health and Human Rights mechanisms.

The question we ask in this chapter is how can the Internet be an empowering tool for Arab women's fight against discrimination? Arab women do not view the latest high-tech communication tool as an urgent priority. Given that the Arab world has a high degree of gender inequality – the illiteracy rate for women is 62 per cent while for men it is 34 per cent, and only 10 per cent of women participate in the work force, there is room to wonder if there actually can be an Internet market for Arab women (Regional Meeting of Arab NGOs, 1995). We could well conclude that the Internet not only does not represent an avenue for Arab women's advocacy but also is not even a tangible possibility to explore. We could end this chapter here, in fact, allowing the Arab region to retain its isolation and hoisting question marks over the reality and effectiveness of the communication revolution ever reaching developing countries.

But let us go back and ask the question again: can the Internet be a tool for Arab women's advocacy? Should we encourage Arab women to use the Internet and how could that help the goal of gender equality?

Arab women's status

The main reason for the subjugation of Arab women is the religious influence on the formulation of legislation in regard to women's status: the Family Status Law (FSL).[1] In order to change this status, women must change the laws, but they can only do that by moderating the religious thought from which the laws are derived. In the absence of freedom of expression and with the widespread influence of religious discourse, it is hard for women to call for moderation in the development of Islamic thought. Not all factions of the Arab women's movement question the religious teaching approach; they prefer to base their arguments on human rights discourse. Nevertheless, it is hard for women to avoid religious discourse totally. Religion is at the base of Arab culture and values: debating women's issues one must confront the religious sphere, from whichever angle.

Another factor that creates a barrier to changes in women's conditions is that women tend to be treated as symbolic of the Arab individual and communal identity. Arab society, led by the elites, has been modernizing gradually over the last two decades towards a Western model of consumption. Such modernization has shown a tendency to remain at the level of the elite, the average Arab citizen being left untouched by such trends. Women from the elite classes adopted Western characteristics (whether economic or social). And it was the 'Westernized' women, rather than the men, who have been criticized. It is the women who symbolize the Arab traditions of their country. Women's move towards the West, specifically towards emancipation, has created cultural and social tensions, reflected in the call for a return to Islamic values, that have permeated all segments of Arab societies. Women constitute the dividing line between the Arab world and the Western one. Arab countries use Arab women's issues as a diplomatic tool. If they want to present themselves as opening up to the modern world and democratic values, then they push for the development of women, but when they want to shun Western interference they point to the differences between the two cultures, evoking the image of the veiled woman. This makes women's leadership role in achieving civil society's goals of social change, development, and democracy even more pertinent. They are the symbolic and actual agents for change.

The Internet and cultural boundaries

If Arab women are to consider the Internet as a tool for their empowerment, they first have to consider the questions their culture raises in the face of the expansion of this medium of global information. The Internet was born in the West and, although a strong argument is made for it as a multicultural tool, it is a creation of Western modernization: the main language used on the World Wide Web is English; freedom of expression is embraced (including pornography); users are part of a global consumer culture, must be PC literate, and live in countries with facilities to access the Internet easily (telephone lines, electricity, etc.).

In the Arab case, however, it is cultural rather than technical and financial issues which are the obstacles. This was evident during the 1990s when media played a major role in promoting Western values, which irritated many Arab protectionists. A regional meeting of Arab NGOs, held in Beirut in July 1994, tabled a request for international media to respect the values of other countries:

> The Arab Regional Meeting recommends that the Social Development Summit calls for respecting the cultural peculiarities of peoples and countries and to free the popular mass media enjoying universal coverage from their subordination to the logic of profit and from the cultural propaganda of patterns that are imposed on people from the outside. These mass media with their power of influencing awareness and life styles, turn into a factor that generates tension and cultural counter-mobilization of the values opposed to them, and therefore fuel violent cultural inadequacy and disregard for the national values of the people and countries (Regional Meeting of Arab NGOs, 1995).

Cultural and religious particularities are the main sources of tension in Arab relations with the West. World media have an immense power to redefine values and impose life styles. The 'receiving' society is often overwhelmed with information; there is seldom enough time to digest all that it receives, leading sometimes to outright rejection.

Protectionism was the response of the Arab world to mass media. Nevertheless, the characteristics of the Internet – free, multicultural, multilingual, where different religions and different minds are all in infinite play – should not be perceived as anti-Arab or purely Western.

The Internet is multicultural, and therefore can represent the different realities in our world, including the Arab world. Meanwhile, studies show that the use of the Internet in Arab countries is growing. The growth rate of users in 1997 has risen by 225 per cent (Alkamli, 1998), one of the highest growth rates of the Internet in the world. The difficulties of language and computer literacy, as well as finance, were overcome. Privatization, the increased importance of education and price decreases paved the way for this growth.

In terms of culture, the Arab region entered the Internet world market with a protectionist attitude, fearing that free access was in conflict with their morals and values. Saudi Arabia, the biggest opponent, allowed only a few connections to universities and public institutions. With even the Saudi market predicted to expand in 1998, we find that in the end, contrary to the reality lived on the other side of the screen, freedom in cyberspace is granted. This suggests that the Internet could be a very positive space for Arab women obliged to silence in public debates. Internet could be a tool for women to break away from the protectionism that has dogged their movement since its inception.

Arab women's voice on the Net

Although the level of repression differs from one country to another, all Arab women experience the lack of a democratic environment. In all Arab constitutions the meaning and extent of 'freedom of expression' is left vague (Azzam, 1996). Thus authorities can intervene and redefine the parameters of the code when needed. It is clear that women need to use the Internet in order to confront the growing influence of protectionism and to open up for discussion Islamic reading of the law. If Islamic thought as it has evolved in past centuries cannot be discussed, it will be hard if not impossible for the Arab world to change towards a more democratic and pluralist society.

The question still remains: how? The illiteracy rate of women is over 60 per cent, so how can we expect them both to be computer literate and to master the English language along with high-tech communication? We should first recognize that there is a dynamic shift in rates of literacy for young men and women. Some schools and universities have begun to adopt the Internet as part of their educational system: Ibn Taymia high school in Qatar;[2] and an educational centre based on the Net.[3] And Arabic is now on the Net from websites to server providers.

Arab NGOs have begun to recognize the usefulness of the Internet.

Women's NGOs established to promote women's awareness and advocacy for gender, political, social and economic equity are more and more using the Internet, although there have been no studies to quantify users. They have realized the importance of this tool for communication, even if it is still largely e-mail and not the WWW (Friedrich-Ebert-Stiftung Workshop, 1997).

Potentially, women working in NGOs can use the Internet to express themselves and their views on these topics, which would be impossible – even dangerous – in the public sphere. The religious debate, as well as other issues relevant to women's rights and democracy and subject to government suppression, can be carried on the Net and Arab women can network in order to develop their ideas and activities further.

Moving from the virtual to the real world

This is an important beginning. It will be harder, though, to move from the virtual world to reality. It would not make sense to announce a plan of action that cannot be carried through. Advocacy is also needed on the international level to break the wall of silence and the isolation that the Arab region has built around its social and cultural concerns.

The process of expanding women's use of the Net can start with the urban-based NGOs, where women are educated and can easily learn to use the Internet, and where connections to the Internet can be provided. The move to involve rural women will take more time, education and training. Even if such a process takes a decade, what is essential is that the potential of the Internet is recognized rather than ignored or postponed to a later stage. The Internet is growing fast and it is crucial that Arab women contribute to the culture being created now in cyberspace. They need to be subjects not objects of a shared cyber-culture that can eventually help to transform their reality.

NOTES

1 Changing the Family Status Law (FSL) is one of the key battles of the Arab women's movement, especially in the Arab Maghreb. Tunisia is the most fortunate in this sense, as the amendments made to the Tunisian FSL have prohibited polygamy, for example, and brought a greater sense of equity between men and women; there is still a state of inequality, however, particularly in the economic sphere.
2 http://www.ibn-taymia.edu
3 http://www.arabuniversity.com

CONCLUSION: LOCAL/GLOBAL ENCOUNTERS
WoN Weaving Together the Virtual and Actual

Wendy Harcourt

A cyborg conversation?[1]

How are we to define this collection of thoughts, stories and visions for *Women@Internet*? The differences in experiences, the multiple visions of how to navigate the cyberworld, the languages used, the hopes expressed – do they add up to a new set of communications by cyborg women and men connecting confidently to the new technoscientific world? How are we to interpret these voices? As cyberactivists? Elites? Feminists? Political intellectuals? Ventriloquists? How are we to understand their coming together as a network across such different geo-political and cultural terrains? Are they the cyborgs of Haraway's 'Cyborg Manifesto' (Haraway, 1991)?

We have a 'delicatessen' offered for the tasting by the Women on the Net (WoN). They present the spice of what these new communication technologies offer and the tempting new ways to experience one another, suggesting a new closeness as women (with men) explore and create a cyberculture. Lurking in these new sensations and experiences are the voices warning us to consider carefully that such a mixture of cultures, hopes and visions might well fragment on the tasting. They are housed in a not so congenial structure, and it is uncertain from just where the ingredients come.

Despite the warnings peppered throughout the book, we are presented with some convincing evidence that the Internet is a tool for creating a communicative space that when embedded in a political reality can be an empowering mechanism for women. We learn that women are building on their strengths – particularly networking and lobbying for women's rights – through the Internet, and that they are moving beyond that to intervene and affect powerful policy agendas on telecommunications and social and economic policies. We see that they are creating and managing new knowledge systems, deeply conscious of the different realities of women from marginalized communities and careful not to take up cyberspeak, analytic jargon and assumptions that a wonderful new world will open at the touch of a button. They are un-afraid to listen to their own doubts. They voice their need to overcome a resistance to technology while they insist that screen to screen contacts can never replace face to face. And they point out that the maleness and the elitism of the tools – the exclusivity, the language barriers, the costli-ness, the Western biases and the divides – run too deep just to be over-come by more information and 'skills'. They embrace the possibilities to break down personal and public divides, to experiment in a mix of per-sonal, political and professional, and to mediate the crossing of boundaries.

Defining mediations

Let us look at which boundaries these women and men find themselves crossing. How does the group perceive the 'here and now'? What language is emerging in the evolving communication? Perhaps we can begin with the gender divide – the majority of the authors of the book and the WoN are women who welcome the interaction with the men joining them in exploring the gendered implications of the Net. Indeed the issue of men as part of the group has not arisen – possibly because at the beginning almost none knew beyond a sense given by the name and place (but then many are no longer situated in their country of origin) what people looked like in the flesh, who they 'were' just on sight. So a vital element of communication – physical attraction – could not enter. Not knowing gender or the look of someone is a virtual robbing of some of the richness of communication. This explains, perhaps, the tolerance but also why some of the language does become personal and even poetic to help people gain a sense of who 'I am really' beyond the typing on the screen.

Perhaps the most obvious and celebrated crossed boundary is the geopolitical one – thousands of kilometres fade in chats across the screen. With just a few hours of time difference, which can be peripheral as access to terminals at all hours in homes or cybercafes, messages reach the Pacific, Asia, Europe, North America, Africa, Latin America and the Middle East instantaneously, at the cost of a telephone call. Something curious and wondrous. But again the continual crossing of the here and now divide brings the need to create a sense of reality and place starts to creep in – at least to say what the weather is like – to give a sense of the humidity of the Zanzibari breeze, the heat of Rome's summer, the deep winter snow of Toronto, the buzz of the people around the clatter of the keyboards. Certainly the cyborg list conversations express the need to embed and to root deeply virtual discussions in the political reality being fought every day. There is an attempt to anchor the happenings of the real life community to the virtual global discourse in order for the cyber communication space to have meaning.

Even so, the sense of community becomes unsettled – where is that community located? In space – which space? Whose space? As Fatma Alloo raises the question in her chapter – where does the Zanzibar community locate itself as people log in throughout the world to discuss *kanga* patterns and learn home news? And as Arturo Escobar and Kekula Bray-Crawford and others mention, where is the fight for Chiapas happening – in Mexican jungles or on the cyber battlefields – or both – and what does this mean? And for those who do not have a fixed physical location, like Laura Agustín and Silvia Austerlic – and potentially all migrant women forced to move from their home to look for work – can virtual communities exist to provide services, information and education, and to build another kind of knowledge base?

Other boundaries being crossed continually in the group and in these pages are those of intellectual and activist, of feminist and women-centred work. Labels become fluid as people find the words to understand each other divorced from concrete ways of judging – there is no actual classroom, no trade union hall, no ancestral ground to defend, no government office to lobby. These remain virtual points of reference that are imagined, not actually embraced and shared. Those who would not meet with professors or high-level policy makers find themselves in correspondence with them through e-mail. Papers that would never have reached an African NGO in rural Senegal are translated and sent within a few days of delivery at a scientific or intergovernmental event. Women who will never meet exchange on a daily basis their worries about the men and children in their lives. Women engrossed in their own battles for survival suddenly find groups living in other countries share the same concerns, and exchange valuable strategic knowledge. Academics and activists engage in a vigorous debate that each will use in different contexts enriched by what they have exchanged.

Then we see the crossing of the personal and professional boundaries. For those able to afford access, and to obtain it easily in terms of time (even if squeezed between family needs) and equipment, the Internet offers a sense of being able to share your life more easily. People provide the personal in an e-mail communication – something that perhaps would never be placed in a fax or letter. There is something wonderful about this – news of a baby born goes out to a never-met transnational group of cyberfriends, breastfeeding problems are discussed among women isolated in rural settings, urgent messages are sent by refugee Afghan women throughout the globe. But there are also the dangers of never-ending conversations running into other issues, messages too quickly sent, tempers flaring, unwisely shared fears and hopes.

Less vital but still worth noting is the boundary of good or bad writing (beyond the issue of English as the dominating language or cyberspeak technical jargon). E-mail is producing the tendency to produce quick and ungrammatical messages sent without rereading – telegraphic in brevity and almost in code, list serve messages left unread by some. This too changes the face of communication.

In mediating these boundaries, at least within the WoN, there is an attempt to delineate the borders and the exciting possibilities in crossing them as women open up new political spaces. Nevertheless it seems a tiny area women are inhabiting, controlled and designed usually by others. The questions remains: are we truly connected or just scratching at the surface of a fast-changing world that is evolving without our design or needs in mind? Hence the attempts by some like Sophia Huyer and Nidhi Tandon to venture into the world of decision making and the setting of the policy agenda on telecommunications and other areas affecting access and use of the Net and Web. In this some brave women are charting the ground into which women are yet to venture as a critical mass. For now, these seem power battles which women are not well equipped to fight. The world of Microsoft, high finance and tele-communications business are not the spaces in which women or those pushing for an alternative agenda easily find a voice.

A sense of identity?

To return to the metaphor of the cyborg. One question which continues to be asked within the group and is echoed in the book is what, if any, sense of identity can be created for women in cyberculture? Can we have a fluid and multicultural communication space which is safe, one from which our visions can be drawn and eventually enacted in reality? What do women from all these countries and backgrounds have in common, beyond the sense that the Internet could be a useful tool for empowering them in their local battles? In order to create a critical mass it is important to find a sense of identity. Perhaps one resides in the metaphor of a feminist cyborg – but for many women, as Pi says in the e-mail conversations reported in the 'Cyborg Melody', this is too removed from their reality and belongs to a sophisticated cyberspeak being produced mainly in Northern feminist (postmodernist) circles. Perhaps it better resides in the sense of political activism that is using the Internet as a global tool for local political needs in the references in the book to the 'politics of place' first raised by Arturo Escobar and illustrated continually in the experiences shared in Part 3.

Local and global encounters

If one can come to a conclusion in the midst of this myriad of information and sharings perhaps it is to focus on this relationship between the local and the global, or 'global delocalization'. The book suggests that the women and men writing here are seeking not to be trapped in the excitement and hype around the cyberworld but are trying to map out virtual reality as closely as possible to their place-based politics. And in this resides some sort of identity in cyberculture.

From which places are the WoN speaking? NGOs, resource centres, academic institutes, UN agencies and homes based in rural and urban Europe, Asia, the Pacific, the Middle East, North America, Latin America and Africa, and those places temporarily occupied by intellectual and visionary migrants on the move. They are an eclectic mix who are involved in women's issues in different ways – as migrant and indigenous rights activists, policy lobbyists, women in development researchers, journalists, technical communication experts, ecologists, anthropologists and policy makers. All are brought together because from their local positions – as they try to fight for change, build their political analysis and skills, sort through the maze of information, the types of knowledge required and the potential allies – they have recognized the power of the Internet. The Internet has become an increasingly accessible learning space, a place to network, and to gain power and strength. They introduce their local needs into the global space of the Internet in order to fight their local battles but also to understand the process and transform cyberspace so that it reflects their own and other women's needs in the creation of a 'glocality'. The notion of place is inherent in these women's lives and struggles.

Building on Arturo Escobar's chapter we can define the meaning of place and gender in relation to cyberculture on several levels. Owing to the gender bias of social and cultural processes, women's bodies are their first environment or place. It is the female body in all cultures that defines women as the other, as the reproductive being, the mother, as the sexually desired. It is the body through which women are primarily to mediate all gendered interactions, including those from which they defend and evolve their identity. The cyborg woman has evolved an identity which on the one hand breaks this notion of biological body by extending communication of self through the sexless machine of the computer and modem. And, on the other hand, cyberculture offers the possibility to celebrate and share the feminine space with other women from many diverse situations, giving credibility to women's bodily experience through an oral medium which encourages a more open personal discourse – if the safe space Gillian Youngs speaks about can be nurtured. It also, in its darkest interface, allows for manipulation and misuse of women's bodies – another area for women to fight against in their struggle against bodily violence.

A second level is the domestic space of the home, which for many women still defines their primary social and cultural identity and lived domain. The home and immediate community are the safe places for women to express themselves, and it is here, potentially, that the possibilities of the terminals in the home, and the personal and political exchanges this potentially facilitates, could change women's political lives. Women, calling on long traditions of flexibility between repro-ductive and productive work, could weave new political spaces while maintaining their reproductive work space. Already Northern women are increasingly working from home, raising on one side the problems of exploitative work conditions but on the other the potential of new feminine spaces from which to launch plans for change.

The third place is that outside the home – the political and social public place, the male-dominated domain to which some women still have no access, and where many women find themselves silenced and few women rule. For many years now the women's movement has been creating diverse avenues for entry into that space, even if the space occupied remains marginal to the pulse of political power. The cyber-culture now being created in this public domain, as several chapters in the book argue, is a new type of political space which has power and impact. Its current accessibility for women suggests a possible opening that could promote women's public political battles and link these three different levels of place: the body; the home; and political and social public space. The critical point is that women have to ensure that they are part of the design and crafting of the cyberculture in order to produce new types of gendered communication spaces throughout the Internet. They need to craft a process where their voices are heard in ways that can penetrate and radically change the public political domain.

This book is propelled by the collective vision of the WoN to use the

potentially globally accessible tool of the Internet to extend the corridors of power outwards and create a new politics emanating from place.
Such a place-based strategy is being mapped out and defined by women
based on their sense of the feminine, their everyday life realities, their
current questionings of hierarchies, resistance to male domination and
confidence in their own creativity.

NOTES

1   Thank you to all the members of the WoN project who sent their comments on
    this chapter.

BIBLIOGRAPHY

ABANTU for Development (1997) *Using Information Technology to Strengthen African Women's Organizations.* Prepared by Gillian Marcelle. ABANTU Publications, London.

Agencia Latinoamericana de Información (ALAI) – Women's Area (1994) 'Global Communications and Access to New Technologies: A Democratic Right for Women'. Paper presented to the Regional Preparatory Meeting of Latin America and the Caribbean for the Fourth World Conference on Women: Action for Equality, Development and Peace (Beijing 95). Mar del Plata, Argentina, September 1994.

Alkamli, A. (1998) 'The Arabs and Internet 1998', *Internet the Arab World* (Arab version), January 1998.

Alston, M. (1995) *Women on the Land: The Hidden Heart of Australia.* University of New South Wales Press, Kensington.

Alvarez, S. E. (1997) 'Latin American Feminisms "Go Global": Trends of the 1990s and Challenges for the New Millennium', in S. E. Alvarez, E. Dagnino and A. Escobar (eds), *Cultures of Politics/Politics of Cultures: Re-visioning Latin American Social Movements*, pp. 293–324. Westview Press, Boulder.

Alvarez, S. E. (1998) '... And even Fidel Can't Change That': Trans/national Feminist Advocacy Strategies and Cultural Politics in Latin America', paper presented at the Department of Anthropology, Mellon Lecture Series on 'Public Culture and Trans-nationalism'. Duke University, 27 October.

APC (Association for Progressive Communications) (1997) *Global Networking for Change. Experience from the APC Women's Programme. Survey Findings.* APC, London.

Austerlic, S. (1997) 'New Tendencies in Design in Latin American', *Organization* Vol. 4 No. 4, pp. 620–27.

Azzam, F. (1996) *Arab Constitutional Guarantees of Civil and Political Rights: A Comparative Analysis.* Dar El-Mostaqbal Al Arabi for Cairo Institute for Human Rights Studies (CIHRS), Cairo, Egypt.

Bautista, R. (1995) 'Linking Women Worldwide', *Annual Report of Isis International.* Isis International, Manila.

Bautista, R. (1996) 'Global Information Through Computer Networking Technology Workshop', paper presented at the UN Conference on Global Information Through Computer Networking Technology, New York, 26–28 June 1996.

Belausteguigoitia Rius, M. (1998) 'Visualizing Places: She Looks, Therefore ... Who Is?' *Development,* Vol. 41 No. 2 (June).

Berger, P. (1974) *The Pyramids of Sacrifice.* Allen Lane, Harmondworth.

Bollier, D. (1996) *Reinventing Democratic Culture in an Age of Electronic Networks.* Report to the John D. and Catherine T. MacArthur Foundation.
http://www.netaction.org/bollier/index.html

Bonsiepe, G. (1991) *Las siete columnas del diseño.* Universidad Autonoma Metropolitana Azcapotzalco, Mexico.

Bonsiepe, G. (1996) 'Educat innovadores', *Revista Tipográfica,* No. 7. Buenos Aires.

Boulding, E. (1990) *Building a Global Civic Culture.* Syracuse University Press.

Bowes, A. (1996) 'Evaluating an Empowering Research Strategy: Reflections on Action-

Research with South Asian Women', *Sociological Research Online*, Vol. 1, No. 1. Available: http://www.socresonline.org.uk/socresonline/1/1/1.html [27 June 1996].

Burrows, J. (n.d.) *Fourth World Documentation Project*. Centre For World Indigenous Studies, Washington DC, USA. (http://www.halcyon.com/FWDP/fwdp.html)

Cabrera-Balleza, M. (1995) 'Asian Women's NGOs Tap New Communication Technologies', paper presented at the Seminar on New Communication Technologies, Women and Democracy organized by the Asian Mass Communication Research and Information Centre in Bangkok, Thailand, 19–21 October 1995.

Cameron, D., F. McAlinden, and K. O'Leary (1993) 'Lakoff in Context: The Social and Linguistic Functions of Tag Questions' in S. Jackson (ed.), *Women's Studies: Essential Readings*. New York University Press, New York.

Castells, M. (1996) *The Rise of the Network Society*. Blackwell, Oxford .

Chen, M. A. (1995) 'Engendering world conferences: the international women's movement and the United Nations', *Third World Quarterly*, Vol. 16, No. 3.

Chernaik, L. (1996) 'Spatial Displacements: Transnationalism and the New Social Movements', *Gender, Place and Culture,* Vol. 3, No. 3, pp. 251–75.

Courier-Mail (1997) 'Niue takes moral stand on sex lines', 20 February 1997.

Cribb, J. (1994) 'Farewell to the Heartland', *The Weekend Australian Magazine*, 12–13 February, pp.10–16.

D'Ambrosio, U. (forthcoming) 'La transdisciplinaridad y los nuevos rumbos de la educación superior'. Presented at the Seminario Latinoamericano de Filosofía e Historia de las Ideas. http://www.ldc.lu.se/UVLA/univ.html

DAW (Division for the Advancement of Women) (1996) 'Women and the Information Revolution', *Women 2000* No.1, October.

Daws, L. (1997) 'An Analysis of the Role of the Internet in Supporting Rural Women's Leadership Initiatives', paper presented to the Sixth Women and Labour Conference, Deakin University, Geelong, 28–30 November.

Dean, J. (ed.) (1997) *Feminism and the New Democracy: Resiting the Political*. Sage, London.

Dean, J. and A. Opoku-Mensah (1997) 'Telecommunications Development and the Market: The Promises and the Problems', *Panos Media Briefing*, No. 23 (March). http://www.oneworld.org/panos/

Delisio, J., e-mail correspondence, 26 April 1995.

Der Derian, J. and M. Shapiro (eds) (1989) *International/Intertextual Relations: Postmodern Readings of World Politics*. Lexington Books, New York.

Descola, Ph. and G. Pálsson (eds) (1996) *Nature and Society. Anthropological Perspectives*. Routledge, London.

Dirlik, A. (1997) 'Place-based Imagination: Globalism and the Politics of Place', unpublished manuscript.

Dirlik, A. (1998) 'Globalism and the Politics of Place', *Development*, Vol. 41, No. 2, pp. 7–13.

Dumelie, R. (1997) Presentation on the GK97 Conference, 22nd World Conference of the Society for International Development (SID).

Ehrlich, S. and R. King (1993) 'Gender-based Language Reform and the Social Construction of Meaning' in S. Jackson, *Women's Studies: Essential Readings*. New York University Press, New York.

Enloe, C. (1989) *Bananas, Beaches and Bases: Making Feminist Sense of International Politics*. Pandora, London.

Escobar, A. (1997) 'Cultural Politics and Biological Diversity: State, Capital and Social Movements in the Pacific Coast of Colombia', in R. Fox and O. Starn (eds), *Between Resistance and Revolution*, pp. 40–64. Rutgers University Press, New Brunswick.

Escobar, A. (1998a) 'Whose Knowledge, Whose Nature? Biodiversity Conservation and

Social Movements Political Ecology'. Paper prepared for the IV Ajusco Forum on 'Whose Nature? Biodiversity, Globalization and Sustainability in Latin America and the Caribbean'. Mexico, DF, 19-21 November 1997.

Escobar, A. (1998b) 'The Place of Nature and the Nature of Place: Globalization or Postdevelopment?' Under review, *Social Text.*

Escobar, A. (1998c) 'El final de salvaje: Antropología y Nuevas Tecnologías'. Presented at the seminar on 'The Sciences and the Humanities at the Dawn on the Twenty-First Century'. UNAM, Mexico.

Esteva, G. and M. S. Prakash (1997) 'From Global Thinking to Local Thinking', in M. Rahnema with V. Bawtree (eds), *The Postdevelopment Reader*, pp. 277–89. Zed Books, London.

Fishman, P. M. (1990) 'Interaction: The Work Women Do' in Joyce McCarl Nielsen (ed.) *Feminist Research Methods.* Westview Press, Boulder, Colorado.

Flores Morador, F. (1996) 'Siete ensayos para la libertad', *Cuadernos Heterogenesis.* Lund, Sweden.

Flores, F. (1994) *Creando Organizaciones para el futuro.* Dolmen Ediciones, Santiago.

Foucault, M. (1979) *Discipline and Punish: The Birth of the Prison.* Vintage Books, New York. Translated by Alan Sheridan.

Foucault, M. (1984) 'The Order of Discourse' (translated by Ian McLeod), in M. Shapiro (ed.), *Language and Politics*, pp. 108–38. Basil Blackwell, Oxford.

Frankson, J. R. (1996) 'Women's Global FaxNet Charting the Way', *Journal of International Communication*, Vol. 3, No. 1, July, pp. 102–10.

Freire, P. (1985) *La Educación como practica de libertad.* Siglo XXI Editores, Argentina.

Friedrich-Ebert-Stiftung Workshop (1997) *Internet as a Strategic Tool for NGOs.* Cairo, Egypt, 14–16 October 1997.
http://dialspace.dial.pipex.com/dmtpruett/FESEgypt/egreport.html

Gates, B. (1995) *The Road Ahead.* Viking, London.

Geertz, C. (1973) *The Interpretation of Cultures.* Basic Books, New York.

Gender Working Group, UN Commission on Science and Technology for Development (1995) *Missing Links: Gender Equity in Science and Technology for Development.* International Development Research Centre (IDRC), Ottawa.

Gibson-Graham, J. K. (1996) *The End of Capitalism (As We Knew It).* Basil Blackwell, Oxford.

Giddens, A. (1990) *The Consequences of Modernity.* Stanford University Press, Stanford.

Gilbert, J. (1997) *Session 7.11 Extending the Reach: The GK97 Virtual Conference.* Workshop report, Conference on Knowledge for Development in the Information Age.

Gittler, A. M. (1996a) 'Taking Hold of Electronic Communications: Women Making a Difference', *Journal of International Communication*, Vol. 3, No. 1 (July), pp. 85–101.

Gittler, A. M. (1996b) 'Learning from IT: IWTC's experience with information technologies', *AWID News*, Vol. 10, No. 2 (June), pp. 6–7.

Gore, J. (1992) 'What We Can Do For You! What Can "We" Do For "You"?: Struggling Over Empowerment in Critical and Feminist Pedagogy' in C. Luke and J. Gore (eds), *Feminisms and Critical Pedagogy*, pp. 54–73. Routledge, New York.

Grace, M. (1994) *Women in Rural Queensland: An Exploration of Cultural Contexts, Educational Needs and Leadership Potential.* Centre for Policy and Leadership Studies, Queensland University of Technology, Brisbane.

Grace, M. and J. Lennie (1997) 'Constructing and Reconstructing Rural Women in Australia: The Politics of Change, Diversity and Identity', paper presented to the XVII Congress of the European Society for Rural Sociology, Crete, August.

Grace, M., J. Lennie, L., Daws, L., Simpson, J., Previte, R. Lundin, and T. Stevenson (forthcoming, 1998) *The New Pioneers: Women in Rural Queensland Collaboratively Exploring the Potential of Communication Technologies for Personal, Business and Community Development.* The Communication Centre/Centre for Policy and Leadership Studies, Queensland University of Technology, Brisbane.

Grace, M., R. Lundin, and L. Daws (1996) *Working and Networking: Women's Voices from Elsewhere.* Centre for Policy and Leadership Studies, Queensland University of Technology, Brisbane.

Guteman, S. and A. Rivera (1990) *Conversations in Colombia. The Domestic Economy in Life and Text.* Cambridge University Press, Cambridge.

Gwynne, S. C. and J. F. Dickerson (1997) 'Lost in the E-Mail', *Time,* 21 April 1997.

Halal, W. E. (1996) 'The Rise of the Knowledge Entrepreneur', *The Futurist,* Vol. 30, No. 6 (November–December).

Hamelink, C. (1997) 'Learning Cultural Pluralism: Can the "Information Society" Help?' in D. Cliche (ed.) *Cultural Ecology: The Changing Nature of Communications.* International Institute of Communications, London.

Hamilton, A. (1997), 'World Watch', *Time Digital* (included in *Time*), 15 December 1997.

Haraway, D. J. (1991a) *Simians, Cyborgs, and Women: The Reinvention of Nature.* Free Association Books, London.

Haraway, D. (1991b) 'Cyborgs at Large: Interview with Donna Haraway' in Penley, C. and A. Ross (eds), *Technoculture,* pp. 1–20. University of Minnesota Press, Minneapolis.

Haraway, D. (1991c) 'The Actors are Cyborg, Nature is Coyote, and the Geography is Elsewhere: Postscripts to Cyborgs at Large' in C. Penley and A. Ross (eds), *Technoculture,* pp. 21–6. University of Minnesota Press, Minneapolis.

Haraway, D. (1997) *Modest_Witness@Second_Millennium. FemaleMan_Meets_OncoMouseTM.* Routledge, New York.

Harcourt, W. (ed.) (1994) *Feminist Perspectives on Sustainable Development.* Zed Books, London.

Harcourt, W. (1998) *Women Working on the Net.* UNESCO/SID, Paris.

Harvey, D. (1989) *The Conditions of Postmodernity.* Blackwell, Oxford.

Häusler, S. (1994) 'Women and the Politics of Sustainable Development' in W. Harcourt (eds) *Feminist Perspectives on Sustainable Development* (pp. 145–55). Zed Books and the Society for International Development, London and Rome.

Hayles, K. (1995) 'Searching for Common Ground', in M. Soulé and G. Lease (eds), *Reinventing Nature?,* pp. 47–64. Island Press, Washington.

Hirsh, J. (1997) *Local Knowledge, Global Wisdom Report.* Workshop report, Conference on Knowledge for Development in the Information Age.

Hogan, E. (1994) 'Making Women Visible: Reflections on Working with Women in Agriculture in Victoria' in M., Franklin, L. Short and E. Teather (eds), *Country Women at the Crossroads. Perspectives on the Lives of Rural Australian Women in the 1990s,* pp. 31–7. University of New England Press, Armidale.

Huyer, S. (1997) *Women's Use of Information and Communications Technologies for Sustainable Development.* International Development Research Centre. Report submitted to the IDRC ACACIA Programme.

Huyer, S. (1998) 'Engendering Science Policy: the Case of the Gender, Science and Development Programme', *Gender, Technology and Development* (Spring).

Inayatullah, S. (1988) 'Listening to Non-Western Perspectives' in D. Hicks and R. Slaughter (eds), *1998 Education Yearbook.* Kogan Page, London.

Inayatullah, S. (1993) 'Frames of Reference, the Breakdown of the Self, and the Search for Reintegration: Some Perspectives on the Futures of Asian Cultures' in E. Masini and Y. Atal (eds) *The Futures of Asian Cultures.* Unesco, Bangkok.

Independent Committee on Women and Global Knowledge (ICWGK) (1997) 'The Canon on Gender, Partnerships and ICT Development.' Paper presented at the

Global Knowledge 1997 Conference, June 22–25, Toronto, Canada.

International Development Research Centre (IDRC), Gender and Information Working Group (1995) 'Information as a Transformative Tool: the Gender Dimension' in *Missing Links: Gender Equity in Science and Technology for Development*, IDRC, Ottawa, pp. 267–93.

International Telecommunications Union (ITU) (1994) *Final Report – World Tele-communication Development Conference*. ITU.

International Women's Tribune Centre (IWTC) (1983) *IWTC and its CPT: The Story of a Small International Women's Organization and its Word Processor*. IWTC, New York.

International Women's Tribune Centre (IWTC) (1993) *Support Skills for Third World Women's Groups: Final Report*. IWTC, New York.

International Women's Tribune Centre (IWTC) (1995) 'What Did Women of the World Achieve in our Struggle for a Suitable NGO Forum site in China?' *Global Faxnet*, 19, 1 (27 June).

IWTC (1997) *Global FaxNet: the Second 50 Issues*. December. IWTC, NEW York.

Jacobs, J. (1996) *Edge of Empire. Postcolonialism and the City*. Routledge, London.

James, M., e-mail communication, 23 January 1998.

Jones, S. (1995) 'Understanding Community in the Information Age' in S. Jones, (ed.), *Cybersociety. Computer-mediated Communication and Community*, pp. 10–35. Sage, Thousand Oaks.

Latour, B. (1993) *We Have Never Been Modern*. Harvard University Press, Cambridge.

Lawrence, G. (1995) *Futures for Rural Australia: from Agricultural Productivism to Community Sustainability*. Rural Social and Economic Research Centre, Central Queensland University, Rockhampton.

Lefebvre, H. (1991) *The Production of Space*. Basil Blackwell, Oxford.

Lennie, J. (1996) 'Gender and Power in Sustainable Development Planning: Towards a Feminist Poststructuralist Framework of Participation', unpublished Master of Business (Communication Management) thesis, Faculty of Business, Queensland University of Technology, Brisbane.

León, O. (1997) 'El desafío democrático de la comunicación', *ALAI Servicio Informativo*, Quito, Nos 248–9, (special 20th Year Edition), 24 March 1997.

Leventhal, M. (n.d.) *Microstate Resources Home Page*. (http://www.microstate.com/).

Long, N. and A. Long (eds) (1992) *Battlefields of Knowledge: The Interlocking of Theory and Practice in Social Research and Development*. Routledge, London.

Makhubu, L.P. (1993) 'The Potential Strength of African Women in Building Africa's Scientific and Echnological Capacity' in *Science in Africa: Women Leading from Strength*. American Association for the Advancement of Science, Sub-Saharan Africa Programme.

Marcelle, G. (1997) *Creating an African Women's Cyberspace*. UNU/INTECH.

Massey, D. (1994) *Space, Place and Gender*. University of Minnesota Press, Minneapolis.

McCulley, L. and P. Patterson (1996) 'Feminist Empowerment Through the Internet', *Feminist Collections*, Vol. 17, No. 2, pp. 5–6.

McLuhan, M. (1996) quoted in *New Internationalist*, special issue 'Seduced by Technology: The Human Costs of Computers', Vol. 286 (December).

McNamara, K., e-mail communication, 16 February 1998.

Mitter, S. (1995) 'Who Benefits? Measuring the Differential Impact of New Technologies' in *Missing Links: Gender Equity in Science and Technology for Development*. International Development Research Centre (IDRC), Ottawa.

Mitter, S., e-mail communication, 12 February 1998.

Morse-Houghten, D. (1997) 'Lost in the E-Mail', *Time*, 21 April 1997.

Moser, C. (1993) *Gender Planning and Development: Theory, Practice and Training*. Routledge,

New York.

Nandy, A (1996) 'Bearing Witness to the Future', *Futures*, Vol. 28, No. 6/7 (September).

Nauth, K. and L. Timmermann (1997) 'Bringing the Web to the Developing World', *New Media*, September 1997.

Negroponte, N. (1995) *Being Digital*. Hodder and Stoughton, London.

Nguyen, D. T. and J. Alexander (1996) 'The Coming of Cyberspacetime and the End of the Polity' in R. Shields (ed.), *Cultures of Internet: Virtual Spaces, Real Histories, Living Bodies*, pp. 99–124. Sage, London.

Oldham, G. (1995) 'Preface' in *Missing Links: Gender Equity in Science and Technology for Development*, International Development Research Centre, Ottawa.

Paterson, N. (1996) 'Cyberfeminism', *Fireweed*, No. 54.

Peterson, V. S. (1992) 'Transgressing Boundaries: Theories of Knowledge, Gender and International Relations', *Millennium: Journal of International Relations*, Vol. 21, pp. 183–206.

Pettman, J. J. (1996) *Worlding Women: A Feminist International Politics*. Routledge, London.

Philippine Daily Inquirer, 15 May 1996.

Plant, S. (1996) 'On the Matrix: Cyberfeminist Simulations' in Shields, R. (ed.), *Cultures of Internet: Virtual Spaces, Real Histories, Living Bodies*, Sage, London, pp. 170–83.

Rahnema, M. and V. Bawtree (eds) (1997) *The Postdevelopment Reader*. Zed Books, London.

Regional Meeting of Arab NGOs (1994) 'Human Development in the Arab World and the Role of Non-Governmental Organizations.' Working paper and recommendations presented at the Social Development Summit, Copenhagen, 1995.

Ribeiro, G. L. (1998) 'Cybercultural Politics: Political Activism at a Distance in a Transnational World', in S. E. Alvarez, E. Dagnino and A. Escobar (eds), *Cultures of Politics/Politics of Cultures: Re-visioning Latin American Social Movements*, pp. 325–52. Westview Press, Boulder.

Robbins, K. (1997) 'The New Communications Geography and the Politics of Optimism' in D. Cliche (ed.), *Cultural Ecology: The Changing Nature of Communications*. International Institute of Communications, London.

Rocheleau, D., B. Thomas-Slayter and E. Wangari (1996) 'Gender and Development: A Feminist Political Ecology Perspective', in D. Rocheleau, B. Thomas-Slayter and E. Wangari (eds), *Feminist Political Ecology*, pp. 3–23. Routledge, New York.

Ronfeldt, D. (1992) *Cyberocracy is Coming*. Taylor and Francis, New York. (http://gopher.well.sf.ca.us:70/0/whole_systems/cyberocracy).

Rushkoff, D. (1997) *Children of Chaos*. Harper Collins, New York.

Sandhya R. and N. Ch. Natesan (1996) 'Internet: Threat or Opportunity for India?' *Media Asia*, Vol. 23, No. 2.

Sandoval, Ch. (1995) 'Re-entering of Cyberspace Sciences of Resistance' in G. Brahm, and M. Driscoll (eds), *Prosthetic Territories: Politics and Hypertechnologies*. Westview Press, Boulder.

Sanger, J. (1994). 'Emancipation, Empowerment or Authorship? Mass Action Research' in M., Laidlaw, P. Lomax and J. Whitehead (eds), *Proceedings of the 3rd World Congress on Action Learning, Action Research and Process Management*, 'Accounting for Ourselves', pp. 199–202. University of Bath, England, 6–9 July.

Sardar, Z. (1996) 'alt.civilizations.faq Cyberspace as the Darker Side of the West' in Z. Sardar, and J. R. Ravetz, *Cyberfutures: Culture and Politics on the Information Highway*, pp. 14–41. Pluto Press, London.

Sardar, Z. (1996) 'The Future of Democracy and Human Rights', *Futures*, Vol. 28, No. 9, November.

Sarkar, P. R. (1959), *Problem of the Day*. Ananda Marga Publications, Ananda Nagar, India.

Sarkar, P. R. (1984) *The Human Society*. Ananda Marga Publications, Calcutta, India.

Schild, V. (1998) 'New Subjects of Rights? Women's Movements and the Construction of Citizenship in the "New Democracies"', in S. E. Alvarez, E. Dagnino and A. Escobar (eds), *Cultures of Politics/Politics of Cultures: Re-visioning Latin American Social Movements,* pp. 93–117. Westview Press, Boulder.

Schuler, D. (1996) *New Community Networks. Wired for Change.* Addison Wesley, New York.

Serageldin, I. (1996) 'Islam, Science and Values', *International Journal of Science and Technology,* Vol. 9, No. 2 (Spring).

Sheldrake, R. (1981) *A New Science of Life.* Blond and Briggs, London.

Sher, J. and K. Sher (1994) 'Beyond the Conventional Wisdom: Rural Development as if Australia's Rural People and Communities Really Mattered', *Journal of Research in Rural Education,* Vol. 10, No. 1, pp. 2–43.

Shortall, S. (1994) 'Farm Women's Groups: Feminist or Farming or Community Groups, or New Social Movements?' *Sociology,* Vol. 28, No. 1, pp. 279–91.

Shute, C. (1996) 'Women With Byte', *Australian Women's Book Review,* Vol. 8, No. 3, October.

Soja, E. (1996) *Thirdspace.* Basil Blackwell, Oxford.

Spender, D. (1995) *Nattering on the Net: Women, Power and Cyberspace.* Spinifex, Melbourne.

Staudt, K. (1990) 'Gender Politics in Bureaucracy: Theoretical Issues in Comparative Perspective', and 'Context and politics in the gendered bureacratic mire' in K. Staudt (ed.) *Women, International Development, and Politics: the Bureaucratic Mire,* pp. 3–34. Temple University Press, Philadelphia.

Tandon, N., e-mail communication, 25 February 1998.

Te Pareake Mead, A. (1996) 'Cultural and Intellectual Property Rights of Indigenous Peoples of the Pacific'. PhD thesis.

Thomas-Slayter, B., E. Wangari and D. Rocheleau (1996) 'Feminist Political Ecology: Crosscutting Themes, Theoretical Insights, Policy Implications', in D. Rocheleau, B. Thomas-Slayter and E. Wangari (eds), *Feminist Political Ecology,* pp. 287–307. Routledge, New York.

Toronto Platform for Action (1995). Adopted at the UNESCO International Conference on Women and the Media: Access to Expression and Decision-Making. Version of 17 February 1995.

Tracey, M. (1997) 'Twilight: illusion and decline in the communication revolution' in D. Cliche (ed.), *Cultural Ecology: The Changing Nature of Communications.* International Institute of Communications, London.

UN (1993) *UN General Assembly Resolution 48/163,* International Decade of the World's Indigenous People, 86th plenary meeting, 21 December 1993.

UNCSTD (1995) 'Taking Action: Conclusions and Recommendations of the Gender Working Group' in *Missing Links: Gender Equity in Science and Technology for Development,* pp. 1–26. International Development Research Centre (IDRC)/ UNIFEM, Ottawa.

UNCTAD (1997) 'Some Major Implications of the Global Information Infrastructure (GII) for Trade and Development'. Paper presented at the Trade and Development Board Commission on Enterprise, Business Facilitation and Development: Expert Meeting On Telecommunications, Business Facilitation And Trade Efficiency. Geneva, 8–10 September 1997.

UNDP (1997) *United Nations Development Programme Report.* United Nations, New York.

United Nations (1995a) *The Platform for Action A/CONF/177/20.* United Nations, New York.

United Nations (1995b) *The World's Women: Trends and Statistics.* United Nations, New York.

United Nations Development Programme (UNDP) (1997) *Human Development Report.*

Oxford University Press, New York.

United Nations University Institute for New Technologies (UNU/INTECH) and the United Nations Development Fund for Women (UNIFEM) (1998) *Gender and Telecommunications – An Agenda for Policy*. United Nations, New York.

Villanueva, P. (1997) 'Wielding New Technologies', *Women Envision*, No. 45 (May).

Virilio, P. (1996) *Cybermonde, La Politique du Pire*. Textuel, Paris.

Virilio, P. (1997) *Open Sky*. Verso, London.

WEDO (1991) 'Action Agenda 21' in *World Women's Congress for a Healthy Planet in Miami*, Women Environment and Development Organization.

Weedon, C. (1987) *Feminist Practice and Poststructuralist Theory*. Blackwell, Oxford.

Whitworth, S. (1994) 'Theory as Exclusion: Gender and International Political Economy' in R. Stubbs, and R. D. S. Underhill (eds), *Political Economy and the Changing Global Order*. Macmillan, London, pp. 116–29.

Women, Information and the Future (WIF) (1994) *Information Statement by 'Women, Information and the Future'*. Schlesinger Library. International Conference 'Women, Information and the Future', Radcliffe College, Cambridge, Mass., 17–20 June.

World Bank (1997a) *Global Knowledge and Local Culture*. Plenary Address, Conference on Knowledge for Development in the Information Age. 24 June 1997. Workshop Report.

World Bank (1997b) *Knowledge for Development in the Information Age: About the Conference*. 20 June 1997. Available on World Wide Web: URL;http://www.globalknowledge.org/text/about_gk97.html

WTO (1997) *The WTO Negotiations on Basic Telecommunications: Informal Summary of Commitments and M.f.n. Exemptions*. Geneva, Switzerland.

Youngs, G. (forthcoming a) 'Breaking Patriarchal Bonds. Demythologizing the Public/Private' in Marchand, M. and A. S. Runyan (eds), *Gender and Global Restructuring*.

Youngs, G. (forthcoming b) *From International Relations to Global Relations: A Conceptual Challenge*. Polity Press, Cambridge.

INDEX